Ethics and Education Research

Research Methods in Education

Each book in this series maps the territory of a key research approach or topic in order to help readers progress from beginner to advanced researcher.

Each book aims to provide a definitive, market-leading overview and to present a blend of theory and practice with a critical edge. All titles in the series are written for Masters-level students anywhere and are intended to be useful to the many diverse constituencies interested in research on education and related areas.

Titles in the series:

Atkins & Wallace	*Qualitative Research in Education*
Hamilton & Corbett-Whittier	*Using Case Study in Education Research*
McAteer	*Action Research in Education*
Mills & Morton	*Ethnography in Education*

Access the additional resources here:
http://www.sagepub.co.uk/beraseries.sp

BRITISH EDUCATIONAL RESEARCH ASSOCIATION

Los Angeles | London | New Delhi
Singapore | Washington DC

Ethics and Education Research

Rachel Brooks, Kitty te Riele and Meg Maguire

Los Angeles | London | New Delhi
Singapore | Washington DC

Los Angeles | London | New Delhi
Singapore | Washington DC

SAGE Publications Ltd
1 Oliver's Yard
55 City Road
London EC1Y 1SP

SAGE Publications Inc.
2455 Teller Road
Thousand Oaks, California 91320

SAGE Publications India Pvt Ltd
B 1/I 1 Mohan Cooperative Industrial Area
Mathura Road
New Delhi 110 044

SAGE Publications Asia-Pacific Pte Ltd
3 Church Street
#10-04 Samsung Hub
Singapore 049483

Editor: Marianne Lagrange
Assistant editor: Rachael Plant
Project manager: Bill Antrobus
Production editor: Nicola Marshall
Copyeditor: Solveig Gardner Servian
Proofreader: Fabienne Pedroletti Gray
Indexer: Anne Solamito
Marketing manager: Dilhara Attygalle
Cover design: Wendy Scott
Typeset by: C&M Digitals (P) Ltd, Chennai, India
Printed and bound by CPI Group (UK) Ltd,
Croydon, CR0 4YY (for Antony Rowe)

© Rachel Brooks, Kitty te Riele and Meg Maguire, 2014

First edition published 2014

Library of Congress Control Number: 2014933235

British Library Cataloguing in Publication data

A catalogue record for this book is available from the British Library

ISBN 978-1-4462-7488-0 (pb)
ISBN 978-1-4462-7487-3

CONTENTS

About the authors   vi

Acknowledgements   viii

1 Introduction   1

2 Ethical theories, principles and guidelines   18

3 Regulatory contexts   44

4 Research design   59

5 Informed consent and reciprocity   79

6 Identity, power and positionality   100

7 Data analysis   117

8 Dissemination   135

9 Conclusions   152

References   169

Index   187

ABOUT THE AUTHORS

Rachel Brooks is Professor of Sociology and Head of the Sociology Department at the University of Surrey in the UK and co-editor of the journal *Sociological Research Online*. She has carried out a wide range of research projects on different aspects of education, with a particular focus on higher education and lifelong learning. Most recently, her research has focussed on: international student mobility; the funding of higher education; and a cross-national comparison of the experiences of university students with parental responsibilities. Rachel also has a strong interest in research methods. She co-authored *Researching Young People's Lives* (Sage, 2009) with Heath et al., and co-edited *Negotiating Ethical Challenges in Youth Research* (Routledge, 2013) with Kitty te Riele.

Kitty te Riele is Principal Research Fellow in the Victoria Institute for Education, Diversity and Lifelong Learning, at Victoria University in Australia. She researches educational policy and practice for disadvantaged young people, with a particular focus on alternative education initiatives. Her research has involved students, teachers and community members as participants. Kitty has supervised doctoral research students from both Australia and Hong Kong on research projects in primary, secondary and tertiary education. She has taught professional ethics for pre-service teachers and has experience as an active member of faculty and university human research ethics committees. Her most recent book *Negotiating Ethical Challenges in Youth Research* (Routledge, 2013) is co-edited with Rachel Brooks. They have also guest-edited two journal special issues (for *Young* and *Youth Studies Australia*) focused on research ethics.

Meg Maguire taught for many years in London schools, including a period as a head teacher. Her research interests include: education policy and practice; social justice issues; the life and work of school-teachers; teacher education; and the challenges of inner-city schooling. She is Professor of Sociology of Education in the Department of Education and Professional Studies at King's College London. She has extensive experience of supervising research with undergraduate, masters and doctoral students in educational studies and has a long-standing concern with ethics in research. Her most recent book How Schools Do Policy: Policy Enactments in Secondary Schools (Routledge, 2012) is co-written with Stephen Ball and Annette Braun. She is lead editor for the *Journal of Education Policy*.

ACKNOWLEDGEMENTS

We would like to thank all the students, co-researchers and other colleagues with whom we have worked for making us think more critically about the ethics of our research. We are also grateful to colleagues who attended our presentations on various aspects of the book and provided valuable feedback. The Visiting International Fellowship awarded by the Department of Sociology at the University of Surrey to Kitty te Riele in 2013 offered major support by enabling the team to work together in person. Thanks are also due to the British Educational Research Association and SAGE for including the book in their series on education research methods.

CHAPTER 1

INTRODUCTION

Following an encounter with an ex-prisoner in his undergraduate Sociology of Education class, Gustav decides to embark on a new research direction to explore the educational opportunities provided within juvenile justice facilities. Gustav has previously conducted research on the educational experiences of young refugees and on students' sexualities. He wants his research to empower and give voice to marginalized groups. For this new project he needs approval not only from his university ethics committee but also from the prison service. The former is concerned about participants disclosing illegal activities and the possibility of Gustav and his data being subject to a court subpoena. The latter wishes to control exactly who he can include in his research before granting access. Is this project just too hard to do?

Andrew is doing a PhD on young primary school children's views about their friendships. Nearly all the parents have consented to their children being interviewed in focus groups. Sean's mother has not given her consent although Ms Briggs, the class teacher, thinks this is because she lost the form or forgot to return it. Andrew takes a small group off to the library

(Continued)

(Continued)

and then sees that Sean is in the group. He is with Mohammed, his best friend. Ms Briggs comes hurrying into the library. 'Oh, there you are Sean', she says. 'Stay with Andrew now you are here.' What should Andrew do?

Sevati was doing some research for her master's degree in Education Management based on a small number of interviews with headteachers about their views on leadership. She was talking about her data and her conclusions with her tutor Alex. 'I only did six interviews with headteachers,' she said, 'and one was no good, so I decided to drop it from my data set.' 'What do you mean no good?' asked Alex. 'Well, what one of them said didn't really match with my literature review, and they didn't think there was such a thing as leadership anyway, so I have decided not to include it in my findings section.' Is it justifiable for Sevati to exclude this interview? What ethical issues are involved in decisions to include or exclude data?

Sam's doctorate is about race relations and education. She has just started conducting fieldwork in one school: visiting the school on three separate days, observing three teachers in their classrooms, and writing down snatches of conversation she overheard in the staff room. Based on these experiences, she describes the school as 'racist' in her field notes. Sam has the opportunity to present at a national conference next month. She's excited that she has some interesting data to report on. What might she need to consider as she writes up her perceptions of this school?

These vignettes illustrate some of the sorts of ethical dilemmas commonly encountered by the education researcher, whether he or she is a student, embarking on a research project for the first time, or a more experienced researcher. In *Ethics and Education Research* we use these vignettes, and others like them, as points of entry to the various ethical debates that are discussed in the chapters that follow. They may also be useful, within their own right, to stimulate debate amongst groups of researchers – within classrooms and elsewhere.

Our aim in *Ethics and Education Research* is to provide a comprehensive overview of the ethical issues associated with conducting research within the discipline of education. In doing so, we take a broad view of education, including learning both within institutions and informally, and across various age ranges. We discuss areas that raise complex ethical issues such as health and sex education, and research with young people with learning difficulties. The structure of the book, exploring ethical issues raised at all stages of a research project – from research design through data collection and analysis to writing and dissemination – is intended to emphasize strongly that ethics is not something to be forgotten once 'ethics approval' has been gained but, instead, needs to inform all of our actions as education researchers. We argue, throughout the book, that there is a need for ongoing ethical reflexivity throughout the process of research, and that researchers must be sensitive to the complex and sometimes unexpected ethical concerns that may arise. This approach serves to highlight responsibilities not only to participants, but also to sponsors of research and the wider community. The following eight chapters of the book discuss the ethical issues faced by researchers using a wide range of methods – including surveys, ethnography, interviews and visual methods. *Ethics and Education Research* is also international in orientation, and draws on examples of practice and academic literature from both the Global North and the Global South. Indeed, emphasis is placed throughout on the importance of contextual specificity, recognizing that ethical issues – and the responses of researchers – may well vary across place and space.

Ethical thinking is intimately connected to practical research skills, which need to be developed and reflected upon (Mauthner et al., 2012). Our aim in *Ethics and Education Research* is therefore to bring together theory and practice, to facilitate reflection and help both beginning and more experienced researchers develop a comprehensive understanding of the ethical implications of their work and the ethical challenges they may face. As indicated above, at the beginning of each chapter we provide a case study – derived from our experiences as teachers and researchers – to illustrate (in what we hope is an accessible and practical manner) some of the dilemmas researchers face in practice. In relation to the core theme of each chapter, we then draw on a wide variety of studies, from various different countries, to illustrate how particular ethical dilemmas are played out in practice. Throughout the book, we are concerned to draw out some of the more theoretical issues that underpin these dilemmas, to encourage reflection on what are frequently complex issues. *Ethics and Education Research* offers no simple 'toolkit' for resolving ethical dilemmas. Instead, we hope that it will inform practice by discussing useful principles as well as practical examples of how researchers have responded to such dilemmas.

In this chapter we provide an introduction to the eight chapters that follow. First, we discuss why ethical issues are important for all those conducting research – from undergraduates embarking upon their dissertation to senior professors co-ordinating complex international projects. We then outline some of the reasons for focusing on ethics in *education* particularly, and identify a number of specific issues that are raised by conducting research in educational settings. We discuss the range of research methods covered in the book before exploring some of the ways in which ethical issues can vary over time and space. Finally, we outline the structure of *Ethics and Education Research*, and provide a brief overview of the subsequent chapters.

The importance of ethical issues

In 1989, in the introduction to his book *The Ethics of Educational Research*, Burgess claimed that ethical questions in education research were largely absent from debate. This is certainly no longer the case. Over recent decades ethical issues have been discussed extensively within education and most other academic disciplines and by government, international agencies, higher education institutions and funding bodies, as well as by researchers themselves. This increasing focus on ethical issues – or 'ethics creep' as Haggerty (2004) calls it – has been driven by a number of changes within wider society. Legislative change in many countries has required researchers to pay greater attention to the way in which data are managed and stored; new technologies have given rise to new research methodologies and new ethical challenges; and, in many parts of the world (although not all), research ethics have become increasingly regulated by research funders and the organizations for whom researchers work. Over the last 30 years, international conventions (such as the United Nations Convention on the Rights of the Child) have given more rights to children, and have thus had an impact on social research – particularly education research, which often focuses on children in schools and other contexts (Danby and Farrell, 2004; Balen et al., 2006; Graham et al., 2013). Hammersley and Traianou (2012b) argue that the fragmentation of social science research along political and philosophical lines has also contributed to the increasing prominence of ethical issues. By this, they mean that the purpose of social research has come to been framed by some researchers in primarily ethical terms: for example, by critical theorists who contend that the purpose of research is to challenge the status quo and achieve political change.

The legislative and regulatory frameworks that now operate in many countries (discussed in detail in Chapter 3) make it imperative that all of us conducting education research take seriously the ethical implications of our work. However, we argue that conducting research ethically is important in itself. Indeed, as Mauthner et al. (2012, p.181) note, if we refuse to adopt an ethical stance in our work 'not only will our peers doubt the value of our work, we will be letting others down who we made a pact with – our participants who '"gifted" their words to us, and the readers of our findings'. Hammersley and Traianou (2012b) differentiate between two approaches to ethics. They maintain that many researchers assume that ethics is primarily or exclusively about the way in which they treat those they study and contrast this with their own approach, which focuses instead on the production of knowledge. From their perspective, they contend that the aim of ethical research is to 'produce conclusions that reach a relatively high threshold in terms of likely validity, and make a worthwhile contribution to collective knowledge' (p.134). In *Ethics and Education Research* we suggest that these two concerns should not be seen as mutually exclusive; indeed, we develop an argument over the next eight chapters that ethical research practice pays attention to the relationships researchers forge with those who participate in their projects, but is also concerned with the quality of the research produced – from the initial design, through data collection and analysis, to dissemination. Moreover, we believe that researchers need to consider the ethical implications of their work for the community of education researchers, educational professionals, sponsors of research, policymakers and the general public – as well as research participants.

Ethics and education

While many of the ethical issues discussed in this book apply to disciplines across the social sciences and beyond, there are several reasons for focusing on *education research*, specifically. First, education research is conducted by a wide variety of people including practising teachers, trainee teachers, undergraduates, postgraduates, academics, employees of government departments, and those working for voluntary agencies. While many of the more generic research texts currently available provide useful advice for students and professional researchers, relatively few grapple with some of the ethical dilemmas faced by those who are conducting research alongside professional practice. By focusing explicitly on education research, this book engages with some of the ethical questions faced by, for example, teachers conducting research in the schools and colleges in which they teach, and students who may be completing an undergraduate or postgraduate qualification before taking up a teaching position. As Bell and Nutt (2012) note, ethical dilemmas are especially likely to occur when researchers who are also practitioners are faced with multiple responsibilities and sensitivities. For example, teacher-researchers are likely to have responsibilities to the students they teach (and the students' parents), the school or college within which they work, the wider teaching profession, as well as to other researchers in their field, those who participate in their research, the scientific community, and perhaps also to society in general, in terms of the human benefit of their research (Iphofen, 2011). While in some cases these responsibilities may be well-aligned, it is entirely possible for the teacher-researcher to feel divided loyalties to the different people who may have an interest in his or her work. Moreover, in some contexts it can be hard for some of these groups (particularly students and parents) to understand fully the role of a teacher-researcher (DePalma, 2010).

Second, much education research is conducted in specific institutional contexts, such as schools, colleges, higher education institutions and workplaces. Such locations often give rise to ethical challenges that are less likely to be encountered in other places. For example, it is usually necessary for a researcher to negotiate access with at least one 'gatekeeper' (such as a head teacher or principal) if she or he wishes to conduct research in a school or college. As we will discuss in later chapters, such negotiations have implications for the way in which students are (or are not) approached and the extent to which fully informed consent is possible (Denscombe and Aubrook, 1992; Heath et al., 2007). The power relationships within educational institutions (related to differences in status and also, often, age) can make it more difficult for students to decline to take part in research. These issues provide an important focus for Chapters 5 and 6.

Third, education research differs from some other types of social research by virtue of its close relationship with policy and practice. A considerable proportion of education research conducted worldwide is sponsored: by government departments, charities, commercial organizations or academic funding bodies. As will be discussed in more detail in later chapters, this can impose certain constraints on the freedom of the researcher 'not only to initiate research, but also to retain control over its orientation and dissemination' (Troyna and Carrington, 1989, p.218). Intervention from sponsors may affect the type of research that is deemed fundable (e.g. favouring quantitative approaches over qualitative methods). In some cases government-commissioned research that fails to support current policy may be suppressed, or research may be funded only to provide support for a policy initiative that is already underway (Burgess, 1989a). Furthermore, as a result of the close relationship between education research and policy and practice, education researchers can sometimes come under more public scrutiny than their colleagues in other areas of social research. In the UK, this was evident in the late 1990s when the government commissioned a review of the quality of education research, which was very critical of the work being conducted in universities and elsewhere (Tooley and Darby, 1998). This scrutiny can be seen still in the current century: in 2013 the British Educational Research Association felt it necessary to publish *Why Educational Research Matters* (BERA, 2013) in an attempt to defend the activities of its members in a relatively hostile political climate. Scepticism can also be experienced at a more local level. Indeed, Torrance (1989) has argued that occasionally some kinds of education research can come to be seen as 'policing' rather than investigating the design and implementation of policy. He writes: '"Evaluation" may come to be perceived as a wholly instrumental activity, offering at best perhaps "intelligence" about where in-service resources might be most effectively deployed, at worst, the appraisal of teachers with regard to their willingness and competence to deliver change' (p.183). Such suspicions may be less common in some other areas of academic enquiry where the links between research, on the one hand, and policy and practice, on the other hand, are less strong.

Methodological diversity

Within the discipline of education, researchers draw on a wide variety of approaches and methods largely because of the range of theoretical traditions and methodological assumptions that underpin their work. As Iphofen (2011) notes in relation to social science more generally, this variety has implications for ethical decision making; because of the divergent views about the nature of the human subject and the form any ensuing investigation should therefore take, more complex dilemmas are raised than are typically found in bio-medical research. For example, education researchers who conduct experiments are likely to face different ethical issues and may well have different ethical perspectives from those who pursue participatory research.

Many research texts focus on the ethical issues specific to qualitative research on the grounds that such methods involve greater engagement with human participants than quantitative approaches, sometimes on a long-term basis, and that relationships with participants are more 'humanistic' in nature, involving more mutual trust and less predictability (Hammersley and Traianou, 2012b; Miller et al., 2012). Nevertheless, we argue in *Ethics and Education Research* that while there may be important differences by method in the type of relationship forged between researcher and participant, all methods have ethical implications – including survey research (Raffe et al., 1989), randomized control trials (RCTs)

(Brady and O'Regan, 2009), and re-studies (O'Connor and Goodwin, 2013). As a result, in the book as a whole, we cover a wide range of different research methods.

Within the chapters that follow, we do, however, explore differences between methods, some of which relate broadly to the variation between qualitative and quantitative orientations. For example, in Chapter 4 we discuss whether education researchers using qualitative methods are more likely than their peers using surveys or other quantitative methods to have their approach questioned by research ethics committees (RECs) (Brown, 2010; Ells, 2011). In the ensuing chapters, we also consider changes to the methodological orientation of education researchers. Some scholars have argued that the dominant paradigm in education research is based on qualitative methodologies, largely because 'there are complex interactive processes operating within the classroom situation requiring investigation and understanding' (Torgerson, 2001, p.316). While this may still be true for research conducted by postgraduate researchers and practitioner-researchers, it is now perhaps less true for those bidding for external research funding. Indeed, as we suggest below and in Chapter 4, over recent years there have been increasing pressures on some education researchers to adopt quantitative approaches.

Variation over time

In the next chapter of this book (Chapter 2, Ethical Theories, Principles and Guidelines), we draw on philosophical literature to discuss some of the principles than underpin ethical approaches to research. In doing so, we emphasize that, despite the recent nature of the 'ethics creep' described above, such principles have a long history. We do, however, recognize that ethical practice has varied significantly over time – as a result of changes to the methods used by education researchers and also our ethical sensibilities. Indeed, over recent decades we have seen shifts in the methodological choices made by education researchers. These have been influenced by a variety of factors, including changes to dominant theoretical frameworks and the wider political environment (Brooks et al., 2013). For example, over the past twenty years or so, quantitative research has been favoured by governments in several nations of the Global North, and increasing use has been made, within education, of RCTs (Delandshere, 2004; Brady and O'Regan, 2009; Ong-Dean et al., 2011). A range of specific ethical issues are associated with RCTs, with which education researchers have had to engage, and these are discussed in some detail in Chapter 4.

Changes to research methods have also been brought about by evolving technologies. Within education research, visual methods have become increasingly common over recent years, in large part due to the availability of cheap, high-quality digital technology. It has become much easier for researchers to use cameras and video-recorders themselves and, in some cases, to provide research participants with such devices. Visual methods have also been seen by some education researchers as a means of reducing power differentials between adult researcher and child respondent, by offering a form of communication that is not word-based (Coffey et al., 2006). Such methods have, however, given rise to new ethical questions. Many of these relate to the dissemination of research findings and the extent to which researchers should ensure that the identity of participants is not revealed in any photographs or film footage. Researchers have responded to such ethical concerns in different ways. For example, the school children in Wood's research used creative ways, such as blurring and over-exposing photographs, to ensure that they were present in the images they took, but unidentifiable (Wood and Kidman, 2013). Other researchers have, however, expressed ethical unease about the use of use blurred images (Coffey et al., 2006; Blum-Ross, 2013). (These issues are discussed in more detail in Chapter 8.) Additional ethical concerns have also been raised, including the way in which taking photographs or recording film may put the person collecting the data (whether researcher or participant) at risk from any people who object to being recorded in this way, and the possibility that visual images can do harm to others by exposing them to embarrassment or ridicule (Hammersley and Traianou, 2012b).

Online research methods have also grown considerably in popularity with education researchers over the past decade, again raising some new ethical dilemmas (Mauthner et al., 2012). For example, it is now not unknown for research participants to provide their own account of being involved in a research project in an online space, accessible to all, which can be seen as compromising the confidentiality of the research data and, potentially, increasing the vulnerability of both participant and researcher (e.g. Miller et al., 2012). One of the most commonly discussed ethical concerns about online research relates to the blurring of boundaries between the private and public. This has been discussed most frequently in relation to social media sites, which are sometimes accessible to the public and yet used for private discussion (Robards, 2013; Young, 2013). Researchers have debated whether informed consent is required if data are collected from such spaces and, if it is, the form in which it should be secured (e.g. Battles, 2010). This topic is pursued further in Chapter 5.

Such issues have also been raised in relation to other new technologies. Hinton (2013), for example, used mobile telephones to conduct some of the interviews for her doctoral research (on choosing to study in Wales for higher education) on the grounds that she did not have the resources (in terms of time or money) to travel to interview all of her participants. She describes how many of those who agreed to take part in her study chose to conduct the telephone interview in a public space, such as a shared living area, a shopping centre or a bus stop. In some cases, they even involved their friends in the interview, by checking specific facts with them. Hinton argues that this blurring of the distinction between private and public spaces challenges taken-for-granted assumptions about the best ways to protect participant confidentiality and personal data during research. She was concerned that her participants' actions compromised the assurances she had previously given to them about the confidentiality of their data, and also that they may later regret their decision to discuss confidential matters in front of friends and/or strangers. As Hinton contends, we should not see new technologies merely as innovative and more efficient ways to communicate with research participants, but rather as the means through which social interactions may be radically reshaped and ethical challenges reconfigured.

Changes to our ethical sensibilities are, to some extent, influenced by the shifts described in earlier parts of this chapter: for example, as a result of increased regulation, new legislation, and more debate (within professional communities and the public at large) about ethical conduct. A good example of this is provided by O'Connor and Goodwin (2013) in their discussion of their research on young people's transitions from education into employment, which drew on a dataset collected in the 1960s. Over ten years ago, they discovered 850 interview schedules that had been stored in an attic office since they were last used in the mid-1960s. The interviews had focused on the experience of leaving school and entering local employment in Leicester in the UK. In deciding whether or not to use this data, O'Connor and Goodwin grappled with a number of ethical dilemmas, some of which related closely to changing ethical standards in the UK over the past 50 years. They describe one of their dilemmas in the following way:

> the richly detailed interview schedules contained a significant amount of personal biographical information about the respondents and their families ... Having access to such detailed personal biographical data would, on the one hand, allow us to attempt to trace the respondents and explore those within-individual changes that had occurred over the

intervening 40 years. On the other hand, this was clearly personal information that would not have been retained (or at least would have been
anonymized) by current standards of ethical practice in social science
research. (O'Connor and Goodwin, 2013, pp.291–2)

They had access to information which, by contemporary standards,
should not have been available to them. Ultimately, however, they made
the decision to use the data and, indeed, contacted the individuals concerned to ask them if they would be prepared to take part in a follow-up
study. Their actions were, they argue, 'best guess' compromises, based
on what they thought would be good practice given the lack of specific
guidance about data reuse and the other issues they faced. They argue
that, while it was necessary to 'reframe' contemporary codes of conduct
on ethical research, throughout they adhered to an ethical approach that
emphasized respondents' rights to confidentiality and anonymity, and
their right to withdraw from the research.

Variation over place and space

Alongside acknowledging changes to ethical dilemmas and practices
over time, *Ethics and Education Research* pays attention to the ways
in which such dilemmas vary across place and space. In the chapters
that follow, we draw on examples from a number of different countries, and from both the Global North and the Global South. We are
also sensitive to differences between countries and cultures in a number of important domains. In his account of ethical decision making
in social research, Iphofen (2011, p.9) argues that while there is not a
global moral order, 'the globalisation of research professional activities
can aid in the spreading of cross-cultural principles and, possibly,
even the setting of a set of universal ethics within the field of research'.
In subsequent chapters, we draw on examples from across the world
to show how a large number of the issues we discuss (e.g. in relation
to issues of power and positionality) are relevant to many different
national and cultural contexts. Nevertheless, it is also important to
recognize the quite significant differences that remain, which raise
questions about the extent to which establishing a set of 'universal
research ethics' is possible.

First, and as will be discussed in some detail in Chapter 4, significant
national differences are evident in what are seen as legitimate approaches
to research and/or foci of enquiry. Such differences can also change over
time. For example, Rex (2010) has argued that, in the USA over the last

decade, education research that is based on relatively small-scale, qualitative work has become much more difficult to pursue because of the privileging of quantitative research (and particularly RCTs) on the part of the government. This government position can be seen as an ethical issue in so far as such pressures may compromise the independence of the researcher. Moreover, the widely accepted principle of justice (see Chapter 2) requires that the benefits and burdens of research are fairly distributed. This is put at risk when the government, as a major sponsor of research, skews what kinds of research can be pursued. Second, different nations have adopted different means of regulating research, and the national legal frameworks that impinge on research practice differ considerably. For example, Tetteh (2013) describes how, during her research with young people in Ghana, she drew on a British ethical code in the absence of a Ghanaian ethics council and a local REC. Such national differences, and their implications for research practice, are discussed in Chapters 2 and 3. Third, different cultural norms can affect the extent to which particular places are seen as safe and ethical spaces in which to conduct research. For example, many western researchers have questioned how free children and young people are to give their own opinions in schools and colleges, given the hierarchical power relations that often structure such institutions (Heath et al., 2007). In contrast, however, Bochow (2012) has argued that, in Ghana, the young people in her research felt able to speak more freely about certain subjects within schools than at home, because such spaces were seen as not subject to 'the rules of intergenerational respectful speech' (S23-4) that pervaded domestic spaces.

Fourth, and perhaps most importantly, there are significant variations in ethical principles across space and place. As will be discussed in Chapter 8, in many parts of the world it is common practice not to reveal the identity of research participants in reports, presentations and other forms of dissemination – primarily to protect them. However, research with Indigenous communities has shown how such approaches are not universally accepted. Drawing on her work with aboriginal groups in Canada, Ball (2005) argues that it is important that researchers do not assume that their participants would prefer to remain anonymous; in many cases, they prefer to be named and credited for their involvement. This is illustrated well in Wood and Kidman's (2013) account of research with a Maori community in New Zealand (also discussed in Chapter 6). The community believed that the responsibility for protecting participants lay with the community itself, rather than the researchers or the university from which they came, so insisted on geographical locations being specified within research reports (the naming of waterways and mountains constitutes a central part of Maori identity) and participants' faces being included in the visual material produced by the project. Cultural differences can also emerge in relation to the ownership of data. Western norms would assume that researchers have intellectual property rights over the data they collect and analyse. Indigenous groups, however, do not always share this view. For example, in the study discussed above, the community group saw the researchers as merely custodians of the data they had collected, and required them to seek permission to use it on an annual basis. Furthermore, while in some parts of the world it may be seen as good ethical practice to destroy data after a specific period of time, such practices can cause distress to some Indigenous groups (Ball, 2005).

Drawing on examples such as these, some scholars have argued that many of the ethical principles that guide research practice in the Global North are based on western values and are therefore far from universal in their scope. For example, the concept of informed consent (discussed in detail in Chapter 5) is based on the principle that research should respect the autonomy of those being studied, and that potential participants should be able to exercise control over their own lives and decide for themselves whether or not they want to be involved in any specific research project. Hammersley and Traianou (2012b) contend that the notion of autonomy is a western concept, influenced by the tenet of liberal individualism that people know better than anyone else what is in their own interests. This belief, they suggest, is not a universal one; it is not, for example, held by various Indigenous communities, who require researchers to seek permission to conduct data collection from the community as a whole, rather than from individuals. A similar argument is made by Alldred and Gillies (2012), who suggest that a number of research practices are underpinned by the ethics of liberal individualism. These, they argue, can have the effect of eliciting performances of a 'modernist self' from participants and suppressing radical differences. They maintain that

> [t]he legal framework [which underpins social research] is founded on the modern subject – to whom individual rights are accorded and from whom rational, cognitive agency is expected. The paradox is that it would be unethical in current conditions not to assume practices that assume the modernist subject, and yet we can see how the ideas underpinning these practices are not ultimately ethical themselves. (p.146)

By this, they mean that interviewees are frequently expected to perform as a reflexive subject and 'narrate themselves through a confessional, self-conscious account' (p.148). Such expectations help to construct linear, developmental accounts, which are inherently modernist in nature.

In this way, the interviewee is very limited in the ways he or she can present him- or herself and 'modernist selves' tend to be reproduced.

Many of the issues outlined above are pursued in more detail in the chapters that follow. However, we are aware of the limitations of our discussion. Our analysis of the wider literature has been limited to texts written in English and is therefore likely to be skewed towards accounts of research that assume many of the western principles and orientations described above. Second, it is notable that, within the English-language literature on research ethics, there is an uneven geographical spread. As perhaps would be expected, there is much more scholarship in this area from countries that have experienced most 'ethics creep' over recent decades, such as Australia, Canada, the UK and the USA. Despite our commitment to including examples from across the world, this imbalance is also evident in our ensuing discussion.

Structure of the book

As we have explained above, *Ethics and Education Research* is underpinned by the assumption that ethical issues need to be addressed at all stages of a research project. While a number of texts address ethical issues at particular stages in the research process, particularly in relation to data collection, other stages – such as analysing data and disseminating findings – remain relatively neglected. To redress this gap, this book adopts a broadly chronological approach, first discussing ethical principles and the regulatory and legal context within which many education researchers now work. It then goes on to consider critically the range of ethical issues that may arise at all stages of a research project – from formulating the initial design, through data collection and analysis, to disseminating the findings to interested parties. We acknowledge, however, that research is rarely conducted in this straightforward, linear fashion. For example, decisions about research design often have to be made 'in the field', in the midst of data collection, not just at the start of a project, and dissemination may start to take place before the analysis is complete. Our ordering of chapters in this way should thus be seen primarily as a pragmatic means of structuring the issues we want to cover, rather than prescribing any particular way in which research should be conducted. Below, we outline in more detail the structure of the book and the content of the eight chapters that follow.

Chapter 2, Ethical Theories, Principles and Guidelines, draws on relevant philosophical literature to outline the main principles upon which much ethical guidance is based, namely harm prevention, respect, and reciprocity and equity. It gives examples of how these are relevant for education research. It does, however, suggest that the application of such principles is not always straightforward: for example, there is not always consensus about the definition of each of the principles and, in some cases, they can be seen to be in tension with one other. The chapter highlights some of the resources that have been developed to support researchers in their ethical decision making (e.g. professional codes of practice), but also engages with some of the significant critiques that have been made of the role of RECs and ethical guidance.

The work of the education researcher may frequently be affected by particular legislation, regulation and/or guidance, and this is the focus of Chapter 3, Regulatory Contexts. For example, he or she may have an obligation to gain parental consent for research involving school students and to report any instances of abuse that are revealed by research participants. There are also specific legal issues that may affect research with particular types of students (e.g. children who are looked after by the state) and in particular contexts (e.g. prisons and health settings). This chapter will give various examples, from across the world, of the types of regulation that may impinge on those conducting research in education, paying particular attention to differences between nations as well as exploring the international implications of the United Nations Convention of the Rights of the Child.

Chapter 4, Research Design, explores some of the ethical issues that need to be considered at the very start of a research project, when the initial design is being formulated. In particular, we focus on the ethical issues associated with: the choice of research topic; the research methods; the design of research instruments; collaborative research (within a research team and with participants); the location of the research; and data archiving. The chapter focuses explicitly on power relationships in the design stage (e.g. with those who fund research), ahead of the discussion of power in relation to data collection in Chapter 6.

Many of the most pressing ethical dilemmas occur during the data collection phase of a project. These constitute the focus of Chapters 5 and 6. Chapter 5, Informed Consent and Reciprocity, discusses processes of gaining informed consent and the way in which information is provided to potential research participants. The chapter considers who has the capacity to give consent, paying particular attention to the position of young children and those with learning difficulties. It then explores the socially embedded nature of decision making and some of the questions this raises about whether, in schools, colleges and other institutional contexts, consent can ever be perceived as freely given. As part of this discussion, we consider the role of those who may act as 'gatekeepers', such as parents and teachers. The chapter then discusses: the extent to which issues related to informed consent differ by research method; various approaches to informing potential participants about research projects; and the ethical issues associated with attempts to establish reciprocity within research relationships.

The ethics of positionality is the focus of Chapter 6, Identity, Power and Positionality. The chapter critically considers power relationships between researchers and research participants, and debates about the extent to which 'matching' social characteristics is important. It explores the ways in which researchers present themselves during the course of a research project, and how they understand the position of those whom they are researching. The chapter also discusses the ethical issues involved in gaining the trust of respondents, and those which are brought into play when research is conducted with one's own colleagues (e.g. within schools, colleges and universities).

In Chapter 7, Data Analysis, we argue that ethical considerations are important in the analysis of data, not only its collection, and that this applies equally to qualitative and quantitative data. The chapter considers a number of the ethical dilemmas that occur in analysing quantitative data, and examines ethical slippages such as concealment and exaggeration. It then explores some of the ethical challenges of analysing qualitative data, with a particular focus on partisanship in personal ethics and frameworks for analysis. The extent to which participants should and can be involved in analysis is also discussed.

Although the dissemination of research may seem unproblematic from an ethical point of view, Chapter 8, Dissemination, suggests that there are a number of important issues that need to be thought about carefully at this stage. It considers the way in which research participants are presented in both written and oral accounts, and the importance of an ethics of inclusion and respect, in which judgemental languages and deficit categorizations are avoided. The chapter also considers the specific issues that are raised by some particular methods: for example, protecting the identity of participants in visual research. The responsibilities of researchers to sponsors of research and to the wider community, and potential dilemmas around authorship, are of particular relevance at this stage and will be discussed in the chapter.

The final chapter, Chapter 9, Conclusions, draws together themes from the preceding chapters of the book, while also considering some of the gaps, shortcomings and unresolved dilemmas in our work. It then makes a number of recommendations for further developments in what we see as the most important part of doing research: the ethical core that shapes everything else.

Although we have chosen to structure the book in this broadly linear fashion, we have written the chapters so that they are also relatively free-standing. In this way, we hope that researchers will use the book as a resource that they can dip into at any stage of the research process, without feeling that they must read the preceding chapters first. In many ways, this reflects our belief that research itself is rarely a linear process, and that ethical decisions often have to be made throughout the life of a research project, not merely at the beginning.

CHAPTER 2

ETHICAL THEORIES, PRINCIPLES AND GUIDELINES

> Anwar has submitted his research proposal to the Research Ethics Committee (REC) at his UK university. For his PhD, he is planning to conduct an exploration of the educational experiences of children in urban boarding schools for rural children. He wants to interview ten students in three such institutions, in his home country: South Africa. He plans to name the sites, to help inform the public about the quality of education children receive in different institutions. He has a letter granting permission from the local education authority, but his REC suggests he also needs to get written consent from the students' parents. However, Anwar explains to his supervisor that he believes these processes are inappropriate in South Africa. He adds that concerns about what happens in these institutions means the research is vital for the benefit of the children.

This book is underpinned by two broad understandings in relation to research ethics. First, we argue for the situated nature of ethical decision making. For this reason we have attempted to include examples across a range of research methods, educational settings and geographical areas throughout this book. As authors we are located in two countries (the UK and Australia) that are characterized by relatively detailed and demanding research ethics frameworks. We acknowledge, however, that these cannot simply transfer to other countries – such as for Anwar's research. This is something we specifically address towards the end of this chapter. Second, we recognize that decisions regarding research ethics often are difficult, and even frustrating, for education researchers. Our view is that engagement with research ethics is at its foundation an educative process for all stakeholders, including graduate students, experienced researchers, Research Ethics Committee (REC) members, research funders and participants. Our intention is that this book will contribute to this process. We agree with Bridges' explanation that

> one of the main ways in which one learns to work with any rule governed system [...] is by using the language in a community, through conversation. It is only through talking through rules and situations that we become clearer about how these inter-relate, what the principles really mean in practice, what practice which is really informed by the appropriate rule governed behaviour might look and feel like. Working with an ethical code is learning to use a language successfully in real social situations, and that is something we need to do socially in conversational communities, not in isolation. (2009, pp.4–5)

This chapter contributes a brief discussion of major ethical theories, an overview of research ethics codes and principles, and engagement with some of the significant critiques that have been made of the role of university ethics committees and formalized ethical guidance. Together with the overview of relevant regulation in Chapter 3, this discussion provides a foundation of knowledge for the remaining chapters that address various stages of a research project.

Theories of ethics

The question 'What ought I to do?' is of fundamental interest in philosophy. The answer varies considerably depending on the ethical perspective one adopts. Ethical theories were developed for thinking about this question more generally, not specifically for research, let alone education research. For our purposes, three philosophical traditions are of most relevance: utilitarianism, deontology and virtue ethics. The first two have informed research ethics principles and guidelines, as we will show later in this chapter. Virtue ethics has been explicitly discussed by (education) researchers as a useful alternative theory for thinking about research ethics in ways that are less common in formalized codes. Most importantly, we argue that it is valuable for education researchers to have a well-informed personal ethical perspective to support their decision making, since the advice from RECs and national or discipline-based guidelines is unlikely to encompass every ethical dilemma that researchers may encounter. This personal perspective may well be informed by a wider range of theories than the ones we have decided to focus on. Three other perspectives are worth considering briefly. These are rights-based theories, ethics of care, and Foucauldian ethics.

First, rights-based theories suggest that ethical actions are based on people's natural rights, most notably liberty, which cannot be taken away by society, and which apply to everyone – leading to another basic right: equality (Freakley and Burgh, 2000; Wenar, 2011). As in deontology, the consequences of an action are considered less relevant than adherence to these rights (or in deontology, to certain duties; see pp. 23–4). A major proponent of rights-based ethics was the British philosopher John Locke in the 17th century. He suggested that 'natural rights put limits on the legitimate authority of the state' (cited in Wenar, 2011, section 6.1, para.2). Contractual rights, such as civil and human rights, are perceived to flow logically from natural rights. According to Wenar, 'Rights dominate modern understandings of what actions are permissible and which institutions are just' (2011, para.2). An obvious application of rights-based perspectives is in the various United Nations' declarations on human rights. In Chapter 3 we discuss several Articles from the United Nations Convention on the Rights of the Child that are relevant to education research. More generally, the notion of academic freedom (e.g. to pursue certain research topics and to publish findings) is based on rights-based ethics and enshrined in research guidelines (e.g. BERA, 2011).

Second, ethics of care was developed initially as an alternative to male-dominated ethical traditions. An ethics of care is well established in education practice and is based on 'the ontological assumption that the more connected the self is to others, the better the self is' (Tong and Williams, 2011, section 2, para.1). Care is proposed as the central moral virtue, rather than justice. In the 20th century, care ethics was championed by Gilligan (1982) and Noddings (1984) who emphasized the importance of establishing and maintaining positive networks of relationships. In research, members of a network would include not only the participants, but also the researchers themselves, their colleagues, sponsors/funders, and the general public. Noddings (1984) distinguished between the 'one-caring' (care-giver) and the 'cared-for' (care-receiver) and argued the former must act on behalf of the latter. All people within a network of social relations have an obligation to care reciprocally, and care for self is also considered important. Trust, compassion, cooperation, community, consensus and empathy are all central to exercising an ethics of care (Freakley and Burgh, 2000; Tong and Williams, 2011). As a result, ethics is perceived to be not just rational, but also to have an emotional dimension.

Third, Foucault's work has some relevance to research ethics. Ball (2013, p.16) explains that, for Foucault, knowledge was 'always an ethical as well as a political practice'. Foucault's (2000) perception of power as relational, mobile and modifiable thus has implications for research ethics: all parties in a research project hold some power (e.g. not just the researcher but also potential participants; see the case study at the beginning of Chapter 6); and power shifts and changes throughout the process of research (so that ethical decisions need to be made not just at the start but on an ongoing basis). Moreover, power is not just a negative phenomenon, it can also be productive (Foucault, 1980) – for example, it can be exerted by teachers and researchers working together to generate positive outcomes for students. In Foucault's later work his exploration of ancient Greek philosophers led him to consider the idea of 'truthful speaking' as central to ethical practice (Gutting, 2013; Robinson, 2013). For researchers this point is especially relevant for how we publish and disseminate our research findings. Foucault also argued for philosophy as a way of life that required care of the self, and elaborated his view of ethics as 'the intentional work of an individual on itself' developing 'its own moral being' (as explained by Robinson, 2013, para.1). This is not an undemanding instruction to follow one's own rules, rather: 'What one is or might be has to be obtained by hard labour and this labour is never done' (Ball, 2013, p.146).

This section on theories of ethics is necessarily brief: not only do we leave out several ethical theories, but we pay only limited attention to differences within each of the three traditions we focus on below: utilitarianism, deontology, and virtue ethics. Our intention is to provide sufficient material to inform the remainder of the chapter and to enable readers to decide whether they wish to explore any theories further through other literature.

Utilitarianism

At its most basic, utilitarianism (or consequentialism) looks to the 'utility' of the consequences of possible actions to decide which action one ought to take (Chappell, 1998; Freakley and Burgh, 2000; Sinnott-Armstrong, 2012). In other words, 'the justification of a particular action is calculated on the basis of foreseeable consequences' (Freakley and Burgh, 2000, p.121). Using the principle of benefit-maximization, this calculation involves working out the potential positive and negative consequences of each possible action, and then choosing the action that maximizes benefit and minimizes harm. This 'majority rules' approach is familiar in educational practice (e.g. pitching the level of a lecture at the majority of students) and education research (e.g. writing a consent form so the average participant will be able to understand it).

In order to carry out the required calculation, we need to know how to define 'utility'. According to John Stuart Mill (1863, pp.9–10), 'actions are right in proportion as they tend to promote happiness, wrong as they tend to promote the reverse of happiness' (although the question of 'whose happiness counts' is controversial; see below). Other possible definitions of 'utility' are pleasure (based on Jeremy Bentham, see Chappell, 1998) or individual welfare (Sinnott-Armstrong, 2012). A variation in what we mean by 'utility' in turn leads to a different calculation of the benefits and drawbacks of a certain action. For example, decisions about what research to undertake are likely to vary if the utility of education research is tied to learning, or to well-being, or to social justice. For Anwar (see our case study at the beginning of the chapter) utility may lie in children's learning, but for the institutions it may lie in their reputation. Once a definition has been chosen, agreeing on a valid way to measure that utility may also prove difficult. For example, happiness is quite vague and does not give us 'one clear, measurable standard of comparison by which to rank the goodness or badness of all options' (Chappell, 1998, p.317).

A further concern is which stakeholders are considered relevant to the calculation: for example, only those immediately affected and/or the public good? In education research, the potential stakeholders include the participants, the research team, the educational community, and society at large. For example, research that introduces an intervention into a classroom tends to be justified for its potential contribution to the educational community even though the impact on the participants is unknown and hence may include negative consequences. In Chapter 4, we refer to a programme which took school children into prisons with the intention to 'scare' them into becoming law-abiding citizens. Even if this had been effective (it was not; see Chapter 4) would the benefit to society have outweighed the potential emotional trauma inflicted on the children?

Utilitarianism holds a certain, common-sense appeal: if the consequences of an action are good, then surely that means the action is good? At a practical level, issues that need to be resolved include how to define and measure good (utility), which stakeholders to include, whether to adhere different weightings to different stakeholders (including the researcher her/himself) or different potential outcomes, and our ability to foresee all the relevant consequences. At a more fundamental level, we may disagree with the approach that 'the end justifies the means'. This is exactly the perspective of deontology.

Deontology

In deontology, certain acts are seen as intrinsically right or wrong and certain moral obligations as applying irrespective of the consequences (Chappell, 1998; Freakley and Burgh, 2000; Alexander and Moore, 2012). The most influential philosopher in this tradition is Immanuel Kant (1724–1804). Kant contrasted the hypothetical imperative of utilitarianism (if you want to achieve X outcome you must do Y) with his own categorical imperative (you must do Y). In order to ascertain which rules are universalizable as categorical imperatives, Kant proposed to draw on reason through an imagined, purely rational, agent. As explained by Chappell (1998, p.329), Kant assumed 'that there are some things that any rational agent is bound to will just because he is a rational agent'. In order to decide what to do, we need to ask ourselves whether we can 'logically will that what I propose to do should become binding on all other agents in similar situations?' (Freakley and Burgh, 2000, p.115). For example, Anwar (see the case study at the start of this chapter) does not want to obtain consent from the parents of the children in his proposed study. Can he 'logically will' that consent is not required for all similar research? This example highlights the complexity of the condition of universalizability: does 'all similar research' refer to all research that interviews children in any country, or could it be interpreted as applying specifically to such research in a particular country or culture?

In addition to the question of universalizability, a core principle for establishing a rule as a categorical imperative is equal respect for persons. Using others simply to achieve our own ends is not acceptable in deontology, regardless of how desirable those ends may be. Moreover, every person has an equal value, regardless of wealth, health, culture or social status. In deontology all people are entitled to respect and dignity simply because they are considered to be fellow rational beings (Hallgarth, 1998). This principle is summed up through the 'golden rule': we must treat others as we would like others to treat us. For example, in Anwar's case, even if he is concerned that the institutional staff may not be providing a high-quality education, he needs to treat them with respect.

Kant's deontology has been critiqued for over-emphasizing rationality and the freedom of our will to do as reason dictates as well as its inability to reconcile conflicting duties (Chappell, 1998; Hallgarth, 1998; Freakley and Burgh, 2000). As a result, his framework has limited practical application. W.D. Ross (1877–1971) extended the principles of deontology to suggest we have certain prima facie duties (Freakley and Burgh, 2000; Hallgarth, 1998). The prima facie duties Ross proposes are beneficence (doing good), non-maleficence (not directly causing harm) and harm prevention (caused by someone else), justice, self-improvement, fidelity (honesty and keeping promises), gratitude, and reparation (making up for having harmed someone) (Hallgarth, 1998; Small, 2001; Garrett, 2004). For example, a researcher has promised a student that an interview about her or his schooling will be confidential, and the student offers some rather negative appraisals of her or his teacher. Later, the student's teacher asks the researcher if the student is happy in his class. The researcher has prima facie duties to keep promises and to tell the truth (two aspects of fidelity) and to prevent harm. Ross suggested that if we are faced with conflicting prima facie duties then we must perform the more important duty. Instead of Kant's purely rational agent, Ross uses (entirely respectfully) the idea of the 'plain man' whose moral intuition informs him which duty is most important (Hallgarth, 1998; Small, 2001). As Alexander and Moore (2012, part 4, n.p.) point out, 'the prima facie duty view is in some danger of collapsing into a kind of consequentialism' because such intuition and the idea of a hierarchy of duties is inevitably based in part on consequences. Nevertheless, Ross' starting point is to establish what is the 'right' thing to do, not what counts as a 'good' outcome (Hallgarth, 1998; Small, 2001). The overarching governing principle for Ross is that 'an act is morally right (i.e. an actual duty), if and only if it is a prima facie duty, and no other conflicting act represents a more stringent duty' (Hallgarth, 1998, p.621).

Virtue ethics

Both utilitarianism and deontology are action-oriented ethical theories – they are aimed at assessing which action we ought to take. In contrast, virtue ethics is agent-based – rather than asking what we ought to do, it asks what kind of person we ought to be (Chappell, 1998; Freakley and Burgh, 2000; Cua, 2001; Macfarlane, 2009; Hursthouse, 2013). The focus shifts from actions to the character of the person (the 'agent') who not only knows what is the right thing to do, but also actually chooses to pursue this course of action. For Aristotle, virtues include courage, temperance, justice, pride, friendliness and truthfulness (Freakley and Burgh,

2000; Harris, 2001; Macfarlane, 2009). Confucianism has as its basic inter-dependent virtues *jen* (concern for human well-being), *li* (rules of proper conduct) and *yi* (reasoned judgement as to what is right) as well as specific virtues such as loyalty, reciprocity, filiality and courage (Cua, 1992, 2001; Chappell, 1998). In relation to research integrity, Macfarlane (2009) refers to the virtues of courage, respectfulness, resoluteness, sincerity, humility and reflexivity. It is important to note that virtue ethics is contextual rather than absolute. Different virtues are included on lists in different eras and locations and each virtue will be interpreted differently as well. For example, courage may mean something different to Aristotle, Confucius and Macfarlane – and to any of us as education researchers.

Naming specific virtues, therefore, is not the main element of virtue ethics. The central focus is on becoming a more virtuous person who is able to work out what is virtuous in a specific case. This makes virtue ethics somewhat vague, as it is reluctant to define virtue, instead suggesting this is work for each of us to do. Learning is therefore considered central: a virtuous character is cultivated through imitation, practice and education (Freakley and Burgh, 2000). Moreover, what matters is that people strive to be virtuous. Virtue ethicists recognize that 'our capacity to act ethically depends on our upbringing, our education and the opportunities we have to develop our "character"' (Bessant, 2009, p.430) and that 'our moral learning has no terminus' (Cua, 1992, p.61). Aristotle emphasizes the development of phronesis: a practical wisdom based on the deliberative, social and emotional skills we develop as we learn (Bessant, 2009; Freakley and Burgh, 2000). Similarly, for Confucius, in order to be virtuous people must develop *yi*: the individual's capacity to respond to 'ethical perplexities' through both 'reasoned judgment of what is the right or fitting thing to do' and 'the courage to carry it out' (Cua, 2001, p.293; also Cua, 1992). Developing phronesis or *yi* depends on learning from our experiences and from others. Both Aristotle and Confucius point to the importance of having a role model to help us decide what to do: a good person (Kraut, 2012, para 5.2) or chun-tzu (Cua, 1992, 2001). For research students this may be their supervisor, but it may also include other 'critical friends' or 'wise elders' to whom they look up. The vital importance of learning in virtue ethics makes it an ethical perspective that is of particular interest for educators and education researchers.

Research ethics codes and principles

Ethical theories are of interest to education researchers for two main reasons. First, they have informed the formulation of research ethics guidelines. As will become clear in this section, common research ethics principles draw on utilitarianism and deontology in various, at times contradictory, ways. Second, ethical theory can support researchers beyond the scope of research ethics guidelines. We agree with Small that

> there is no substitute for the individual's development of the capacity to make ethical decisions about the design and conduct of his or her project. In the end, it is everyone's responsibility to ensure that educational research is ethical research, and the better prepared we are to address this task, the better our research will be. (2001, p.405)

As we move on to analysing research ethics principles and guidelines, we ask that you keep in mind this additional role of 'moral self-cultivation' (Cua, 1992, p.61). We will return to this later in the chapter, as part of our discussion of critiques of research ethics guidelines and RECs.

Brief overview

As a historical background to the development of research ethics guidelines, it is common to refer to notorious examples of what is considered unethical research. These include Nazi experiments in concentration camps during World War II, the Tuskegee syphilis study, and the obedience research by Milgram (e.g. see Farrimond, 2013; Israel and Hay, 2006; Macfarlane, 2009). Apart from this brief acknowledgement, we will not discuss these examples, partly because they are of little immediate relevance for education research but mainly because they may actually get us off on the wrong foot:

> When only outstanding and scandalous cases are defined as matters for ethical concern, then the daily perplexities, interactions and decisions occurring in the field may well be perceived as merely 'personal'. Ethics then becomes an academic subject, consisting primarily of abstract concepts counterposed by shocking violations. (Cassell, 1980, cited in Burgess, 1989b, p.61)

Rather than portraying research in terms of the risk of major ethical misconduct, our argument is that ethical dilemmas are as common in research as they are in life, and require careful consideration and professional judgement rather than 'policing'. As Small (2001, p.389) puts it, 'the task [is] one of education rather than enforcement'.

The Belmont Report (DHEW, 1979) is widely recognized as providing the first formalized guidelines for research involving people as participants (or as the report put is, as 'subjects'). It continues to be the primary human research ethical framework in the USA and has had widespread international influence through its articulation of specific ethics principles and the establishment of institutional review boards (IRBs, or as we call them in this book: Research Ethics Committees, or RECs) charged with implementing research ethics guidelines. The Belmont Report focused on biomedical and behavioural research, and this scope has been reflected in some countries (e.g. in continental Europe; see OHRP, 2012) where national formal regulation of research ethics through RECs is mostly limited to health-related research. However, in the USA as well as several other English-speaking countries, the principles and procedures that flowed from the Belmont Report are also applied in guidelines for the social sciences, including education research. The Belmont Report outlined three ethical principles (respect for persons, beneficence and justice) as well as three applications (informed consent, assessment of risk and benefits, and selection of subjects). This distinction between foundational principles and practical implications is also reflected in some subsequently developed research ethics guidelines (e.g. in Canada: CIHR, NSERC and SSHRC, 2010; and in Australia: NHMRC, ARC and AVCC, 2007). The applications of principles will be taken up in Chapters 4 to 8 of this book. Here we focus on the ethical principles themselves.

The approach taken in research ethics guidelines following the Belmont Report is referred to variously as 'principlism', 'principalism' or 'principled ethics' (Halse, 2011; Macfarlane, 2009; Small, 2001). The assumption is that it is possible to start with universal moral principles which, through deductive logical reasoning, leads to specific decisions (critiques of this are examined in the final section of this chapter). This privileging of abstract principles seems to draw on deontology and is made visible through the positioning of principles at the start of the Belmont Report and other guidelines. It is interesting to note that the committee developing the Belmont Report actually began with consideration of concrete cases, and that the articulation of the basic principles was conducted afterwards. As Small argues:

> the presentation of The Belmont Report lends itself to misunderstanding. By beginning with the basic principles of beneficence, non-maleficence, justice and respect for persons, it suggests that its approach is a 'Euclidean' strategy of starting with definitions, postulates and axioms, and proceeding to derive theorems from those. Instead, the general principles appear to have been abstracted from the collection of particular judgements contained in the report's detailed recommendations. (2001, pp.401–402)

Whether intended by the Belmont Report committee or not, a principalist approach to research ethics is now widespread. Next, we turn to consider these principles in some more detail.

Principles

The Belmont Report stipulated three basic principles for ethical research: respect for persons, beneficence (and non-maleficence) and justice. The first of these is clearly reminiscent of Kant's deontology, both in his insistence that people may not simply be used as a means to an end and in his conceptualization of people as rational, autonomous agents. In the Belmont Report, respect for persons has two elements: 'the requirement to acknowledge autonomy and the requirement to protect those with diminished autonomy' (DHEW, 1979, part B.1). Acknowledging autonomy means that research participants should be enabled to make up their own mind about taking part, for example by providing sufficient information about the project. Providing protection applies to research participants who are considered vulnerable because they are perceived as not being fully autonomous, such as children (this premise has been contested: see Chapters 3 and 5). The Belmont Report advises that 'The judgment that any individual lacks autonomy should be periodically reevaluated and will vary in different situations' (DHEW, 1979, part B.1). In education research it is common to rely on the decision of someone else who is considered to have full autonomy, such as a parent or guardian, in order to adhere to this principle. This can be seen as a practical solution, but it is not necessarily always ethical, especially if applied to all children of a certain age regardless of the specific project and the child's maturity (te Riele and Brooks, 2012; Farrimond, 2013). For example, Anwar (in our case study at the start of the chapter) may argue that the rural children attending the boarding schools where he plans to conduct his research are better placed to consent (or dissent; see Chapter 5) to participation than their parents.

Beneficence and non-maleficence refer to, respectively, actively doing good and avoiding (the risk of) harm. These are both prima facie duties in W.D. Ross' deontology and therefore according to his theory both are required unless they are in conflict (see p. 24). Commonly, however, they are treated in a more utilitarian sense of balancing the potential benefits and risks of participating. The Belmont Report expresses it thus: 'investigators and members of their institutions are obliged to give forethought to the maximization of benefits and the reduction of risk that might occur from the research investigation' (DHEW, 1979, part B.2). Benefits may apply directly to participants, to the group or community represented by the participants (e.g. early childhood teachers, or students on a particular course at a specific institution), or at its most general to the public good. Harm may be physical, psychological or social, and assessment of the risk of harm includes both its likelihood and its severity. In education research, neither the benefits nor the risks of harm may be as dramatic as in some medical research which may lead to lives being saved or lost. In our introductory case study, Anwar's research may have the benefit of leading to an improved quality of education for children in his research sites as well as in other similar institutions. However, the children he interviews may be penalized by institution staff if they are (wrongly or rightly) seen to have voiced critical comments, institution staff may lose their jobs, and institutions may have their reputation damaged and perhaps even be closed down. RECs tend to scrutinize closely the balance of benefits and harm, and advise researchers on ways to minimize harm, for example through the practical application of confidentiality of participants (see also Chapters 6 and 8).

Finally, in Ross's deontology, justice refers to a fair distribution among people of burdens and benefits (Garrett, 2004). This is closely reflected in the Belmont Report's discussion of the principle of justice, which is applied especially to the selection of research participants. The Belmont Report recognized that what is considered a fair distribution may vary: for example, if based on the formula 'to each person an equal share', 'to each person according to individual need' or 'to each person according to merit' (DHEW, 1979, part B.3). As a result, disagreement about inclusion and exclusion criteria for research participation are common. Considering Anwar's proposed research again, should he randomly select both his research sites and interviewees within them (to each an equal share), select children in sites where the quality of education is known to be low (to each according to need) or where the quality of education is known to be high (to each according to merit)? As a general rule, the Belmont Report points out that it is unjust (and therefore unethical) to select systematically some groups of people for research 'simply because of their easy availability, their compromised position, or their manipulability, rather than for reasons directly related to the problem being studied' (DHEW, 1979, part B.3). At worst such (unjust) selection may involve exploitation of vulnerable people. More commonly, it is to do with convenience. The latter is apparent, for example, when young people are sourced for research participation through schools although the research topic has nothing to do with education. Insider research may also be considered controversial in relation to this principle of justice (see also Chapter 6).

With some modifications, these principles have informed the development of guidelines for researchers across disciplines and countries. Ethical research codes are especially strong in the English-speaking world, including the USA, Canada, the UK, Australia and New Zealand. Table 2.1 demonstrates the continuing resonance of the Belmont Report principles as well as ways in which they have been adapted and augmented. The table is not intended to be comprehensive, but rather offers an overview from a variety of international and disciplinary contexts of relevance for education researchers.

The stated principles in some of these documents (e.g. ESRC, 2012) are more like the Belmont Report's applications rather than what it refers to as principles. The role of legislation (see RESPECT Project, 2004 in Table 2.1) will be addressed in Chapter 3. The main additional principle of

Table 2.1 Principles in selected ethical research guidelines

Source	Principles
The Belmont Report (DHEW, 1979)	Respect for persons Beneficence and non-maleficence Justice
Australia (NHMRC, ARC and AVCC, 2007, p.11)	Research merit and integrity Justice Beneficence Respect
Canada (CIHR, NSERC and SSHRC, 2010, p.8)	Respect for persons Concern for welfare Justice
Europe (ESF and ALLEA, 2011, p.5)	Honesty Reliability Objectivity Independence and impartiality Duty of care Fairness Responsibility for future generations
Europe (RESPECT Project, 2004)	Upholding scientific standards Compliance with the law Avoidance of social and personal harm
International: World Conference on Research Integrity (Singapore Statement, 2010)	Honesty in all aspects of research Accountability in the conduct of research Professional courtesy and fairness in working with others Good stewardship of research on behalf of others

Source	Principles
UK (ESRC, 2012, pp.2–3)	Integrity, quality and transparency Full information Confidentiality of information and anonymity of respondents Voluntary participation Avoidance of harm to research participants and researchers Independence of the research
UK (BERA, 2011, p.4)	An ethic of respect for: The person Knowledge Democratic values The quality of educational research Academic freedom
USA (AERA, 2011, pp.146–7)	Principle A: Professional competence Principle B: Integrity Principle C: Professional, scientific, and scholarly responsibility Principle D: Respect for people's rights, dignity, and diversity Principle E: Social responsibility

Note: Table constructed by Kitty te Riele from the specified sources

interest in this chapter is to do with the quality of the research, mentioned in several codes and explicitly addressed in the American Educational Research Association's *Code of Ethics* (AERA, 2011, pp.146) and the Australian *National Statement on Ethical Conduct in Human Research* (NHMRC, ARC and AVCC, 2007, p.11). The following excerpts explain this principle:

> Education researchers strive to maintain the highest levels of competence in their work; they recognize the limitations of their expertise; and they undertake only those tasks for which they are qualified by education, training, or experience. [...] They consult with other professionals when necessary for the benefit of their students, research participants, and clients. (AERA, 2011, p.146)

Research that has merit is:

(a) justifiable by its potential benefit [...];

(b) designed or developed using methods appropriate for achieving the aims of the proposal;

(c) based on a thorough study of the current literature, as well as previous studies. [...];

(d) designed to ensure that respect for the participants is not compromised by the aims of the research, by the way it is carried out, or by the results;

(e) conducted or supervised by persons or teams with experience, qualifications and competence that are appropriate for the research; and

(f) conducted using facilities and resources appropriate for the research.

(NHMRC, ARC and AVCC, 2007, p.11)

This principle of research quality or merit explains why RECs may apply particular scrutiny to applications by new researchers, including research students. REC attention to research quality is quite controversial because critics argue that REC members lack the necessary expertise to judge research quality for proposed projects outside their own discipline or research paradigm (see later in this chapter).

BERA guidelines

Research ethics codes and guidelines vary in their origin and scope. At one end of the spectrum, guidelines may apply to all research across all disciplines. This is the case in Australia, where the National Health and Medical Research Council has responsibility for the guidelines as well as for overseeing the official registration of the RECs who implement those guidelines. Although the Australian Association for Research in Education does have its own research ethics guidelines, these have far less authority and have not been updated substantially since 1993 (see AARE, 1993). In contrast, in the UK, national guidelines are characterized by relatively technical protocols and requirements (e.g. the *Framework for Research Ethics*, ESRC, 2012) or by aspirational statements and commitments (e.g. the *Concordat to Support Research Integrity*, UUK, 2012). Professional associations contribute significantly to informing national discussion and documents as well as to the work of institutional RECs, and produce their own guidelines. Such bodies include, for example, the British Sociological Association (BSA, 2002), the Social Research Association (2003) and the British Educational Research Association (BERA, 2011). Since this book is published through the book series developed between SAGE and the British Educational Research Association (BERA), we will examine BERA documentation further here. Not all countries have such detailed guidelines and the implementation of codes varies not only between countries but also between institutions within countries, and between disciplines within institutions. The applicability of ethics guidelines to different national and cultural contexts is one of the issues we will take up in the final section of this chapter.

The key source for the British Educational Research Association is *Ethical Guidelines for Educational Research* (BERA, 2011). In addition, BERA has published several online resources, the most relevant of which is *Ethics and Educational Research* (Hammersley and Traianou, 2012a). It is worthwhile regularly checking the BERA website, as documents are updated or added. Before exploring these two documents, it is important to note that official procedures for applying for ethical review and approval (also referred to as 'favourable ethical opinion') to carry out research are channelled through RECs at universities and research institutions in the UK, not through BERA. Each REC has its own specific forms and processes, informed by relevant legislation (see Chapter 3) as well as by national guidelines (ESRC, 2012; UUK, 2012; RCUK, 2013). Discipline-specific organizations such as BERA play a central role in informing such national documents as well as informing the practice of education researchers. For example, the ESRC framework includes the BERA guidelines as one of its 'useful links to professional associations' (ESRC, 2012, p.43). Highlighting the role of professional guidelines, Ransome (2013, p.50) gives the example of his own university which 'simply refers social researchers back to the codes issued by the appropriate professional bodies'.

The current (2011) BERA guidelines have evolved from the first draft developed in 1992 through reviews in 2002–2004 and again in 2008–2010. It is a living document, subject to debate among BERA members and Council (BERA, 2011, p.11). The most recent revision was developed by a working party chaired by Professor David Bridges. The review had a specific focus on potential tensions between contract research (i.e. research commissioned and funded by an interested party) and BERA's ethical principles of democratic values and academic freedom (see Table 2.1). Neither of those principles is elaborated – they are simply listed in both the previous and current versions of the guidelines. The working group noted that in the contemporaneous version of the ethical guidelines 'the principle of democratic values seems to disappear as soon as they have been declared' (BERA Working Group, 2009, p.2). As a result of the deliberations by this working party, the 2011 BERA guidelines include an additional section, the fourth one in this list:

1. Responsibilities to Participants
2. Responsibilities to Sponsors of Research
3. Responsibilities to the Community of Educational Researchers
4. Responsibilities to Educational Professionals, Policy Makers and the General Public

The first section addresses the most familiar ethical issues, such as voluntary informed consent, potential detriments from research participation, and privacy. The second section outlines both duties and rights of researchers, for example in relation to written agreements, methods and publication. The third section attends to misconduct and authorship. The fourth, new, section delineates the responsibility of researchers to communicating results from their research for the benefit of wider audiences. In addition to the guidelines, BERA has published an online resource to support education researchers to make ethical decisions in the course of their research (Hammersley and Traianou, 2012a). This is based on principles reminiscent of the Belmont Report: minimizing harm, respecting autonomy, protecting privacy, offering reciprocity and treating people equitably. The resource addresses complexities in relation to the principles and their application, especially through 'informed consent'. We agree with the argument by Hammersley and Traianou that such complexities require the researchers to make his or her own, well-informed and situated judgements. The resource also includes detailed appendices providing overviews of literature on ethics in education research, on philosophical perspectives on ethics, and on ethical regulation. It thus serves as a useful complement to the official BERA guidelines.

At a general level there is broad agreement among social researchers regarding principles that underpin ethical research conduct. The details of how these are explained and applied within research ethics guidelines, however, vary considerably. This may be a matter of emphasis, interpretation or requirements. In relation to the latter, while countries such as the USA, Canada, the UK, Australia and New Zealand require formal applications for ethics approval of education research through RECs, in other countries (such as in continental Europe) education researchers are expected and trusted to implement such principles themselves. Critique of research ethics procedures and committees, as discussed in the next section, stems mainly from researchers in the former list of countries, and also from researchers in non-western countries required to adhere to the same (culturally bound) procedures.

Critiques of research ethics guidelines and committees

As pointed out by Schrag (2011), social researchers started airing complaints about research ethics regulations almost as soon as these began to be implemented for research in the social sciences and humanities in the 1960s. Enforcement of such regulations for social research became much more stringent in the 1990s and 2000s, however, and the literature that critically discusses research ethics regulation has corre-spondingly expanded during the past two decades. Philosophical objections focus on contradictions between the utilitarian and deonto-logical origins of research ethics codes, as well as on the inappropriate use of concepts from those theoretical traditions (Small, 2001; Macfarlane, 2009). At a more practical general level, critiques of research ethics guidelines and institutional RECs tend to be based on the premise that since codes and committees were established within the context of health and medical research, they do not suit the disciplinary context of education and other social science research (e.g. Schrag, 2011; Dingwall, 2012). Within the field of education, some go further and argue that RECs cannot adequately judge education-based projects if their members come from other disciplines (Scott and Fonseca, 2010). We disagree, and consider such rejections too easily dismissive of colleagues' expertise.

A closer analysis of the extensive literature that critically examines formal research ethics products and processes (in education research and in the social sciences more generally) leads us to identify three major areas of concern: restrictiveness; undermining professional reflec-tion; and lack of cultural relevance. We will discuss these in turn below. Commonly, critiques focus on the application of ethical guidelines by RECs, although some critiques also propose flaws in guidelines them-selves. We also note that literature advocating on behalf of research eth-ics processes is less common than critiques. As Sikes and Piper explain in the editorial to their special issue for the *International Journal of Research and Method in Education*:

> Our aim is to re-present and reflect educational researchers' lived experi-ences of ethical review committees and procedures. [...] Perhaps inevita-bly, given both the wording of the call and the propensity of people to feel moved to complain about bad experiences rather than to praise good ones, the majority of responses concerned troubles, disagreements, barri-ers and prohibitions. (2010, pp.205–206)

Restrictiveness

For the category of concerns regarding 'restrictiveness' we consider, first, the focus of formal ethics review. RECs are charged by some critics with being more concerned with protecting the university than with protecting participants or researchers (Scott and Fonseca, 2010; Sikes and Piper, 2010; Dingwall, 2012). Halse (2011, p.250), an education scholar reflecting on her experiences as a REC chair, acknowledges that

RECs have 'responsibilities to an institution as well as to researchers and research subjects, and the interests of these different groups do not always comfortably align'. In the context of legislation (such as privacy, data protection, freedom of information and mandatory reporting; see Chapter 3) and litigation it may be understandable that university senior executives perceive REC processes as part of a suite of risk management strategies. We argue that while this may form one function of research ethics review, it has a lower priority than ethical commitments to participants, researchers and the general public.

Second, our category of 'restrictiveness' includes critique of the ways in which the key aspects of risk and harm as well as informed consent are interpreted through RECs. Some scholars argue that there is little evidence of major, or even minor, harm to participants (Scott and Fonseca, 2010; Schrag, 2011; Dingwall, 2012; Hammersley and Traianou, 2012a). We suggest that this may in part be due to a lack of public reporting, rather than reflecting the actual absence of harm occurring due to education research. More serious are charges that the focus by RECs on minimizing even minor harm and on the protection of 'vulnerable' populations may reduce the usefulness of research (Hammersley and Traianou, 2012a) and deny certain groups a voice (Scott and Fonseca, 2010). On the other hand, O'Neill (2010) explains that sometimes the REC simply wants to see more evidence that potential risks of harm have been considered by the researcher, rather than intending to veto certain aspects of a research project. There is a shared responsibility, we argue, by RECs for more clearly communicating this desire and by researchers for helping RECs to understand their proposed research. In relation to consent, the main critique is of the use of consent forms. The listing of all possible (however unlikely) risks on such forms or their accompanying information statements as well as the requirement to sign the consent form may be unnecessarily off-putting or worrisome to some participants, especially in certain cultures (Bridges, 2009; Sikes and Piper, 2010; see also later in this chapter). The use of consent forms can also lull a researcher into believing they have fully informed the participants, even though this is impossible within a short form provided in advance; and even though in practice many participants may not fully read or understand the information on the form (Hammersley and Traianou, 2012a). We take this up in more detail in Chapter 5, arguing that consent may be provided in various modes (not just written) and that it is better perceived as a process rather than a one-off, up-front product.

Third, 'restrictiveness' refers to the gatekeeping role of RECs, restricting certain research (in terms of participants, topics or methods) from being conducted. Dingwall is particularly vocal about the risk of growing and systematic ignorance about population groups whose circumstances may be precisely those about which we should [...] least want to be ignorant or who most need to have their voice articulated by reasonably disinterested advocates. [... and] the promotion of ignorance about important social issues, or the abandonment of investigations to people outside the academy whose particular motives and voices will go unquestioned and unchallenged by the disciplined evidence-gathering of the social sciences. (2012, pp.18–22)

None of Dingwall's examples relate to education research, but Scott and Fonseca (2010) claim that research with school children is constrained by RECs that do not always understand the context of schooling. If such situations occur, we argue that they afford a role for researchers to assist the understanding of REC members. For example, researchers may help RECs to understand the implications of Article 12 in the United Nations Convention on the Rights of the Child (UNCRC), which highlights children's right to participation (see Chapter 3).

In relation to methods, RECs are commonly charged with not understanding – and therefore preventing or unreasonably modifying – the use of qualitative research methods, especially ethnography, action research, participatory research and visual research (Scott and Fonseca, 2010; Sikes and Piper, 2010; Schrag, 2011). Such methodological gatekeeping is likely to depend on the specific practices of a particular REC, shaped by the distinctive research strengths of the institution, and may not be as common as some critics imply. Sikes and Piper (2010, p.211) acknowledge that, despite their concerns about the regulatory emphasis of RECs, they 'suspect that the vast majority of applications for ethics review are passed with no or very minor amendments'. O'Neill (2010) provides evidence from the REC at his university in New Zealand indicating that in the period 2003–2008, between 83–91 per cent of applications were given immediate or provisional approval, with the latter requiring only minor revisions. Moreover, most of the 'deferred' applications (requiring major revisions) benefited from the REC feedback and were subsequently approved. He argues that

in contrast to the apparently wide-spread view that increasingly bureaucratized institutional ethics committees hold all the power and voice, my experience is that committee members and, especially, committee chairs are acutely aware that their knowledge of the ethics of doing research in particular disciplines, settings and contexts is almost always partial and provisional. They also appreciate that in order to maintain committee credibility, their decisions must secure the broad endorsement of the research communities in which they function. For the most part, discussions take place between the committees and individual researchers or, occasionally, particular research groups, rather than the University academic community as a whole. Nevertheless, these understandings have encouraged a view among the committee chairs of ethical review as, ideally, a supportive, dialogical and educative process. (O'Neill, 2010, p.231)

It is unfortunate if the procedures used by RECs and/or the perceptions of researchers lead to a 'them versus us' approach, rather than such an educative process within a collegial community.

Undermining professional reflection

Our next category focuses on critique that research ethics review processes undermine professional reflection on ethical issues by researchers. At their most strident, such critiques assert that strict ethical guidelines and their implementation by RECs are evidence of a lack of trust in researchers (Schrag, 2011; Dingwall, 2012). Without going that far, we concur with the argument made by Hammersley and Traianou (2012a, p.7) that 'the situated nature of practical decision making within research makes clear that sound judgments about what it is best to do cannot be made simply by following instructions or applying rules'. If researchers are to be responsible for such ongoing decisions then 'they must be free to make them' (Hammersley and Traianou, 2012a, p.7) – and to be given this freedom we must be responsible. BERA's principle of respect for academic freedom is also relevant in these debates.

This leads to the second, more vital, concern in this category: that research ethics review protocols may prevent ongoing ethical reflection by researchers once the project has been approved. Obtaining 'ethics approval' may be perceived as the end-point of ethical consideration for a research project, rather than merely one step in an ongoing process. Halse (2011, p.249) quotes Derrida (1995) to warn that relying on principles and rules through a research ethics framework 'manages to irresponsibilize our decisions and our singular responsibility for them'. As we argued in Chapter 1, ethical considerations do not cease to be relevant once 'ethics approval' has been gained but, instead, ongoing ethical reflexivity is required throughout the process of research. In other words, ethical considerations arguably are even more relevant during the practice of research.

A constructive proposal for encouraging ongoing professional ethical reflection comes from several education scholars who draw on a virtue ethics approach to supplement research ethics codes and RECs (Pring, 2001; Bridges, 2009; Macfarlane, 2009). Rather than suggesting that social researchers simply ought to be trusted (as Schrag, 2011, and Dingwall, 2012, seem to do), this approach encourages explicit efforts to cultivate virtue so that ethical principles become internalized and researchers are empowered to negotiate ethical dilemmas as they occur. As Bridges argues,

> such virtue may render the codes redundant, but the codes will never dispense with the need for their virtuous interpretation and application. [...] I do not want to say that codes have no function, but they need to be employed by people who have, independently of the code, a deeply embedded sense of and commitment to the moral and intellectual values which underpin academic work. (2009, pp.6–7)

Moreover, such 'virtue cultivation' would apply not only to (postgraduate) researchers but also to their colleagues who serve as the members of RECs. This aligns with our view that ethical codes and the work of RECs are resources that can enable research to be more ethical, both by preventing some ethical concerns from occurring and by supporting researchers to deal with unexpected ethical challenges throughout the research process.

Lack of cultural relevance

Our final category of critique addresses arguments that research ethics protocols lack cultural relevance beyond the Anglo-American (and going back further, Hellenic) world from which they stem. It has been argued that RECs and researchers from 'western' countries may fail to recognize the value-ladenness of their principles and procedures (Viete, 2004; Bridges, 2009; Halse, 2011; Hammersley and Traianou, 2012a). A common obstacle identified in terms of cultural inappropriateness is the use of written consent forms based on 'western' assumptions (Harold, 2004; Viete, 2004; Bridges, 2009). Bridges offers an example based on his supervision of a group of Ethiopian postgraduate researchers:

> They understood that they had to treat research participants with respect and to honour their wishes with respect to the research, but the idea of approaching them (some of them in any case illiterate) with forms or documents was laughable if it were not also offensive. 'They will think we are trying to acquire their land' said one 'or that we are government tax officials!' suggested another. (2009, p.5)

In contrast to these postgraduate students, Hamid (2010) – a Bangladeshi academic conducting his PhD research in Bangladesh but enrolled through an Australian university – had an almost opposite experience. His research explored the experiences of English-language education in a disadvantaged community in northern Bangladesh, requiring permission from national education authorities as well as participants. He explains that in Bangladesh, official documentation is expected to be decidedly formal and verbose. However, the Australian REC advised him that:

> A few of the committee members feel that the consent and information sheets are overly wordy and not necessarily socio-culturally appropriate. The committee requests that you consider more user-friendly and simple language for your information packet. It is important to create documents that can be genuinely read, understood, and signed. At present some members feel the wording is too dense. (REC report cited in Hamid, 2010, p.263).

Hamid (2010, p.264) notes the irony that 'documents prepared by a local researcher for local use were judged "socio-culturally inappropriate" by a non-local IRB [REC] who had little knowledge of the society or the culture in question'. The contrast between Bridges' example and Hamid's experience highlights that 'western' RECs must be careful not to jump to conclusions about what is a suitable way of obtaining consent in 'non-western' countries. For Anwar (in our case study at the start of the chapter), this means having a conversation with the chair of his university REC as well as with research experts in South Africa. The Australian guidelines recognize that written consent is not always appropriate, stating that:

> Consent may be expressed orally, in writing or by some other means (for example, return of a survey, or conduct implying consent), depending on: (a) the nature, complexity and level of risk of the research; and (b) the participant's personal and cultural circumstances. (NHMRC, ARC and AVCC, 2007, p.19)

The REC perception of participation in research as an imposition may contrast with a local perception of research participation as a valuable opportunity and even as an honour (Hamid, 2010). For pilot testing of his instruments, Hamid selected only a small sample of school students, which was perceived as a breach of the principle of justice by their peers:

[A] few students who were not selected asked me why I had deprived them of the opportunity to participate. My explanations of the purpose of the pilot test did not prove convincing, and their understanding was that they had been denied an experience that their friends alone would be able to relate to family and other locals. (2010, p.265)

A further cultural issue that is raised by critics is the difference between individualist Anglo-American and communitarian non-western orientations. In their resource for BERA, Hammersley and Traianou (2012a, p.10) point out that in relation to consent the opinion of 'the head of a kin group or a community leader' may have greater weight than individual autonomy to consent to participate (see also Suaalii and Mavoa, 2001). Viete (2004, p.10) notes that in some societies the high status and authority of teachers to make decisions relating to students means that 'the notion of parental consent serves only to prompt suspicion about the "sinister" nature of the research that should require such an unusual measure'. A similar argument may well apply to Anwar's situation.

In addition, the gender of researchers and participants may require additional measures in 'non-western' countries compared to the expectation of 'western' RECs. For example, as a male researcher, Hamid (2010) had to invite a parent or sibling to be present when he interviewed female students: cultural appropriateness outweighing considerations of confidentiality. Harold (2004) recounts her experience of working with two local female graduate research assistants (GRAs) in the Middle East, who needed permission from their parents or husband to work on the project. In addition, 'My unmarried GRA was not comfortable with interviewing male teachers and in those cases we paired her with me or my female colleague' (p.6).

Concerns about the relevance of 'western' ethical codes and procedures are not limited to (western and non-western) researchers working in 'non-western' contexts. Indigenous researchers have also raised alarm bells. Māori (New Zealand Indigenous) scholar Tuhiwai Smith (1999) offers a powerful critique of the imposition of western research methods on Indigenous peoples. The wariness of research among Indigenous communities, based on a historical imbalance between bearing the burdens of research participation versus receiving its benefits, is now widely acknowledged in countries such as New Zealand, Australia and Canada, and each has guidelines specifically for conducting research in Indigenous communities (NHMRC, 2003; CIHR, NSERC and SSHRC, 2010; Pūtaiora Writing Group, 2010; AIATSIS, 2012). For example, the guidelines by the Australian Institute of Aboriginal and Torres Strait Islander

Studies present 14 principles that highlight Indigenous people's 'rights to full and fair participation in any processes, projects and activities that impact on them, and the right to control and maintain their culture and heritage' (AIATSIS, 2012, p.1). In addition, a guide by the National Health and Medical Research Council (NHMRC, 2003) is widely used in Australia beyond health research for its articulation of the values of reciprocity, respect, equality, responsibility, survival and protection, and spirit and integrity. Australian university RECs now require researchers to adhere to the values and principles outlined in documents such as the AIATSIS and NHMRC guidelines. Indigenous people themselves are also more aware of their rights:

> We know you university people have to go through your own ethics, but we have to go through our own process too before the project goes ahead you know, we have to go talk to community and the elders first, make sure the community and the elders approve of this project first, otherwise we can't start anything. (Indigenous community organization representative, cited in Minniecon et al., 2007, p.25).

Such a process of researchers being hosted into a community is relevant for research in non-Indigenous settings as well.

Conclusion

In this chapter we have provided an overview of ethical theories, discussed research ethics principles and guidelines, and examined critiques of such guidelines and their implementation by RECs. In relation to the latter, at their most serious, such critiques raise the concern that ethical guidelines and RECs may make research less, rather than more, ethical. Our view is that (alongside ethical theories) formal guidelines and RECs serve a valuable function to assist research integrity, but that care is required to ensure that they meet this purpose and to ward off the concerns discussed in this chapter. Halse (2011, p.246) queries 'the conditions of possibility for becoming/being an ethical researcher in the academy' and argues that rather than blaming postgraduate students or RECs, this points to 'the imperative for a broader moral concept of responsibility in the relationship between student/supervisor/university'.

Returning to our point at the start of this chapter, we suggest that an educational approach is necessary to support mutual learning. Many universities offer workshops on research ethics and integrity, however, the ubiquity of REC forms and processes (at least across the USA, Canada, the UK, Australia and New Zealand) means that these may focus more on practical advice (how to complete the form) than on critical reflection regarding ethical challenges in research. Rather than rejecting the forms and processes, Bridges (2009, p.4) argues that what is needed is some type of 'community of practice' in which postgraduate research students and early career researchers can share and discuss their experiences because 'the principles themselves will always need to be applied intelligently or wisely in the light of particular features of a situation'. This would be of assistance not only to a postgraduate researcher such as Anwar (see our case study at the start of the chapter) but also to his supervisor, as well as to REC members, funding bodies, government agencies and research participants.

Another set of resources to discuss through such a community of practice and to inform education research is provided by international and national regulations and legislation. These are examined in the next chapter.

CHAPTER 3

REGULATORY CONTEXTS

Following an encounter with an ex-prisoner in his undergraduate Sociology of Education class, Gustav decides to embark on a new research direction to explore the educational opportunities provided within juvenile justice facilities. Gustav has previously conducted research on the educational experiences of young refugees and on students' sexualities. He wants his research to empower and give voice to marginalized groups. For this new project he needs approval not only from his university ethics committee but also from the prison service. The former is concerned about participants disclosing illegal activities and the possibility of Gustav and his data being subject to a court subpoena. The latter wishes to control exactly who he can include in his research before granting access. Is this project just too hard to do?

In Chapter 2 we outlined some of the guidelines for (educational) research and the work of Research Ethics Committees (RECs) in implementing such guidelines. In addition to such regulations specifically aimed at research, the ethical work of the education researcher may be affected by international and national legislation and policies. In this chapter we begin by exploring the implications of the United Nations Convention on the Rights of the Child, as this is a framework that affects education research across most countries. In terms of national (or even state, province, regional or municipal) legislation and policies there are substantial differences, especially in terms of specific requirements that impact on researchers. Our approach for this chapter, therefore, is to discuss two broad types of relevant regulations (which may or may not be formalized in law) with examples from various countries as illustration. First, there are regulations that have a gatekeeping role: stipulating procedures for researchers gaining access to certain institutions and participants. Second, some regulations are related to the principle of confidentiality, such as legislation to do with privacy, mandated reporting of suspected child abuse, compelled disclosure through subpoenas and freedom of information requests, and data sharing.

The United Nations Convention on the Rights of the Child

A rights-based approach to ethics (see Chapter 2) is reflected in various international human rights conventions. For education researchers across the globe, the United Nations Convention on the Rights of the Child (UNCRC), which was initially adopted in 1989, is of particular relevance as it enjoys near-universal ratification. The UNCRC (UN, 1990) sets standards for nations in relation to education as well as health care and legal, civil and social services (UNICEF, 2013). The status of the UNCRC as a legally binding international human rights instrument combined with its widespread visibility and recognition make the UNCRC a fundamental document for education research involving children. Its rights-based nature directs our attention to the rights, well-being and human dignity of children, whether as participants in or intended beneficiaries of education research. The 54 Articles (UNICEF, 2013) address:

- *The guiding principles*: non-discrimination, the best interest of the child, basic rights to life, survival and development, and respect for children's own views (Articles 1, 2, 3, 6 and 12). These are then further explicated through the next three sets.
- *Survival and development rights*: life, survival and development of one's full potential (Articles 4–10, 14, 18, 20, 22–31, 42)
- *Protection rights*: keeping safe from harm (Articles 4, 11, 19–22, 32–41)

- *Participation rights*: having an active voice (Articles 4, 12–17)
- *Implementation by governments and international organizations* (Articles 43–54).

All of these may be of interest to education researchers depending on the specific project topic, aims and participants. Articles 28 and 29 outline the right to education and goals of education. These may be used merely as context, or more specifically (for example) to suggest specific topics worthy of research such as 28 1(e) 'measures to encourage regular attendance at schools and the reduction of drop-out rates' or 29 1(d) 'the development of respect for the natural environment' (UN, 1990, p.8 and 9). Of specific relevance for education researchers are Articles 3, 12, 36 and 42. The UN Committee on the Rights of the Child emphasizes that the Convention should be considered as a whole (UNICEF, 2007). Nevertheless, for ease of discussion we will consider these Articles separately below.

Article 3 articulates the guiding principle of 'the best interests of the child', encouraging adult decision-makers in governments, public and private organizations actively to consider and prioritize those interests. This is attractive at a 'common sense' level but does not address what exactly we mean by children's best interests and how they can be determined. It is not surprising, therefore, that the concept of 'the best interests of children' has received extensive attention in education research in relation to various contexts and in countries around the world (e.g. Thomson and Molloy, 2001; Vojak, 2003; Cumming et al., 2006; Bergström, 2010). Common across such literature is the concern that the best interests of the child may be at odds with the best interests of adults (parents, teachers – and we would add researchers) or other children. This is of relevance in research, which may not be directly in the best interests of the participating child although it may be in the interests of children as a group, or in the interest of adults. For example, it is important to study whether and how a new educational programme works before expanding it to more schools. If the programme turns out to be ineffective or even counter-productive, the children who participated in the research suffer harm, but children in general benefit because the programme will (presumably) be stopped (see also Chapter 4 on RCTs). In our case study at the beginning of the chapter, Gustav's research might uncover deficiencies in educational provision within juvenile prisons. This could lead to improvements that benefit future young offenders, but may also expose his participants to reprisals by prison authorities unhappy with the findings.

The UNCRC implementation handbook clarifies that the Convention stipulates the best interests of the child are 'a', not 'the' primary consideration and recognizes that 'there may be competing or conflicting human rights interests, for example, between individual children, between different groups of children and between children and adults' (UNICEF, 2007, p.38). This does not provide an excuse for researchers to override children's rights. Not only must researchers demonstrate that they have taken children's interests into account as a primary consideration (UNICEF, 2007, p.38), but this must be done within the spirit of the entire Convention and of the other guiding principles. At the very least, researchers should not allow their own interests (e.g. to pursue a particular topic or for career advancement) to override the interests of children. In relation to the Convention as a whole, it is not permissible to interpret 'best interests' in a relativist manner that goes against rights guaranteed elsewhere in the Convention (e.g. the right to privacy, and to access information). A legal (rather than research) example comes from the USA, where a group of parents brought a lawsuit against the local board of education because the parents objected to content in the compulsory set textbooks on the basis of their religion (Vojak, 2003). The parents' interpretation of what was in their children's interests was very different from the interpretation by the state. The children themselves were caught in the middle:

> The interests of the child are not always easily separated from those of the parent. Although the parent may believe that he or she always acts in the child's best interests, the child may disagree. A parent's best intentions do not always serve the best interests or outcomes for the child [...]. Likewise, school officials may cite the child's best interests to explain why they teach about nineteenth-century feminists and women's rights, while the child finds that those ideas cause serious parent-child conflicts at home. (Vojak, 2003, p.406)

In relation to the guiding principles of the UNCRC, a key implication is that children should be able to contribute their own views (see Article 12) in order to establish what is in their best interests, for example by becoming co-researchers in projects.

Article 12 addresses the need for respecting the views expressed by children themselves in all matters that affect them. The Committee on the Rights of the Child emphasizes that children should be actively involved in this process and it has noted the impeding effect of traditional, paternalistic attitudes towards children in countries such as Chile, Burkina Faso, Morocco, India, Algeria, Hungary and Tanzania (UNICEF, 2007, pp.150–51) as well as the barrier of children not being adequately informed of their right under Article 12 in countries such as France, Iceland and Belgium (p.152). Education is explicitly mentioned as an arena in which children should be heard. In education research, this has been taken up most explicitly in youth-led and youth-participatory

research approaches. For example, Tuck's research on early school leavers used participatory action research as

> a way for young men and women who are marginalized by race and eth-
> nicity, class, gender, and sexuality to demand not only access to the con-
> versations, policies, theories and spaces to which we/they have been
> systematically denied, but better yet, demand that our research informs
> and inspires these efforts. (2012, p.33)

The connection between research and advocacy is more explicit in this
kind of research than is usually the case. For Gustav, in our case study,
similar sentiments are reflected in his wish to empower his participants
and enable their voices to be heard. Research with children, rather than
on children, is less common in developing than in developed countries
(Powell et al., 2012). We argue, however, that Article 12 applies to all
research involving children and young people, regardless of methodology. When children are research participants the research clearly is a
matter that affects them. This means researchers should be alert to the
views of children about the topic of the research, even if their perceptions are not part of the research aims. In particular, all research should
ensure that children themselves (not just their parent or guardian) are
fully informed about the research and have the right to assent or dissent (see Chapter 5) in advance of, as well as during, the course of the
research. Respect for children's views is central to ensuring that such
efforts are genuine rather than tokenistic or even manipulative (UNICEF,
2005, p.3). In collectivist cultural and societal contexts such respect
would include involvement of family and community (Suaalii and
Mavoa, 2001). Researchers need to be aware of the risk, however, that
young people may be 'unable to exercise their independent choice free
from the influence of their adult guardians' as Ahsan encountered in
her doctoral research about children's participation in decision-making
processes in Bangladesh (2009, p.393). Various adults, such as teachers
and NGO staff, acted as gatekeepers to the young people. Ahsan provides examples of young people being selected for participation by
these adults, of gatekeepers completely blocking access to some sites,
and of misinformation about the research being provided to young
people. Her frustration is palpable, as she claims, in relation to the latter: 'the very first condition of my ethical methodology (empowering
the participants with appropriate information for their voluntary participation) was therefore largely compromised and negated' (Ahsan,
2009, p.304).

The UNCRC, in Article 12 and elsewhere, acknowledges that the child's
age and maturity play a role in the extent to which they are able to

express themselves. However, no lower age limit is set and the Committee on the Rights of the Child vigorously asserts the rights of 'even the youngest children' to express their views (UNICEF, 2007, p.154), offering this advice:

> To achieve the right of participation requires adults to adopt a child-centred attitude, listening to young children and respecting their dignity and their individual points of view. It also requires adults to show patience and creativity by adapting their expectations to a young child's interests, levels of understanding and preferred ways of communicating. (2007, p.153)

For researchers, this may involve transforming research information into child-friendly language or pictorial representation, adapting their own body language and being aware of children's body language, meeting children in places they are familiar with, respecting children's preference not to be involved in the research and adapting data collection strategies (Graham et al., 2012). For example, in relation to enabling young people to communicate in their own preferred ways, Setyowati and Widiyanto (2009) used visual methods, role play and letters, as well as interviews, for their research on violence in schools in Indonesia.

Finally, it is useful to briefly consider Articles 36 and 42. Article 36 addresses children's protection from any forms of exploitation that are not named elsewhere in the UNCRC. In its explanation of Article 36, UNICEF (2007, p.544) explicitly includes research, stating that: 'Children can also be exploited by researchers or experimenters, for example by breaches of their privacy or by requiring them to undertake tasks that breach their rights or are disrespectful to their human dignity'. Article 42 can help prevent such exploitation as it focuses on ensuring that children are aware of their rights under the UNCRC. For education research, this places a responsibility on researchers to help children understand their rights as they are relevant for the study (Graham et al., 2012), including voluntary participation. Danby and Farrell (2005) offer detailed insights in the processes they used to gain and confirm informed consent from children aged 5–11 in Australian primary schools. They refer to the 'pedagogic work of the researcher' (p.57) to help children understand permission forms that locate them as active decision-makers. Such pedagogical and ethical work shifts the focus from children simply 'having' certain rights to supporting the realization of such rights (Roose and Bouverne-De Bie, 2007).

Not all education research involves children. The rights discussed above are also reflected in other conventions, such as the overall Universal Declaration of Human Rights, the Covenant on Civil and

Political Rights and the Convention on the Rights of Persons with Disabilities. A rights-based approach to ethical education research therefore can apply to all participants and intended beneficiaries, not just to children.

National legislation and regulation

In this section we now turn to legislation and regulation at the national (or state/province) level. These regulations may be directed specifically at research, such as in the case of protocols for accessing certain group of participants. These are addressed in the section on gatekeeping below. Other regulations apply more generally and research may not even have been a major consideration in the decisions made by legislators or policymakers. We discuss several such regulations here in terms of their effect on confidentiality.

Gatekeeping

Regulations that serve a gatekeeping role include protocols for gaining access to particular institutions and/or to particular participants. The role of individuals, such as parents and head teachers, as gatekeepers is addressed in Chapter 5. Here we focus on the ways that gatekeeping has been further formalized in certain jurisdictions, by way of illustrating issues that may also apply in other countries. We focus here on access to education, health and prison settings, and to children and Indigenous people.

In relation to education settings, we draw on Australian protocols for research in schools as our examples. In Australia most state governments have regulations governing research access to government schools, such as the Research In Schools and Early Childhood (RISEC) application in Victoria and the State Education Research Approvals Process (SERAP) in New South Wales. Researchers need to submit a proposal for research in government schools to the State Department of Education and gain formal approval, following the guidelines provided. These procedures encompass familiar ethical issues, such as consent and confidentiality. However, they also require researchers to address the benefit of the research to the Department and to schools, the potential disruption the research may cause to the core educational role of schools, and the potential burden imposed on school staff for facilitating the research (NSW DEC, 2012; Victorian DEECD, 2013). The RISEC guidelines (Victorian DEECD, 2013, p.8) list the following criteria used to judge applications to conduct research in schools:

- benefit and value to the Department, sites and participants
- burden on sites and participants
- appropriateness of methodology for the setting
- ethical design and conduct, which includes issues such as informed consent, confidentiality, privacy and protection from harm.

The RISEC guidelines also list types of research that may not be approved, including proposals that 'potentially lead participants to unreasonably incriminate themselves' or that 'have the potential to adversely affect the Department of Education and Early Childhood Development or the school' (Victorian DEECD, 2013, p.13). Both the RISEC and SERAP guidelines indicate that a rejected proposal may be revised and re-submitted. Complexities occur when the changes required by the Department contradict what has been approved by the university Research Ethics Committee (REC). Moreover, research of a critical nature may never be approved. Even if the proposal passes smoothly through the Departmental approval process, it may add a month or more to the project timeline before data collection can commence.

Education research, however, does not only take place in schools but also in other settings. Formalized ethics guidelines are most widespread in relation to health and medical research. As a result, health institutions may apply their procedures to all researchers, even when the project is focused on education rather than health. In the UK, for example, this requires researchers, including student-researchers, to apply to a REC of the National Health Service (NHS), which usually includes attending the REC meeting in person (National Research Ethics Service, 2010). Education research in health settings may include research on education for sick children including in hospital schools (Bolton, 1997; Carstens, 2004; Akiko, 2005; Nisselle et al., 2011) and research on the workplace learning of health professionals (Jubas and Knutson, 2012; Manidis and Scheeres, 2012). For her Master of Education research on teachers' experiences in a hospital school in South Africa, Carstens (2004) had to obtain ethics approval from the Faculty REC in her university, from the provincial Department of Education and from the REC of the hospital.

Education research may also take place in prisons and the ethical dilemmas this creates in relation to gatekeeping and monitoring have been recognized by researchers (e.g. Pascoe and Radel, 2008; Dalen and Jones, 2010; James, 2013). In Australia, State Departments of Corrective Services have protocols similar to the ones used by Departments of Education (see above). The New South Wales guidelines (NSW DCS, 2011, p.2) highlight concerns about privacy of inmates and also warn that 'Exploratory research where no hypotheses have been formulated and the researcher is seeking ideas rather than testing hypotheses will not be considered'. As a result more open-ended qualitative research, such as life history or ethnography, may not even pass the first hurdle. In the UK, the National Offender Management Service considers applications to conduct research and encourages research 'whenever it has the potential to increase the effectiveness of operational policy/delivery' (NOMS, 2013, n.p.). Prison authorities can be very powerful gatekeepers, which impacts on the education research that is enabled within prison settings. An example is provided by Pascoe and Radel (2008) in relation to their research on the education experiences of Indigenous men in custody in Australia. Although Indigenous people are considered a vulnerable group for research in Australia and elsewhere (see below and also Chapter 2), the main barrier for their research was gaining ethics approval from the Department of Corrective Services (DCS) research committee. DCS forms were complex, included various time-consuming requirements (such as obtaining a new criminal history check, even though the researchers had already passed this as part of their teaching work with the same men), and had a pro forma Deed of Agreement including a clause that would infringe the intellectual property rights of the researchers. Removing the latter was a condition of approval by the university. The resulting struggle between satisfying both the DCS and the university was finally resolved by the DCS deleting the clause and granting intellectual property rights to the researchers. The advice provided by Pascoe and Radel (2008) is of use to our case study researcher, Gustav. They point to the importance of lobbying, support networks and relationships with key people for enabling them to gain all the necessary approvals. This took nine months for Pascoe and Radel, suggesting that perseverance and patience are also required.

Gatekeeping may also apply to specific groups of participants. At a general level, regulations commonly require parental or guardian consent for children and young people under a particular age (usually 16 or 18) to take part in research (see also Chapter 5). Governing bodies of institutions such as schools, hospitals and juvenile prisons may implement consent procedures especially strictly when the children are considered to be vulnerable. For example, in the UK, research with 'looked after children' (elsewhere referred to as 'children in residential or foster care') may require permission from several gatekeepers, such as birth and foster parents, case managers and social services organizations. Heptinstall (2000, p.868) explains that 'Looked after children are often perceived by adults as particularly vulnerable – and therefore in need of protection – because of their previous adverse experiences'. As a result, gatekeeping institutions such as schools and social services have tended to emphasize the protection of these children at the expense of children's right to participate and have their views heard (Heptinstall, 2000). The UNCRC also recognizes this tension between children's right to protection and their right to participation, while Ahsan (2009) refers to this as the tension between vulnerability and agency.

Indigenous people are also given special consideration in ethics regulations in countries such as Canada, Australia and New Zealand. The Canadian *Tri-Council Policy Statement: Ethical Conduct for Research Involving Humans* (CIHR, NSERC and SSHRC, 2010) dedicates an entire chapter to research involving Aboriginal peoples. This highlights the gatekeeping role of Aboriginal organizations and leaders, such as tribal and hamlet councils, First Nation/Inuit/Métis* associations, Aboriginal service agencies as well as local elders and knowledge holders. The policy recognizes that there may be diverse interests within Aboriginal communities and that critical research may be valuable. Article 9.10 of the Canadian policy states that 'researchers may seek REB [Research Ethics Board] approval for an exception to the requirement for community engagement, on the basis of an acceptable rationale' (CIHR, NSERC and SSHRC, 2010, p.121). The default expectation, however, is for community engagement and input. This may extend beyond giving permission for research to take place, to participation 'in the design and execution of research' and 'in the interpretation of the data and the review of research findings' (CIHR, NSERC and SSHRC, 2010, p.126 and p.127). The First Nations Centre (2005) explains the principles of what is known as 'OCAP': ownership of, control of, access to, and possession of research processes and data in relation to Aboriginal communities. The First Nations Centre (2005, p.i) articulates this as 'an expression of self-determination in research' in the context of 'colonial research practices' (see also Chapter 2). Education researchers whose projects focus on Aboriginal students therefore need to incorporate into their research planning both time and opportunities for extensive dialogue with relevant communities.

We argue that gatekeeping regulations may serve (unintentionally) to produce ethical concerns, at the same time as intending to ensure that research is ethical. When protocols state that the research should benefit the department or institution, this may preclude important research of a more critical nature. Researchers may also self-censor by deciding to avoid including certain settings or participants. In Australia, for example, it is not

---

*Métis refers to people of mixed First Nations and European heritage; they are recognized as a specific Aboriginal group in Canada represented through national and provincial Métis councils.

uncommon for students preparing for a thesis in an undergraduate or Master's degree to be advised against research in government schools due to the lengthy process of gaining both University and Education Department permission. As Scott and Fonseca (2010, p.291) argue, 'supervisors "in the know" will steer their students towards simple replications and research designs'. In the UK, the National Offender Management Service explicitly states: 'Due to the potential volume of applications from undergraduates it is impractical for NOMS to assist with these' (NOMS, 2013, n.p.). As a result, education research in highly restricted settings (such as juvenile prisons and hospitals) continues to be relatively rare. Researchers whose participants are young people may exclude those under 16 or 18 (depending on the nation) from taking part in order to preclude having to gain consent from parents or guardians. All these omissions and exclusions threaten the vital democratic role of social research to understand, explain and scrutinize society, by keeping certain aspects of educational practice largely invisible. In terms of the ethical principle of justice, it also leads to an unfair over-reliance on those who are easier to access to carry the burden of research participation.

Confidentiality

The second set of regulations that affect education researchers relate to the principle of confidentiality. Of particular relevance are privacy legislation, child protection legislation, subpoenas and freedom of information legislation, and regulations around data sharing. We have purposively chosen to discuss examples here from countries where such regulations are most prominent, and where possible we include some key differences. Nevertheless, the specific legal context obviously varies between jurisdictions, and will also change over time in relation to the specific regulations we discuss below.

Legislation in relation to privacy in some countries focuses on people's personal health information and by extension on health and medical research (e.g. Australia: ALRC, 2008; the USA: HSS, 2007) while other countries take a broader view of sensitive or personal information for both privacy regulation and its application to research (e.g. Canada: Canadian Government, 1985; the UK: UK Government, 2000). In general, privacy legislation reinforces the requirement to respect people's right to confidentiality. This applies especially to a duty to protect personal information about people from disclosure and misuse. For researchers, this translates to safeguarding data both during and after data collection, for example through the use of password-protected computer files. Data protection and confidentiality may be fairly easily achieved with quantitative data, but are more complex with qualitative data, especially if the research involved focus group discussions because 'participants will know who else was there and indeed what they said' (Ransome, 2013, p.40). Some countries also have more specific regulations, for example in Greece consent is required for photographing people in public spaces, while others (such as the USA) have a more lenient approach to privacy. Subject to certain conditions (such as the data not being used in a way likely to cause substantial distress), Canada, the UK, New Zealand and the Council of Europe allow personal information to be disclosed by organizations and companies for research purposes, without requiring the consent of each individual included (ALRC, 2008, Section 65). In other words, various forms of privacy legislation on the one hand increase the onus on researchers to ensure that they preserve the confidentiality of their own data, and on the other hand provide researchers with access to data collected by others.

While privacy and data protection legislation to some extent bolster research ethics protocols for confidentiality, other regulations complicate confidentiality. For education researchers the most obvious example is in relation to requirements to report child abuse. Although researchers are unlikely to be specifically named as a group mandated to report, they are included when all citizens are mandatory reporters (such as in the Northern Territory in Australia and most Canadian provinces) or they may hold a parallel role as, for example, a teacher or child care worker and be mandated or encouraged to report suspected abuse in that role (NHRPAC, 2002a; Mathews and Kenny, 2008; Child Welfare Information Gateway, 2012; Australian Institute of Family Studies, 2013). Mandated reporting is well established in the USA, Canada and Australia, while many other countries (such as Brazil, Hungary, Malaysia and South Africa) have established generic reporting duties (Mathews and Kenny, 2008). The UK does not have a specific mandatory reporting law; however, government guidelines specify that:

> Everybody who works or has contact with children, parents and other adults in contact with children should be able to recognize, and know how to act upon, evidence that a child's health or development is or may be being impaired – especially when they are suffering, or likely to suffer, significant harm. (cited in NSPCC, 2010 p.1)

Some countries have more specific legislation. For example, in Norway professionals are obligated by law to seek to prevent female genital mutilation if they have reason to believe a girl is at imminent risk (Hauge, 2013). These kinds of regulations for mandatory reporting override any promise or duty of confidentiality. This is of particular relevance for education researchers because their 'befriending role' may prompt disclosure of abuse by children in their research (Furey and Kay, 2010, p.121). Fisher (2009) offers her experience of conducting research on academic achievement after the transition from middle to high school in the USA, working with a group of 11 female students. After a final 'reunion' meeting, one of the girls disclosed that she had been sexually abused by a relative. Fisher recounts in detail the emotional turmoil of deciding to file a formal report, and her subsequent interactions with the girl and with other professionals such as the school counsellor. She concludes that:

> When studying vulnerable populations, children especially, the purview of researcher must be expanded. [...] At times we bear witness to things we wish we hadn't. It is at this moment when although we are not legally mandated to report disclosures of abuse, we must realize that out moral mandate is still present. (Fisher, 2009, p.31)

Although many education researchers will never have such an experience, they would do well to heed the warning from colleagues such as Fisher and be prepared in advance. This includes clarifying to underage participants the potential limitations to confidentiality. Care is needed, however, to do so 'without appearing unduly alarming or off-putting' (Felzmann, 2009, p.106). For example, Danby and Farrell (2005, p.67) included the phrase 'It is okay by me that [...] Ann, Susan or Kathy might talk to someone responsible if they are worried about my safety' on their consent form for primary school children.

At a more general level, researchers may be required to breach confidentiality and provide access to their data due to Freedom of Information legislation or to a subpoena from a court of law. The extent to which education researchers have been subject to court-ordered subpoenas is unclear. The potential certainly exists, especially for research on controversial topics. If Gustav, our case study researcher, uncovers information about thus far undetected illegal activity by his participants, he may be subject to a court subpoena (as feared by his university REC) or perhaps to a Freedom of Information (FoI) request by a journalist. As another example, Australian legislation introduced in 2013 gives the Australian Sports Anti-Doping Authority

> the ability to issue a 'disclosure notice' compelling persons of interest to assist ASADA's investigations. This notice can require a person to do one, or more of the following:

- attend an interview to answer questions;
- give information; and/or
- produce documents or things (a legal term meaning pretty much any thing).

(ASADA, 2013)

The final bullet point includes research data. In relation to education research, this may impact on projects investigating junior athletes in schools as well as projects on workplace learning by sports people and their support persons (such as coaches and health professionals). A central ethical concern about this kind of compelled disclosure of data is that the researcher loses control over how data may be used and made public (O'Neil, 2010). For example, data may be misinterpreted (thus threatening the integrity of research) and may lead to the identification of participants (thus undermining confidentiality).

FoI laws usually enshrine processes by which the general public may gain access to information held by governments. In the UK, however, publicly funded universities and research institutions are subject to FoI legislation. Privacy laws apply, so that personal information is exempted from FoI rights. Nevertheless, researchers have expressed concerns about data management, intellectual property and confidentiality (Charlesworth and Rusbridge, 2010; Jubb, 2012; Wilson, 2011), since the request can include research data.

Connected to this, in countries such as Australia, the UK and the US, researchers are encouraged by major research funders to make their data available to fellow researchers through public use files and shared repositories (NHRPAC, 2002b; ESRC, 2010; ANDS, 2012; see also OECD, 2007). In the UK, the high-profile government research funding agency the Economic and Social Research Council (ESRC, which applies to education research) makes explicit that it 'recognizes publicly funded research data as valuable, long-term resources that, where practical, must be made available for secondary scientific research' (ESRC, 2010, p.2; see also Chapter 4 on data archiving). The ESRC requires data to be offered to its archive and will only approve waivers of this requirement in exceptional circumstances. The difference between such planned data sharing and compelled provision of data through subpoenas or FoI requests is not only that the sharing occurs at a time chosen by the researchers (usually after the project has been completed and findings have been published), but also that data are expected to be de-identified before they are made available (NHRPAC, 2002b; OECD, 2007; Van den Eynden, 2008; ESRC, 2010; ANDS, 2012). For example, in the USA the recommendation is that:

> When IRBs [Institutional Review Boards] are satisfied that a protocol involves the collection of data in anonymous form or on unknown persons, these data should be classified as public use data files. When IRBs are asked to authorize public data files from data originally collected with identifiers, [several] factors should be considered by the IRB to be certain the data files has been effectively de-identified for analysis by secondary users. (NHRPAC, 2002b, p.2)

These recommendations assert that removing participant names is not sufficient – for example, researchers also need to remove references to other people made by participants and variables that would identify a person, and to combine categories if the number of people in a category is so small that this could identify them (NHRPAC, 2002b). The ESRC (2010, p.7) suggests that even 'sensitive and confidential data can be shared ethically' as long as researchers prepare for this in relation to consent procedures, anonymization of data and access restrictions as part of their data management plan.

Conclusion

This chapter has highlighted that a variety of international, national and regional regulations may impact on the ethical conduct of education research. We have chosen to highlight the United Nations Convention on the Rights of the Child as our international example, as well as regulations from specific countries that affect education research through gatekeeping or in relation to confidentiality. These regulations illustrate issues that are likely to be pertinent to most education researchers, but our discussion here could not possibly address all potentially relevant legislation and policies. Not only are there differences between jurisdictions, but within a specific jurisdiction, policies will change over time.

It is vital that education researchers are aware of the specific regulations that apply to their local context and to the nature of their project. In some countries there may be little national regulation, for example in relation to mandatory reporting or data protection, and researchers will need to draw on their own morality and their knowledge about local customs in order to decide on appropriate strategies. Such preparation in advance will enable researchers to plan ahead rather than be caught by surprise. For example, Gustav (from our case study) needs to be aware of the role of corrective services authorities as gatekeepers for research access, and also be prepared for the possibility that his data may be subject to a subpoena or FoI request. Such awareness and preparation will inform the first stage of the research: the design.

CHAPTER 4

RESEARCH DESIGN

Sara is a student on a pre-service teacher education course. She has to do a small-scale study in the school where she is teaching as part of the course requirements. She wants to use visual methods to explore students' views about sexuality. However, her mentor, Mrs Armstrong, an experienced teacher in the school, tells her that she would be 'sensible' to do research into a less ethically sensitive area. Mrs Armstrong then suggests a completely different area – one more directly related to the school curriculum. What, if anything, can Sara do?

In the case study above, the ethical issues facing Sara, as a relatively inexperienced researcher, are similar to those that are encountered by many education researchers – even those who have considerably more experience of designing and conducting research. First, Sara needs to decide on the topic of her research. Should she press ahead with researching sexuality, even though it may prove to be a sensitive issue to discuss with the students? Or should she defer to her mentor, and go along with what Mrs Armstrong suggests? Here, we are introduced to ethical debates about researching potentially controversial topics, and about the extent to which we are able to choose our topic independently. Second, Sara must make a decision about the methods she will use. While visual methods are increasingly common in education research, research funders often favour quantitative approaches, which again has implications for the independence of the researcher, and also, potentially, for the specific methods she or he deploys – although Sara's research is not externally funded. These dilemmas, and others related specifically to the design of education research projects, are the focus of this chapter.

In reflecting on developments in education research, Hammersley (1999, p.18) has contended that an increasing emphasis on ethics has led to the neglect of research technique, with 'ethical considerations ... treated by some as constituting the very rationale of research'. We argue, in this chapter, that good research technique and ethical practice should not be viewed as in tension but, instead, as closely intertwined. Indeed, in common with many other social researchers, we suggest that poorly designed research is by definition unethical since it is likely to waste participants' time and risks exposing them to unnecessary and possibly harmful intrusion into their lives to no useful end (Rosenthal, 1994; Heath et al., 2009). This is reflected in the national Australian research ethics guidelines' (AARE, 1993) inclusion of the principle of 'research merit and integrity'. Furthermore, as Iphofen (2011, p.39) notes, poorly designed research may 'discourag[e] participants from future research engagements, which may be of better quality', thus affecting the wider academic community. Ethical considerations should inform research design, but they should not *determine* research design.

In this chapter, we argue that it is important to think carefully about the ethical implications of research from the very earliest stages. As Sara's dilemma above suggests, even the choice of topic cannot be considered an ethically neutral act and, in the first part of the chapter, we discuss the range of pressures that come to bear on a decision about what to research. We then outline the ethical considerations that may impinge upon a researcher's choice of methods, and use the example of one particular method – the randomized control trial (RCT) – to illustrate some of these in more detail. We then explore ethical practice in relation to the design of particular research instruments (such as questionnaires and interview of schedules) and the construction of collaborative projects. Finally, we recognize that making a decision about what will happen to data at the end of the project is becoming an increasingly important part of research design, and we conclude the chapter by discussing some of the ethical implications of data archiving.

Choice of topic

As we suggest throughout this book, conducting research is a political act. In part this is due to the way in which power relationships often structure research encounters (a theme that is taken up, explicitly, in Chapter 6, but which also pervades other chapters); it also relates, however, to the topics we choose to research and the methods by which we investigate them. As N. Mauthner (2012, p.172) contends, 'We cannot be bystanders, innocently deploying our methods. Rather, we must take responsibility not only for what we bring into being but also for how we do this, because the two are inseparable'. Indeed, our understanding of ethical practice needs to be sufficiently broad so that it encompasses the political objectives and/or intentions of our research (Gillies and Alldred, 2012).

Some education research is clearly motivated by specific political concerns. For example, much feminist education research (e.g. Read et al., 2011) has sought to understand better the experiences of girls and women within schools, colleges and other educational institutions, with the aim of challenging gender oppression and improving women's lives (Gillies and Alldred, 2012). Other research has set out to improve the educational experiences of students from minority ethnic backgrounds (e.g. Leonardo, 2009), disabled students (e.g. Mutua and Nicholls, 2013), lesbian, gay and bisexual students (e.g. Epstein, 1994), and those from working class families (e.g. Lehmann, 2013). Recently, education research has focused on the way in which different structural characteristics intersect, and the means by which the inequalities associated with such intersections can best be addressed (e.g. Reay, 2008). Various scholars have argued that such political aims should be made explicit. Indeed, writing almost five decades ago, and in relation to social research more generally, Becker (1967) suggested that all researchers should provide a clear statement of their relationship to those they are researching such that the goals and anticipated consequences of the research for those being studied are made explicit. More recently, Iphofen (2011, p.19) has argued that it is inevitable that we will take sides in our research, but what is important is that we 'make clear to ourselves and others which side we are on'. While Becker and Iphofen were referring to social researchers in general, others have argued that education researchers have a particular duty to conceive research as a political project and, within their work, to assume a normative stance. A strong statement of this position is provided by Rex in her discussion of how we should go about choosing what to research:

In an era in which migration, globalization and digital ubiquity co-exists with test-driven policies and curriculums, and questions about how to educate teachers to work successfully with students unlike themselves, we researchers, no matter where in the world we do our work, are challenged to locate normative, contributory and critical stances for what we produce. Concepts and values like freedom, social justice, human rights and democracy are our societal heritage. (2010, p.3–4)

Rex's argument is based on the assumption that education researchers typically focus on social phenomena such as teaching, learning, failing, achievement and progress, which are deeply ideological in nature, 'in the sense that dispositions, beliefs, values and desires are implicated in their creation, sustenance and transformation' (2010, p.5). She contends that, as a consequence, the researcher has no choice but to engage with ideological positions and political debate.

This position is not held by all researchers, however. Particular research methods, such as RCTs (discussed later in this chapter), are usually predicated upon an ostensibly 'value-neutral' approach to research. Moreover, even researchers who may themselves have a clear political position on the topic under investigation may not always think it wise to publicize this. In their account of developing educational surveys, Raffe and colleagues (1989) describe how they chose not to identify the sponsors of their research in the questionnaire that young people were asked to complete. This was mainly, they state, because of their desire to minimize bias: they believed that a survey that was visibly identified with the Scottish Education Department and the Manpower Services Commission (the sponsors) might give rise to biased answers about some of the topics respondents were asked about – particularly in relation to experiences of schooling and youth training schemes.

In choosing a topic for investigation, education researchers are influenced not only by their own interests and personal political commitments. Although the independence of the researcher is a value which is usually considered intrinsic to social research (Hammersley and Traianou, 2012b), there are a variety of external pressures and priorities that come to bear on the choice of what to research (such as Mrs Armstrong's attempt to influence Sara's choice of research topic in the case study at the beginning of the chapter). In some cases, these pressures may threaten the researcher's autonomy to decide upon the focus of the research and the most appropriate methods to use. First, education researchers may experience pressure from the institution in which they are employed. Universities and other organizations that conduct research may, for example, discourage or even prevent research that they believe may damage the reputation of the institution. They may also strongly incentivize (or even require) researchers to seek external funding for their research activities (Hammersley and Traianou, 2012b), and encourage them to bid for work that seems to stand a good chance of being funded (Thomas, 2013).

Second, pressure may be exerted by those who commission research. Indeed, Iphofen (2011) warns of the dangers of conducting research for government departments that may wish not to contribute genuinely and impartially to the knowledge base in a particular area, but to generate evidence to support an already predetermined policy direction. He goes on to argue that, 'In educational research ... there are many examples of research evidence being exploited to initiate and/or discontinue policies leading to considerable instability in educational systems and unnecessary stress on educators and students alike' (p.25). Conducting research for what is perceived by potential respondents to be an 'untrustworthy' sponsor may also affect participation rates and/or the way in which research findings are viewed (Iphofen, 2011).

While education researchers may want to pursue research funded by government departments and other external sponsors for ethical reasons (e.g. a desire to contribute directly to the formation of education policy), it can often be difficult within such projects to pursue the kind of politically committed research discussed earlier in the chapter. Indeed, within the UK, the USA and Australia there has been a clear policy emphasis over recent decades on commissioning research that is user-oriented and useful to policymakers and politicians, and prescribing particular (usually quantitative) methods (Rogers, 2003; Mayer, 2006; Brooks et al., 2013). As Luke (2010, p.178) notes, this has had the effect of constructing a binary distinction: 'Between qualitative "critical work" which has been portrayed as scientifically "soft", politically correct and ideological by the press, politicians and educational bureaucrats – and empirical, quantitative scientific research, which is presented as unbiased, truthful and the sole grounds for rational policy formation.'

In the USA, for example, the No Child Left Behind educational reform programme has been associated with a shift towards a positivist 'scientifically proven' curriculum (Luke, 2012). Rex (2010, p.2) maintains that, as a result, 'the volume of critical theorists' voices in the US has lowered considerably'. Pursuing a similar argument, Rogers (2003) maintains that this favoured quantitative model of doing research – and the research topics it facilitates and closes down – has filtered down from large-scale evaluations of government programmes to much smaller-scale research in individual classrooms. Indeed, she argues that even practitioner research in American schools 'runs the risk of being incorporated into models congruent with technical rationality... [which will then] lead to its bureaucratisation and blunting of any critical force it has to transform educational practices and institutions' (Rogers, 2003, p.68).

More generally, this privileging of quantitative methods by research sponsors has been critiqued on the basis that many questions within education cannot be settled simply by assembling good evidence, as 'good evidence is always interpreted through the belief lens of the interpreter and then used in different ways' (Mayer, 2006, p.15; see also Adley and Dillon, 2012). Moreover, allowing one's research agenda to be determined by the topics the government and other research sponsors put forward has additional risks. As T. Edwards (2010, p.304) has argued, conducting research in this way 'takes the problems which government brings to it, contributes to their solution, and refrains from adding new ones or further complicating old ones'. Thus, researchers can become drawn into narrow agendas connected to school and student failure, and increasingly less likely to recognize the influence of wider, structural explanations for educational inequalities (Rogers, 2003).

Although a single researcher is likely to have little influence on a government's orientation to research or the type of research it chooses to fund, some steps can be taken to limit the extent to which sponsors can compromise the independence of the research once a particular project is underway. Raffe et al. (1989) suggest that, when researchers are negotiating contracts, they should ensure that research funders do not have a right to confidentiality, nor should they be allowed to inhibit the publication of research findings. In addition, researchers should ensure that intellectual property rights are made clear, monitoring procedures are not overly burdensome, the funding offered is sufficient for the work to be undertaken, and any suggested research design is not so rigid as to restrict the researcher's professional judgement (Raffe et al., 1989). Nevertheless, given the pressures on many academics to bring in research income, it can be hard always to insist on such safeguards. While the postgraduate student rarely has to worry about this type of constraint, concerns about the effect of sponsors in relation to contract and commissioned research were the impetus for the revision of the BERA research ethics guidelines in 2011 (see Chapter 2).

Finally, in some cases, the topic of research can be limited by a desire not to threaten the beliefs and/or values of a particular group. While Hammersley and Traianou (2012b) contend that it is not necessarily unethical to pursue research that touches on private matters and which may be viewed as threatening by potential respondents, they acknowledge that such judgements are frequently difficult. They argue that 'in our view, assessments of the legitimacy of investigating a particular topic depend not only upon assessments of its sensitivity in relation to privacy, and in other respects, but also on weighing these against the value of the proposed research into the topic' (p.109). An example of such sensitivities is provided by Dale (2001) in his historical account of the sociology of education in the UK. He suggests that the desire of researchers not to threaten the values of their colleagues had an important bearing on the topics they pursued, and those they chose not to take up. Indeed, he argues that the institutional location of the majority of sociology of education – within education departments, rather than departments of sociology or social policy – has been particularly influential. As researchers have tended to be working alongside colleagues involved closely with teacher education, few have been keen to subject the work of teacher educators – or even the work of teachers more generally – to critical scrutiny. If we accept Dale's analysis, in this case, an ethical commitment to the endeavours of colleagues foreclosed an area of enquiry and, in effect, limited the independence of the researchers concerned.

A further example is discussed by Sikes (2010) in the context of her own research on sexual relationships between school teachers and students. She suggests that such work confronts taken-for-granted beliefs and assumptions through

> critiquing the dominant belief that youngsters do not lie about sexual abuse by presenting evidence which indicates that sometimes they do; or raising concerns about, and questioning the ways in which, those who are alleged ... to have abused are dealt with; or suggesting that young women who fall in love with a teacher have not always been exploited. (2010, p.148)

Sikes acknowledges that, in questioning dominant narratives about appropriate relationships between teachers and students, such research may have the effect of weakening the protection of children. She notes that a possible consequence of conducting research on this topic is that children may not be believed in the future, or that some young people will be psychologically damaged because they fear that abuse stories they have told will no longer be considered authentic, or that some abusers may be erroneously found not guilty. Nevertheless, she concludes that there is also a strong ethical basis for proceeding with such research – to help protect teachers from false allegations. More generally, she argues that 'avoiding taboo, controversial and/or sensitive topics solely because they are that ... can ... be considered to be a basic abrogation of ethical and moral responsibility' (2010, p.146). Indeed, when aspects of educational practice remain unexamined by research, the resulting invisibility potentially allows problems to remain unchallenged.

Choice of method

Linking topic, methods and ethics

Ethical considerations also impinge on the choice of research methods to be used. As we have suggested above, wider political imperatives may come into play here – influencing the methods chosen as well as the topic of the research. For example, within the USA, government funding has been closely tied to the use of quantitative methods and to experimental approaches in particular (Delandshere, 2004; Mayer, 2006). In contrast, some feminist researchers have had a political commitment to using qualitative methods, and rejected quantitative techniques which they have seen as privileging a 'male way of knowing' (Reinharz, 1984; Oakley, 2000). However, for many contemporary education researchers, the topic itself – and how it is expressed through specific research questions – is likely to have an important bearing on the choice of research methods. For example, even staunch supporters of RCTs (discussed below) recognize their limitations, and acknowledge that qualitative methods are often more helpful to us in understanding *why* an educational invention works (or does not work) (Goldacre, 2013). It is also important to ascertain at an early stage of the design process whether or not the research requires the collection and analysis of primary data. If data already exist that address the research topic, it may well be considered unethical to engage in further primary research, to avoid causing 'interview fatigue' (Ball, 2005) among particular communities, for example. In such cases, secondary data analysis may be a more appropriate methodological choice.

Formal ethical review procedures may themselves put (unethical) pressure on researchers in relation to their choice of research method. This has assumed increasing importance over recent years with the emergence of institutional RECs in many countries across the world (although, as we argued in Chapter 3, there are significant geographical variations in the extent to which research is regulated). The experiences of researchers suggest that, in places where such committees are in operation, not all methods are always treated equally. For example, drawing on her experience of serving on RECs in Canadian universities, Ells (2011, p.881) notes that 'researchers using qualitative methodologies appear to be particularly prone to having the quality of their study design called into question' (and is perhaps a particular problem for those conducting master's or doctoral-level research). She suggests this is often because reviewers have inadequate understanding of the research topic and the proposed methods, and a biased view about what constitutes 'good science'. In addition, the institutional criteria given to reviewers are sometimes inappropriate to qualitative design. As a result, she maintains that many Canadian qualitative researchers have come to view gaining REC approval as the major hurdle in conducting their research. Although Ells (2011) provides guidance to qualitative researchers to help them negotiate such boards – for example, 'follow statements that could raise a red flag to research ethics reviewers with justifications' (p.886) – her work suggests that rather more fundamental reform of ethical review procedures may be necessary.

Such problems seem particularly pronounced for those wishing to conduct practitioner-based education research. P. Brown (2010) describes how a graduate student at her university, who had submitted a proposal for a teacher research project to her institutional ethics committee, received a list of corrections to make before the research was approved: 'One of the "corrections" was that she should transplant the research to another setting because it would be impossible to avoid coercing her own students to participate. The student wrote a rebuttal based on the illogical a priori rejection of teacher research and her research project was approved' (p.278).

Experiences such as those recounted by Ells (2011) and Brown (2010) may encourage researchers – particularly student researchers (such as Sara in the opening case study) and/or those with less experience of working in research institutions – to choose methods that they believe will be acceptable to and/or not unduly held up by RECs. Within the UK, two of the authors of this book (Brooks and Maguire) have supervised education dissertations in which students have chosen to use text-based methods, rather than those requiring contact with participants, primarily to avoid having to submit their research proposals for ethical scrutiny and thus the risk that their research may be delayed (making it more difficult for them to complete their research by the dissertation deadline). It is also the case that there is considerable variation between RECs – particularly in their expertise in relation to qualitative methods (see Chapter 2).

Although the choice of research methods should not be driven by assumptions about the priorities and preferences of RECs, it is equally important that methodological choices do not prioritize the collection of data over ethical considerations. As Heath et al. (2009, p.22) argue, 'not all research data is fair game, regardless of the insights thus gained or the brilliance of the research design'. To illustrate this point, they discuss Hey's use of discarded notes exchanged by girls in classrooms in her ethnographic study *The Company She Keeps*:

Although the notes undoubtedly provided a wonderful source of naturally occurring data, Hey grappled with the issue of whether it was ethically appropriate to fish these notes out of bins into which they had been thrown and then to use them as research evidence, (initially) without the girls' knowledge. She concluded somewhat ambivalently that it was legitimate to use them, and subsequently some of the girls even handed their notes directly to her, but other researchers might well have reached rather different conclusions depending on their personal code of ethics. (Heath et al., 2009, p.22)

There are often thought to be significant ethical differences between qualitative and quantitative methods because of associated differences in relationships with research subjects. As Iphofen (2011, p.24) notes, the relationship between researcher and researched common to qualitative research, 'tends to be of a more humanistic nature' than the relationships characteristic of quantitative methods, as it 'remains methodologically closer to the values, meaning, intentions, aspirations and goals of the human subject'. There are certainly some important ethical issues that are associated with particular qualitative methods. For example, fully informed consent is frequently difficult to secure in ethnographic or longitudinal projects, where researchers typically do not have a clear idea where the research will head (Burgess, 1989b; Levinson, 2010), while visual methods are sometimes seen as ethically problematic because of the potential for causing harm to those who are photographed or filmed (Coffey et al., 2006; Pope et al., 2010). However, 'this does not mean that those engaged in quantitative methods are immune from the need to consider their trust relationship with society and with those from whom the data they are analysing was generated' (Iphofen, 2011, p.24). Experimental methods, in particular, while adopting a quantitative approach, often involve close contact with research participants. Education-focused neuroscience, for example, aims to access real-time information about the brain to enable better understanding of cognitive functions that relate to learning such as attention, memory, language and speech. Lalancette and Campbell (2012) describe various ethical dilemmas with which the neuroscientist has to grapple, including those related to consent and the possibility of incidental findings (of an unexpected pathology). They also discuss the stigmatization that is associated with the value-laden language sometimes used within neuroscience to describe brain structures and function – and outline their concern if some of this terminology (such as the word 'normal' in diagnoses) is transferred pejoratively to educational practice. To illustrate in more detail some of the arguments that relate to quantitative research specifically, in the following section we focus on one method that has gained particular prominence within education research over recent years: the RCT.

An example: randomized control trials

RCTs provide a good illustration of some of the points made above about the politicized nature of education research (in common with social research, more generally). Goldacre, one of the most well-known proponents of this method in the UK, has defined RCTs in the following way:

> Where they are feasible, randomised trials are generally the most reliable tool we have for finding out which of two interventions works best. We simply take a group of children, or schools (or patients or people); we split them into two groups at random; we give one intervention to one group; and the other intervention to the other group; then we measure how each group is doing, to see if one intervention achieved its supposed outcome any better. (2013, p.6)

While some feminist researchers have viewed RCTs, along with other experimental methods, as constituting 'a "super-masculinisation" of rational knowledge' (Oakley, 2000, p.39), recent years have witnessed an increasing interest in this method on the part of politicians and policymakers alike (Torgerson, 2009). The US federal government, for example, has promoted RCTs since the early 2000s; in 2005, the American Secretary of Education stated that experimental methods using RCTs should be implemented in education evaluations wherever possible (Ong-Dean et al., 2011). Moreover, various initiatives tied programme funding to a requirement to use RCTs for the associated evaluation (Ong-Dean et al., 2011), and a dissemination unit was established to promote the findings of RCTs (the 'What Works Clearinghouse', Delandshere, 2004). Ireland has followed a similar path, with policymakers arguing that RCTs should be 'the method of choice for demonstrating cause and effect' (Brady and O'Regan, 2009, p.265). In the UK, government funding has not been tied to specific methods in quite the same way. Nevertheless, recent years have seen an increasing interest in experimental approaches. Goldacre was commissioned by the UK government to write a report on the use of experimental methods within education, *Building Evidence into Education*, published in 2013. In response to this, the Department for Education underlined its commitment to: setting up a UK 'What Works Centre' (following the US example); raising awareness of RCTs among civil servants and ministers; and 'driving behaviour and culture change across the Department to increase the use of evidence [derived from RCTs] in policy and delivery' (DfE, 2013, p.2).

This promotion of RCTs by policymakers in the USA, the UK, Ireland and elsewhere has, however, provoked considerable controversy, and many of the ensuing arguments – made by both opponents and proponents of this method – have hinged on ethical concerns. First, proponents of RCTs have argued that they offer an important means of freeing educational practice from political ideology. Goldacre (2013, p.4), for example, has argued that RCTs have the potential to empower teachers and set the profession 'free from government, ministers and civil servants who are often overly keen on sending out edicts, insisting that their idea is the best in town'. Instead, he draws an analogy with the medical profession to suggest that the evidence provided by RCTs will allow teachers to choose the intervention that works best, and provide a firm basis for resisting political interference. Proponents also argue that RCTs offer an important means of avoiding harm to children and others within the education system (Oakley, 2000; Torgerson, 2001). A frequently quoted example is the 'Scared Straight' programme, in which children were taken into prisons and shown the consequences of criminal acts, in the hope that it would motivate them to abide by laws when adults (Goldacre, 2013). However, RCTs suggested that the programme was actively harmful, with children who had taken part in it more likely to engage in criminal acts (Goldacre, 2013). RCTs have also shown that some costly interventions have had no effect: Torgerson (2001) cites the example of an anti-smoking curriculum that had been used for over five years before the RCT took place (thus constituting a considerable waste of resources).

The ethical concerns raised by opponents of RCTs are, however, more multi-faceted. A first set of concerns relates to the research participants, and focuses on the ethics of randomization. Discussing the young people involved in their youth mentoring and informal education RCT in Ireland, Brady and O'Regan (2009) express concern that those who were assigned to the control group (rather than the intervention group) may have been deprived of something beneficial which, in other circumstances, they could have expected to receive. In response to such criticisms, proponents of RCTs argue that, 'if we do not know whether the intervention works, or is even detrimental to outcomes, we are in an ethically neutral scenario when randomising' and that, if we do know that it works, then 'no evaluation is necessary, and we should not be randomising' (Hutchinson and Styles, 2010, p.5). Moreover, those assigned to a control group can, in many cases, be offered the intervention a few months later, once the trial has ended (Goldacre, 2013). Equally, however, *perceptions* of the ethics of randomization may affect the results – particularly if those agreeing to be randomized do not form a representative sample and/or differential attrition occurs as a result of those not receiving the intervention dropping out of the sample (Brady and O'Regan, 2009; Allen, 2013). To respond to this particular problem, Hutchinson and Styles (2010) recommend that research designers discuss the principles of RCTs with those who will be implementing them (in schools, colleges or other institutional locations) at an early stage of projects. They argue that if participants understand why they are being randomly allocated, they are more likely to take part. In some RCTs, however, for the experiment to work properly, the information partici- pants are given may have to be tightly controlled, thus raising additional ethical concerns about the extent to which fully informed consent can be given.

A second set of ethical concerns about RCTs focuses less on the par- ticipants and more on the wider education research community. Delandshere (2004) has argued that the shift in government funding in the USA, to privilege RCTs, had the effect of marginalizing those who are engaged in other forms of research. Moreover, and in contrast to the claims made by Goldacre (2013) outlined above, she contends that within this particular paradigm of education research, teachers and edu- cators become positioned very much as the consumers of research prod- ucts rather than actors engaged in the intellectual work of teaching and learning. She suggests that the current climate is likely to further depo- liticize education and 'reposition teachers as bureaucrats who execute or implement teaching to increase test scores … rather than as intellectual and social agents who participate in the construction and transformation of education to address social problems as they emerge' (Delandshere, p.248). This connects to a further criticism of RCTs, that researchers using this method misunderstand the nature of educational institutions – assuming that they are relatively stable and reliable organizations when, in fact, the complexity of their social and cultural composition gives no assurance that an intervention that is effective in one location will have the same results in another school, college or workplace (Delandshere, 2004; Smith, 2008; Allen, 2013). Finally, opponents of RCTs have sug- gested that it is important for policymakers and others commissioning and designing research to recognize that there are many important ques- tions within teacher education and other forms of education research that cannot be answered by empirical research alone; data always need to be interpreted, and the lenses through which interpretation occurs are not always the same (Mayer, 2006).

While these broader questions about the impact of RCTs on the wider educational community cannot be easily resolved within a research context in which high political priority is accorded to this particular methodology, work has been done by some researchers using RCTs to try to address the ethical concerns about the impact on individual participants. As part of their RCT of a youth mentoring service in Ireland, Brady and O'Regan (2009) ensured that both intervention and control groups were offered a basic youth service; the mentoring was then framed as an 'add-on' service for the former group. In addition, the young people in the control group were put on a waiting list for the mentoring service once the trial had ended, and the target age range for the service was extended to ensure that all who wanted to would have a chance to be matched with a mentor. They also negotiated what they called a 'free pass' system with the youth service staff who were involved. Any young person who staff deemed vulnerable and in need of mentoring support, and who they were not comfortable with possibly being randomly allocated to the control group, could be forwarded for the intervention and thus not included in the study.

Design of research instruments

We argued above that researcher independence can be threatened by the pressure that is sometimes applied by the sponsors of research. This can apply to the design of research instruments as well as to the topic of research and the methods that are deployed. Raffe et al. (1989) suggest that researchers undertaking survey research may come under particular pressure from the sponsors of the research – because survey data are easily made available, often have considerable generality, and may require high levels of funding. They note that pressure may be applied to prevent 'unwelcome' data being collected in the first place, rather than preventing publication of sensitive findings and that, in their experience, disputes with sponsors 'where they take place, tend to focus on survey design, and on the content of questionnaires or interview schedules' (p.28). Mark et al. (1999) make a similar point in relation to evaluation research, in particular, arguing that funders sometimes 'censor in advance' by restricting researchers from collecting a prospective outcome variable. In cases such as these, they strongly recommend that researchers describe and explain the decisions that were taken within their end-of-project evaluation reports.

Ethical issues impinge on the design of research instruments in other ways, too. For example, for survey researchers, using an online tool rather than a paper-based questionnaire may have advantages in terms of potentially reaching a larger population and obviating the need for manual entry of data into analysis software. However, the absence of any means of identifying individual respondents in such surveys is likely to make it harder, if not impossible, for respondents to withdraw their data at a later date, if they decide they do not want to be part of the study. It is also difficult, with online surveys, to ascertain if participants were able and/or allowed to consent for themselves (e.g. if the survey is intended for those over 18) and for the researcher to respond appropriately if any problematic issues are disclosed by participants during the research (see Ruiz-Casares, 2013). Survey researchers using paper-based question-naires are not immune from such issues, however. Some may choose not to include any identifiers on their questionnaires – which leads to similar problems as those discussed above if a respondent decides that he or she wishes to withdraw their data from the project. Other researchers may give each questionnaire a unique numerical reference number, which is matched with a specific name in an overview document. There may also, sometimes, be reasons for asking respondents to write their name on the questionnaire. In his national evaluation of out-of-school classes for highly attaining students, Lambert (2008) asked respondents to write their names on the questionnaires so that he could ask their primary schools for their results to help examine the relationship between the classes and academic attainment. However, given that the survey was administered by the teachers who ran the out-of-school classes, rather than by Lambert himself, he acknowledges that 'an overly inquisitive teacher could fairly easily find out what had been written' (p.72), and that this lack of confidentiality may have affected the students' responses.

Survey researchers also alert us to the importance of making sure that the questions that comprise a questionnaire can be answered by those who are being asked to complete it. In reflecting on their own survey-based research in schools, Denscombe and Aubrook (1992) explored the comments that their respondents wrote at the end of the questionnaires. In relation to research they conducted on the use of alcohol, tobacco and other drugs, they argue that the comments

> seemed to indicate that some of the pupils felt distinctly uncomfortable about being faced with questions they could not answer. The most obvious example comes from the comments of Muslim and Hindu girls about their difficulty with questions about 'going out'. These comments convey a feeling of discomfort stemming from their frustration at not being able to complete that part of the questionnaire accurately. (1992, p.67)

Within interview-based research, the format and nature of the interview schedule or 'topic guide' that is used will depend, to some extent at least, on the researcher's theoretical position and the methodological underpinnings of the study – which may themselves be informed by ethical concerns. For example, within participatory research, the researcher may deliberately choose to forgo control of the research, and pass it to participants who are the focus of the project (Birch and Miller, 2012). Here, research is likely to be conceived as a shared enterprise, based on the exchange of ideas and understanding, and structured research instruments are likely to be eschewed in favour of a list of a small number of topics to be covered over the course of a research conversation (Oakley, 1981).

Collaborative design

When making a decision about the methods that will be used in a project, the scale of the research and the extent to which other researchers can or will be involved may well be influential. This can relate to collaboration with research participants (participatory research) and also to collaboration between researchers (team research). In line with some of the arguments that have been made earlier in this chapter about the close relationship between ethical and political judgements, some researchers may build collaboration with others into their research design because of specific political commitments (as discussed in the preceding section). For example, it is a well-established precept of feminist social research that research participants should be fully involved in the research process: 'they should help set the research agenda … and have an opportunity to influence its design, analysis and dissemination' (Oakley, 2000, p.18). Over recent years, this participatory approach has been extended to research with children as well as adults and, in some projects, children have made important contributions to research design in addition to data collection and analysis. Bélanger and Connelly (2007) recount the central role children assumed in their research, which sought to understand how students become identified as having difficulties in elementary schools in Ontario, Canada. After critiquing the methods that the two researchers had initially planned to use, the children helped to revise the methods of both data collection and analysis: for example, deciding what the project's observations should and should not cover, and offering their own 'insider' accounts of events that disrupted the researchers' initial interpretations.

Researchers working with Indigenous communities across the world have developed similar participatory approaches with the aim of redressing power differentials, generating new knowledge and, in many cases, establishing 'significant engagement with Indigenous people, based on trust and inclusion' (Ball, 2005, p.84). Moreover, it is argued by some that researchers in the Global North have an ethical responsibility to those in the Global South to involve their colleagues in collaborative research – particularly when the research focuses on countries in the Global South itself (Mama, 2007). Jeanes and Kay (2013), for example, describe how, in their research with young people in Zambia, focus group participants introduced role-plays, dances and poetry to express their views and opinions. This, the authors argue, highlights the 'potential for alternative, culturally relevant modes of expression to be incorporated within the research if the participants deem it appropriate' (p.28).

While there is now a relatively large literature on participatory research and associated ethical issues, few scholars have written about the ethical challenges of *team* research. Such challenges can, however, be significant, particularly in cross-cultural research, when researchers may be used to working to different ethical norms, and in multi-disciplinary research, when researchers may bring different disciplinary traditions and practices to bear (Del Monte, 2000). Several of these issues are illustrated well in Gibson's (1985) account of the ethnography she undertook in California, which focused on the educational opportunities open to Punjabi children living in the area. She put together a diverse team of researchers in terms of age, gender, ethnicity and background, but ended up embroiled in a series of serious disagreements about the theoretical underpinnings of the study, the methods to be used and the ways in which data were to be analysed and written up. While such tensions may be impossible to avoid altogether in a team project, Del Monte (2000) suggests that during the design phase steps can be taken to mitigate them. In particular, she recommends that a 'team compact' is drawn up, which specifies the methods of data collection and analysis to be used, ownership of data, a publication policy and, perhaps most importantly, how disagreements within the team will be handled.

Location of the research

In much education research, the location of the study is determined by the underpinning research questions. For example, an action research project is often conducted in the researcher's own classroom, while a study of workplace learning is likely to take place within specific organizational spaces. Nevertheless, accounts of research that has been conducted in schools and other educational institutions raise interesting questions about the extent to which the location of the study affects what respondents choose to say, how comfortable they are about answering particular questions, and whether they feel able to be honest in their responses. For example, in her research with young people in Ghana, Bochow (2012) argues that her respondents found it much easier to talk to her freely (about relationships, love and sexuality, which was the focus of her study) in schools than within their homes. She argues that within Ghanaian society 'claiming to love somebody in the presence of an older person is seen as evidence of a premature presumption of social maturity and therefore as a violation of the rules of intergenerational respect' (S23); as a result, respondents were uncomfortable about discussing such issues within the home. In contrast, schools were viewed by respondents as spaces in which they could resist parental authority and freely exchange their experiences of relationships and views about sexuality. Various UK-based studies have revealed rather different issues, however; indeed, some British scholars have suggested that conducting research within schools may reduce pupils' capacity to decline to become involved, or their willingness to be honest in the replies they give, because of the hierarchical relationships that pervade many educational institutions (Pole et al., 1999; Heath et al., 2007; Lambert, 2008). This is discussed in more detail, in relation to informed consent in particular, in Chapter 5.

The location of the research also has relevance for researcher safety. The ethical guidelines produced by the Social Research Association (2003) argue that social researchers have a moral obligation to protect themselves, and any other researchers for whom they are responsible, from risk of harm. This may affect decisions about whether data are collected in public or private locations. While travelling to people's homes to collect data may be the ethical course of action in some circumstances (e.g. when interviewing respondents about very sensitive matters), in other cases it may be more ethical to meet respondents in public spaces. As Kenyon and Hawker (1999) note, despite acknowledging that the chance of a dangerous encounter is low, social researchers report that fears about their own safety do arise during periods of fieldwork (and that such fears can affect the quality of data collected). A decision to conduct research in people's homes can also affect the sample that is achieved: for example, as will be discussed further in Chapter 5, in an Australian study on family experiences of transition to school, the gatekeeper chose not to pass on details of families that had a history of violence – because he or she was aware that interviews may be conducted within participants' homes (Dockett et al., 2009). Presumably this decision was taken out of concern for the safety of the researchers but, as Dockett et al. (2009) note, it had ramifications for both data analysis and the outcomes of the whole study.

It is not always the case that 'appropriate' or 'inappropriate' locations for education research can be anticipated in advance. This is illustrated well in Hudson's account of her decision not to visit 'the ditch' during her school-based ethnography (Hudson, 2004, cited in Hammersley and Traianou, 2012b). This was a place on the school's premises but out of the sight of teachers, which was popular with students and where many congregated at lunchtime and break-times. The teachers at the school, however, viewed it primarily as a space where illicit activities took place. Hudson was invited by some of the students to visit 'the ditch' and, presumably, such a visit would have offered an opportunity to collect potentially rich and revealing data. However, she declined the invitation, as she believed that to do so would be seen by staff as condoning what were seen as unacceptable student activities. In this example, we see the ways in which ethical judgements (about not wanting to condone particular types of behaviour) can often be closely intertwined with pragmatic considerations and power relationships in the field; it is possible that if she had indeed visited 'the ditch', the teachers at the school may have been less inclined to facilitate other parts of her research. Hudson's work also shows how ethical issues relating to research design often have to be made in the midst of data collection – not just at the very beginning of a project.

Data archiving

Although the archiving of research data typically occurs at the end of a project, a decision about how this will be done frequently constitutes an important part of initial research design. In the UK, for example, researchers are currently required to include a 'data management plan' as part of any research proposal submitted for funding to the Economic and Social Research Council. This requires them to address a series of questions about data archiving, as well as about the security of data throughout the duration of the project.

While offering to deposit a dataset in a national or institutional repository can be viewed as good research practice on the grounds of openness, transparency and ensuring that maximum use is derived from data, some scholars have problematized this practice. With respect to qualitative data in particular, Mauthner (2012) questions whether it is ethical (or indeed meaningful) to ask respondents to give informed consent to share their stories for future uses that they have not been informed about. Indeed, she suggests that, as informed consent is usually given 'within specific relational terms and conditions' (p.158), potentially harmful effects may follow from seeing one's story interpreted through different lenses or used for different purposes entirely.

This shift towards data archiving is a relatively new development, facilitated by the growth of new technologies, and is not commonplace across the globe, even in the Global North. Indeed, in Canada and Australia, for example, it is still more usual for data to be destroyed after a specific number of years has elapsed. Here, too, however, tensions may occur. Indeed, drawing on her work in Canada, Ball describes the distress experienced by some Indigenous communities on hearing that research data are usually destroyed:

> Indigenous community leaders have been distressed at the prospect that valuable information, such as Elders' testimonials, might be treated as so trivial as to be discarded: Elders would be expending precious time and energy in their final years to transmit their knowledge for the research project. A community may request that interview transcripts are stored in the community, for example in a cultural centre, rather than at the research institution, with the intention that these data never be destroyed. (2005, p.89)

Ball suggests that one way in which a research project can 'give back' to such participants is by collecting and retaining Indigenous knowledge for continued community use.

Conclusion

In this chapter, we have outlined some of the ethical considerations that impinge upon the design of an education research project – from the very first stage of choosing the topic through to archiving data at the end of a project. We acknowledge, however, that not all ethical decisions can be made at the start of a research project. As we have noted above, some research methods – particularly ethnographies and longitudinal qualitative studies – are, by the very nature of their design, open-ended, making it difficult to predict the course the research will ultimately take. Furthermore, even the most well-designed research sometimes throws up events and disclosures that could not have been anticipated in advance. Thus, while it is important to ensure that ethics are given due consideration when designing a research project, they cannot be forgotten once the research has commenced. Indeed, as the subsequent chapters of this book demonstrate, ethics needs to inform all our actions as education researchers – from design through to dissemination.

CHAPTER 5

INFORMED CONSENT AND RECIPROCITY

Andrew is doing a PhD on young primary school children's view about their friendships. Nearly all the parents have consented to their children being interviewed in focus groups. Sean's mother has not given her consent although Ms Briggs, the class teacher, thinks this is because she lost the form or forgot to return it. Andrew takes a small group off to the library and then sees that Sean is in the group. He is with Mohammed, his best friend. Ms Briggs comes hurrying into the library. 'Oh there you are Sean', she says. 'Stay with Andrew now you are here'. What should Andrew do?

Andrew's dilemma in the extract above introduces us to a number of important themes that relate, broadly, to the notion of informed consent. First, it alerts us to the power relationships inherent in conducting research in educational institutions – in this case between Andrew, as the researcher, and Ms Briggs, the teacher: does Andrew have the authority and/or right to send Sean back to class, if he believes that, ethically, it is the correct course of action? Second, it emphasizes the socially embedded nature of decisions whether or not to take part in research projects:

was Sean's apparent eagerness to be involved motivated by his desire to be with his friend Mohammed? Or perhaps, instead, he was keen to miss the lesson in which the rest of the class were involved. Third, it raises questions about whose consent is needed for education research: does it matter that Sean's parents had not signed the relevant form, if Sean himself was keen to be involved? And fourth, we are introduced to debates about the way in which consent is demonstrated: can Sean's eagerness to take part be accepted as sufficient evidence of consent, or is some formal record always required?

These questions form the basis for much of the discussion in this chapter. After first providing a definition of informed consent, and outlining some of the legal imperatives that underpin it, we consider who has capacity to consent, paying particular attention to the position of young children and those with learning difficulties. We then explore the socially-embedded nature of decision making and some of the questions this raises about whether, in schools, colleges and other educational institutions, consent can ever be considered as freely given. Here, we focus, particularly, on the role of parents, teachers and other 'gatekeepers'. We then move on to considering the way in which issues related to informed consent may differ by research method, before exploring the means by which potential participants can be informed about research. Finally, we consider various ways in which researchers have tried to establish reciprocity within research projects, and the implications these may have for informed consent.

What is informed consent?

The concept of informed consent is closely associated with the ethical principle of ensuring 'respect for persons' (as discussed in Chapter 2). It is generally understood to be underpinned by three important principles (Thorne, 1980). First, that it should be based on adequate knowledge: prospective participants should thus be provided with information about the research project that is 'sufficiently full and accessible for their decision about whether to take part to be considered informed' (Crow et al., 2006, p.83). Second, it is important that a decision to consent is voluntary, and that people are free to decline to participate or withdraw during the research without the fear of any adverse consequences. Third, the decision should be made by people who are competent to choose freely. The concept was originally developed to protect patients from abuse by medical researchers but is now considered an important principle for research across the social sciences as well, and is addressed explicitly in ethical codes. Indeed, *Ethical Guidelines for Educational Research* produced by the British Educational Research Association (BERA, 2011) and the American Educational Research Association's (AERA, 2011) *Code of Ethics* both emphasize the importance of gaining informed voluntary consent for all research involving human participants.

As with many of the other ethical principles discussed in this book, the principle of informed consent articulates concerns about the way in which power relations can be played out in research relationships. Drawing on her experience of conducting research in schools and elsewhere, Thorne (1980, p.294) has argued that informed consent 'offers some protection to the powerless simply by extending a right to be left alone which the powerful have always claimed for themselves'. In her analysis, to be powerful is to be able to guard one's own interests. Informed consent can also, it has been suggested, lead to more equal relationships between researcher and respondent, in which the latter is more aware of the nature of the project, and his or her rights to withdraw. This, Crow et al. (2006) maintain, can have a positive impact on the quality of data that is collected: as participants' confidence in the process in which they are involved increases, so too, they suggest, does their willingness to be open about the aspects of their lives that are being researched. The emphasis on informed consent is not, however, driven solely by concerns about power relationships and data quality. Indeed, as will have been clear from previous chapters, significant institutional pressures are also implicated, particularly the concern of universities and other organizations in which education research is carried out to protect themselves from any possible legal consequences (Homan, 1991; Edwards and Mauthner, 2012).

The legal context – and the capacity to consent

The legal context is important, not only in helping to explain the increasing emphasis organizations have placed on their researchers gaining informed consent, but also in informing the way in which researchers themselves understand the concept. This is particularly relevant in relation to children – and thus to all researchers collecting data in schools, youth clubs, playgrounds and other venues in which children are likely to be present. The last quarter of a century has seen the introduction, across the globe, of legislation that has aimed to assert the rights and protect the interests of children. This has included the 1989 United Nations Convention on the Rights of the Child (see Chapter 3) and Article 10 of the UK Human Rights Act, introduced in 1998 (which gave everyone the right to freedom of expression). Such legislation has emphasized the importance of involving children in decisions that affect them, and ensuring that their voices are heard (Morrow, 2005; Balen et al., 2006). From this perspective, it is argued that children themselves should have as much say as possible in whether or not they participate in any research study. Such arguments have also emanated from within the academic community, particularly from sociologists of childhood (e.g. Hutchby and Moran-Ellis, 1998). Within the UK, this position has been strengthened by what has become known as 'Gillick competence'. As a result of a legal judgment in the 1980s about the rights of under-16s to be prescribed contraception (which found against Victoria Gillick, the mother of an under-16-year-old daughter, who had brought the case to court), it is now accepted within social research that young people are able to consent to participate if they have sufficient understanding to enable them to comprehend fully the likely nature of their involvement, and that assessment of their understanding has been conducted on an individual basis (Balen et al., 2006; Heath et al., 2009). Although this legal framework is clear, as we will demonstrate below and in later parts of the chapter, the way in which it is played out in schools and other educational contexts is not always straightforward.

In line with the Gillick ruling, researchers in the UK are usually expected to assess whether, assuming full information is given, respondents have the ability to 'understand, retain and analyse that information, come to an independent decision and express that decision clearly and effectively to the researcher seeking consent' (Iphofen, 2011, p.72). There are, however, two main problems with this approach. First, it assumes that only some people lack the capacity to consent when, in practice 'more of us lack this capacity than we care to admit' (Iphofen, 2011, p.72). For example, we may not fully understand the implications of particular research methods or, indeed, have a clear view of what is in our own best interests (Gallagher et al., 2010; Hammersley and Traianou, 2012b). Second, it assumes that those with 'less capacity' do not wish to be able to choose for themselves whether or not to become involved in a research project. With respect to young children, this assumption can be seen to reinforce a 'developmental approach' in which children are seen as developing, incomplete versions of adults, rather than competent social actors in their own right (Morrow, 2005). An alternative perspective is put forward by Danby and Farrell (2004, p.35), who argue that researchers should start from the premise that children are 'competent interpreters of their everyday worlds' and that understandings derived from this position can demonstrate how young children undertake 'complex and competent interactional work'.

Within education research, although much of the discussion of the capacity to consent has focused on young children, researchers have also been concerned with the rights of those with disabilities (and learning difficulties, in particular). Indeed, there is evidence that children with disabilities are sometimes excluded from school-based research because of a concern, on the part of some head teachers or principals, that inviting them – but not their non-disabled peers – to participate would serve to highlight their disabilities and thus be contrary to policies of inclusion (Connors and Stalker, 2003). Cuskelly (2005) notes that when working with children with a learning difficulty it is often difficult to know their level of understanding, and thus their capacity to consent, until assessment has been undertaken – and yet such assessment, itself, requires consent. Moreover, she suggests that, as some children with a learning difficulty are more likely than their non-disabled peers to acquiesce when asked a question, it is important that researchers pay attention to the way in which questions about consent are phrased, and that an acquiescent response is not taken necessarily to indicate understanding.

The socially embedded nature of decision making

As discussed above, the concept of informed consent is based on the assumption that research should respect the autonomy of those being studied, and that people should be free to decide for themselves what is best for them and thus whether or not to participate. Although it is enshrined in most ethical codes (in education and other areas of social enquiry) worldwide, some scholars have argued that the concept is underpinned by a very particular understanding of human nature that is fundamentally western and masculinist (Hammersley and Traianou, 2012b). This understanding, it is suggested, is not necessarily in line with more communitarian perspectives, which place greater emphasis on the rights of communities and groups, rather than those of individuals (Thorne, 1980; Hammersley and Traianou, 2012b). For example, Wood and Kidman (2013) have shown how, in their research with Indigenous communities in New Zealand, consent had to be negotiated with the community as a whole, rather than with individuals (see also Ball, 2005). The critique of the liberal individualistic basis of the concept of informed consent has been made particularly clearly by some education researchers who have highlighted the ways in which social settings, such as schools and colleges, can have a significant impact on processes of decision making.

While some education research is conducted in relatively open spaces such as playgrounds (e.g. Taylor, 2007; Richards, 2012) or in private places such as homes (e.g. Walkerdine et al., 2001; Brooks, 2005), a considerable proportion is carried out in institutional locations – particularly schools, colleges and universities. Indeed, conducting research within educational institutions is often seen as a very effective means of recruiting a large number of respondents of a particular demographic profile and ensuring a high response rate (Denscombe and Aubrook, 1992). For this reason, such institutions are frequently used to access young people by researchers whose substantive area of enquiry is not education related (e.g. Pole et al., 1999). While educational institutions may offer the researcher many practical advantages in terms of access, the social nature of the setting also raises important questions about the extent to which consent can be considered as always freely given. Children and young people may, for example, feel pressure to consent through a desire to please, win favour with a teacher, be polite to a school 'visitor', and/or because they fear the consequences of being seen not to be cooperative (Malone, 2003; Heath et al., 2007). Equally, they may consent, not through any particular wish to take part in the research, but to get out of a particular lesson (Gallagher et al., 2010) or to be with their friends – perhaps Sean's motivation in the case study at the beginning of the chapter. Moreover, questionnaire surveys, in particular, may carry connotations of a school test, with the implicit expectation that all students take part and that questions are answered 'neatly, fully and correctly' (Denscombe and Aubrook, 1992, p.126). Morrow (2005) suggests, however, that while students may sometimes conform to peer-group norms, they can often find less obvious ways of indicating their unwillingness to be involved or what she calls 'informed dissent': 'My impression is that if children in a whole-class situation are asked for their consent they all tend to say yes, but a minority of them will simply not participate at all, will write minimally and/or say virtually nothing in discussion' (p.158). This two-way nature of power relationships is explored further in Chapter 6. The social context of educational organizations, and schools in particular, may also make it harder than in other settings for prospective participants to become sufficiently informed about the research. Indeed, as Gallagher et al. (2010, p.69) note, stigma may be attached to admitting that one does not understand or require further information – particularly in educational settings 'where children are routinely expected to listen, pay attention and affirm that they have understood'. Moreover, they suggest that many children are well-practised at acting as though they have understood – developed as part of sophisticated strategies for evading teaching (strategies that can also be adopted by adults).

Children's and young people's relationships with adults in particular social settings may also make it more difficult to achieve freely given consent. Drawing on their health-focused research in Australian schools, Balen et al. (2006) argue that many children and young people expect to comply rather than disagree with professionals, which then often makes it hard for them to decline to participate in a project. They go on to suggest that, to mitigate such problems, researchers need to spend time explaining relevant aspects of the research to potential participants, and emphasizing that their views matter: 'this requires the adult, through "dialectic" rather than "didactic" discussions with children, to demonstrate that a different point of view is possible ... that free the child from any expectation of compliance to adults' (p.44).

Gatekeepers

When collecting data in early childhood settings, schools, colleges, universities and other educational institutions, researchers are often required to liaise with multiple sets of 'gatekeepers' (such as head teachers, principals, heads of department and lecturers) who facilitate access to the institutions and thus, eventually, to the individual research participants. Here, again, we can see possible tensions between the role such gatekeepers often take, and the principles of individual autonomy, upon which the concept of informed consent is based. As Hammersley and Traianou (2012b, p.87) have suggested, 'the considerations that inform decisions by gatekeepers are likely to extend beyond the assumed interests of individual members, and perhaps even beyond what are taken to be the collective interests of the group or organisation'. Moreover, even when a gatekeeper does make a decision in the interests of the group as a whole, it may well not be in line with the interests of all individuals within it.

The gatekeeper's role is discussed in Dockett et al.'s (2009) account of their research in Australia on family experiences of transition to school. The project sought to explore families' diverse and multiple experiences of transition, as a means of facilitating a greater degree of familial engagement in education. The academic researchers worked with two partner organizations that had links with a wide range of families and acted as gatekeepers for the project. While grateful for the support and access provided by the partner organizations, the researchers acknowledge that the decisions taken by gatekeepers had an important bearing on who was represented in the research: 'In one site the partner organisation manager indicated that, because there was the potential for interviews to be conducted in family homes, she had omitted families where violence was an issue' (p.63). This, they suggest, affected not only the composition of the sample – and whether individual families were allowed an opportunity to participate – but also the outcomes of the project. The gatekeeper's role is also discussed by DePalma (2010) in relation to research she conducted investigating attitudes to lesbian, gay, bisexual and transgender (LGBT) inequalities in English primary schools. She recounts the way in which the research team's plans to use videos as part of the project had raised serious concerns on the part of the head teacher (principal) in one of the participating schools. These were 'based on the very real danger that parents might withdraw their children from the school which would have serious financial consequences for an already stretched school budget' (p.221). Although in this particular project pupils were allowed to opt into this component of the research, the quotation illustrates well the various interests gatekeepers often have to consider, and that protecting the group or institution may, in some cases, come at the cost of allowing group members the opportunity to participate.

While gatekeepers may effectively exclude some potential participants, in other cases their decisions may make it harder for potential participants to *decline* to become involved. Indeed, by providing access to less powerful groups, in particular, they may in effect (and unknowingly) authorise consent (Miller and Bell, 2012). Although this is discussed most frequently in relation to children and young people and their less-powerful position within the social organization of schools and colleges, gatekeepers' decisions can also make it harder for adults to decline to become involved in research. For example, Burgess (1989b) provides a candid account of his ethnographic research within a school in the 1980s. As part of his data gathering, he sat in on various job interviews. Although all candidates were told about the research beforehand and asked to consent to being observed, as Burgess notes, 'it is dubious whether this situation can be regarded as constituting informed consent given the power relations involved in the situation' (1989b, p.65). It can be assumed that many interviewees would not want to do anything to jeopardise their chances of being offered the job.

Parents often assume an important role in determining the extent to which their son or daughter is able to consent freely to research participation. Despite the notion of 'Gillick competence' discussed above, in practice, many UK schools do not assess competence to consent on an individual basis but tend to use age as a proxy for developmental stage (and thus capacity to consent). As a consequence, researchers are often required to seek parental consent, not just for research with those who cannot be judged competent to understand what is being asked of them, but all those under a particular age (usually 16) (David et al., 2001; Heath et al., 2007). Such practices have been criticized for being essentially adult-centred and reinforcing normative views of children as dependent and in need of protection (Danby and Farrell, 2004). They also potentially impinge on the right of children to be heard – particularly in cases in which they are keen to take part in research but parental consent is not given. For example, in the opening case study, if Sean had been keen to participate in Andrew's research, some researchers would argue he should be allowed to join in, irrespective of whether or not his parents had returned the relevant form. The situation in Australia is similar. The national guidelines state that 'An ethical review body may approve research to which only the young person consents if it is satisfied that he or she is mature enough to understand and consent, and not vulnerable through immaturity in ways that would warrant additional consent from a parent or guardian' (NHMRC, ARC and UA, 2007, pp.56–57). In practice, however, Research Ethics Committees (RECs) and researchers themselves tend to refer to biological age to determine the necessity for parental consent, rather than make an assessment of young people's maturity. This contradicts the explicit argument in the Australian guidelines that 'It is not possible to attach fixed ages to each level [of maturity]' (p.55).

Placing emphasis on parental consent can be seen as problematic not only for the reasons outlined above. For example, in some cases, it is not always clear who should be providing such consent. 'Looked after children' (i.e. those who are looked after by the state) may have relationships with multiple adults, including those from social services and local authorities, as well as foster parents and their own biological parents (Driscoll, 2013). Furthermore, in some contexts, young people may live independently without an adult present. Jeanes and Kay (2013) describe how this was the case for many of the young people in Zambia who they were keen to recruit for their research: many were orphans and several, although under the age of 18, were heads of household, with caring responsibilities for younger siblings. As they were performing adult roles, Jeanes and Kay argue that requesting consent from adult gatekeepers was 'potentially disrespectful of the competence and responsibility the young people displayed in their everyday lives' (p.22).

The requirement of parental consent may also act to limit both response rates to social research and the topics that such research is able to explore. For example, Heath et al. (2007) describe how a doctoral student had been keen to investigate young gay men's experiences of schooling, through conducting interviews at youth clubs. However,

[t]he student's university ethics committee had insisted that consent be gained first from parents, an insistence which [the doctoral student] viewed as 'completely unethical'. The opportunity to explore this topic

was consequently lost through an insensitive approach, one which demonstrated a lack of understanding of the specific research context and of the broader ethical issues concerned. (p.411)

Similarly, in Balen et al.'s (2006) research on contraception and sexual activity conducted with young women in Australian schools, the requirement for parental consent for those under 16 significantly reduced the sample size: 200 flyers about the research were distributed, but only 12 young women eventually took part in the interviews. The researchers conclude that the requirement for parental consent 'effectively meant that the participants would comprise only those who were interested in being in the research themselves, who were willing for their parents to know that they were interested in discussing contraception and sexual activity, and who then returned a parental consent form to school' (p.40). Researchers are, however, sometimes successful in securing ethics approval for projects with under-16s that do not require parental consent. Indeed, Balen et al. describe a second case study – of an evaluation of a UK school-based counselling service. In this example, where it was thought not appropriate, for reasons of confidentiality, to ask for parental consent, a young person's counsellor provided assent, based on their view that participation would not inflict any harm. A detailed leaflet was produced by the research team for discussion with the young person beforehand.

How should the education researcher respond to these critiques of the notion of freely given informed consent? On the one hand, some suggest that researchers should make greater efforts to recruit participants from outside of institutional settings to avoid some of the problems discussed above (Heath et al., 2007). On the other hand, others argue that, particularly with quantitative studies, the quality of data collected is likely to suffer considerably if researchers move away from recruiting their sample through schools and colleges (Denscombe and Aubrook, 1992). Indeed, some suggest that the possible gains to children, overall, as a result of specific school-based research projects can outweigh a lack of fully informed consent. In relation to their research on paid work in late childhood, and their decision to recruit participants through schools, Pole and colleagues (1999) acknowledge that the structures through which they negotiated access were ones that exercised power over the children concerned. Nevertheless, they go on to argue that

> [a]t worst these are structures that deny the agency of children, or at best temper it. The imperatives of our research, however, meant that we were prepared to work within the existing structures and to engage in a compromise which, by giving us access to appropriate children, would allow us to place them at its centre. (p.48)

Difference by method?

The discussion so far in this chapter has focused, primarily, on issues that are common to many different types of education research. There are, however, some ethical dilemmas to do with consent that are more specific to particular approaches, some of which relate to the broad differences between qualitative and quantitative methods. For example, the outcomes of research are often harder to identify in advance when using qualitative approaches, because of the flexible nature of such methods. Thus, it is frequently difficult, or even impossible, to inform potential participants in any detail about that to which they may be consenting (Thorne, 1980; Gallagher et al., 2010; Alldred and Gillies, 2012). Indeed, the researchers themselves may not know the direction the research will take. Some qualitative researchers have gone as far as to argue that, for this reason, the concept of informed consent is largely unworkable, and should be replaced by an 'ethics of care', in which emphasis is placed on care and responsibility for respondents within the context of specific research relationships, however the research eventually unfolds (Edwards and Mauthner, 2012). Others have suggested that consent needs to be renegotiated on an ongoing basis throughout qualitative research projects, particularly in ethnographies and studies that have a longitudinal element (Gallagher et al., 2010). In his account of his 12-year longitudinal ethnography on learning and identity, for example, Pollard (2007) describes how consent was secured in different ways and on a regular basis throughout the project, taking account of both the changing age of the children/young people and the evolving focus of the research. For example, at the start of the study, when the children were beginning primary school (and so 4 or 5 years old), consent was gained from their parents. However, later on in the study, when the children moved to secondary school, they were themselves asked to consent to further participation as, by this stage, they had developed a good understanding of the nature of the research.

To illustrate further some of the method-specific issues that impinge on the principle of informed consent, we focus below on three research methods that are popular with those conducting research on education-related topics: ethnography and other forms of participatory research; action research; and research in online spaces.

Ethnography and participant observation

Ethnography is typically understood as the study of people in naturally occurring settings by methods of data collection that capture their ordinary activities and the social meanings that are attached to these (Heath et al., 2009). Examples from education have included studies of: student culture within medical schools (Becker et al., 1976); girls' friendship groups within school (Hey, 1997); setting, streaming and other forms of school organization (Hargreaves 1967; S. Ball, 1981); prom nights (Best, 2000); and, perhaps most famously, the responses of working-class boys to formal education (Willis, 1977). Ethnographers usually do not give extensive information to everyone they observe on the basis that it is often not possible to specify in advance what data will be collected and how it will be used (Burgess, 1989b) and that a large number of participants may be involved. As a result, few ethnographies offer participants a specific 'moment of choice' about whether or not to become involved. Instead, researchers often tend to assume that 'if their presence is tolerated, if they aren't told to leave, consent has been granted' (Thorne, 1980, p.290). For example, in relation to his ethnographic research on sexuality and the construction of masculinities in schools, McCormack (2012) explains that, while he acquired informed consent for the interviews he conducted, he did not do so for the general interactions he observed while 'hanging out' with young men in common rooms and other social spaces in schools. He describes his general approach in the following way:

> When meeting new students, either in lessons or the common room, I would introduce myself by saying I was a university student 'writing a book on what it means to be a guy in school today'. I said that I wanted to hear their opinions and views, and to get to know them as well. The extent of participants' knowledge of my research (beyond my introduction) was dependent on how much they asked. (McCormack, 2011, p.89)

Dilemmas about how much information to give to research participants, and when such information is best given, are particularly common in participant observation, when the researcher takes on a role as an active participant in the social setting: for example, Bigler's (2010) study of an adventure playground. Here, those who are being researched, even if they have provided informed consent at the start of the project, may sometimes forget about the researcher's presence and be unaware of the extent to which their body language and informal utterances may be construed as data (DePalma, 2010). Moreover, some education researchers have described how, once they have been trained to conduct observations, it is difficult to 'turn off' their researcher's gaze when projects have not yet started and/or informed consent has not yet been given (DePalma, 2010). Finally, the typically long length of the period of data collection can also result in friendships being formed between researcher and researched, such that the latter may forget they are part of a research project (Eglinton, 2013). The establishment of friendships can also make it harder for the researcher to leave the field at the end of a period of data collection, through fear of causing harm to participants, while such bonds may not have been anticipated by participants, themselves, when they initially agreed to take part (Eglinton, 2013).

Action research

Teachers conducting action research may include participant observation as part of their broader focus on collecting data about how their particular schools operate, how they teach and/or how students learn (Nolen and Putten, 2007). However, a distinguishing feature of this approach to research is that the researcher typically continues to assume their original role (usually as a teacher, but sometimes as an administrator or another professional with an interest in teaching and learning) throughout the period of the research. The multiple responsibilities and sensitivities associated with occupying two roles within the classroom can raise particular dilemmas with respect to a range of ethical issues (Bell and Nutt, 2012). In relation to informed consent, it can be difficult for action researchers to assume that students' consent has been freely given: they may feel an obligation to participate because of the power relationships discussed earlier in this chapter, and also a concern that their school marks may suffer if they decline (Nolen and Putten, 2007). Moreover, in some cases, it can be difficult to explain the role of a teacher-researcher as, in the minds of many parents and children, research is not always construed as something intertwined with classroom practice (DePalma, 2010).

In common with some of the ethnographic approaches discussed above, some action researchers have worked on the assumption that is it not necessary to gain informed consent from all individuals who may be involved in such a project. DePalma (2010), for example, reflects on how, for her participatory action research project investigating attitudes to lesbian, gay, bisexual and transgender (LGBT) equalities in English primary schools, she and the other academics in the research team secured consent only from the head teachers of the schools involved and the teacher-researchers who carried out much of the data collection and analysis. She notes that she and the research team did consider, during the project, whether they should have gained consent from the children who were involved, and their parents. They were also concerned, however, that

> [w]ell-meaning attempts to 'inform' might backfire, constructing the project as experimental and dangerous, and reinforcing the very homophobic

assumptions we were trying to undo. After all, we were trying to find a space where the silenced could speak and be heard, and we were well aware of the tendency for these marginalised voices to be heard as shouts and unreasonable rants when they first break the silence. (DePalma, 2010, p.219)

While the research team itself did not seek consent from children or parents on any systematic basis, the individual teacher-researchers in the 16 schools in the study made their own choices about consent. In some cases, they consciously refrained from informing parents on the grounds that their action research was akin to curriculum development, and that they would not have asked for parental consent before introducing a new mathematics curriculum, for example (DePalma, 2010). Others, however, made different choices, and informed parents fully through meetings, newsletters, discussions at parent governor meetings, and invitations to view the work that children produced as part of the project. Many of these activities were pursued because the teacher-researchers feared an angry response if they had introduced such a 'sensitive' topic in the classroom without having kept parents informed.

Action researchers have also found informed consent problematic because, like ethnography and other forms of qualitative research discussed above, the nature of the proposed classroom 'action' may not be known at the start of a project (Nolen and Putten, 2007). Furthermore, even in cases where informed consent has been given, it can be unwise to assume that all those involved always remember that they are part of a research project. Indeed, reflecting on her role in the 'Girls into Science and Technology' action research project in the 1980s, Kelly (1989) argues that the dual nature of the project – as both action and research – may have dulled the teachers involved into a false sense of security, with the result that they became less guarded than they would have been in a more conventional research project about what they revealed of themselves to the researcher.

Research in online spaces

While both ethnography and action research are now both well-established as research methods within education, with large associated literatures, the use of online methods has a much more recent history. Moreover, it is only relatively recently that education researchers have started to explore the ethical implications of internet-based research. Much of the debate about ethics, to date, has focused on the growing ambiguity between demarcations between the private and the public in the online world (Snee, 2008; Mauthner et al., 2012; Young, 2013), and this has particular significance for our understanding of informed consent.

While some contend that data such as blog entries and posting on particular social networking sites are in the public domain and thus should be considered secondary data (Snee, 2010, 2013; Collins, 2012), others argue that as 'the ethical expectations of researchers are far higher that the expectations of those operating and publishing in [online] environments … simply appropriating content because it is public and accessible is questionable' (Schuck et al., 2010, p.241). Thus, in many cases, education researchers have sought both to inform potential participants of the nature of the research and gain their informed consent. Battles (2010) outlines some of the ethical conundrums she faced in her research on informal health education that was taking place through postings on an internet message board about the human papilloma virus vaccine.* The message board she used was publicly viewable, and yet she was concerned that the young people who used it may have understood it in different terms – as a private, or at least a semi-private, space. She considered whether informed consent should be sought from the individuals who had posted messages, the community as a whole and/or the organization that owned the website. Ultimately, she decided that as the information was publicly available, she would not seek the permission of users' parents. She did, however, send a message to all 72 of the people who had posted messages, telling them about how she was intending to use the information, and providing them with an opportunity to withdraw their own data from the study. Permission was also sought from the website's administrative team.

The accounts of those who have conducted education research in online spaces indicate that processes of securing informed consent are rarely as straightforward as in off-line environments. If researcher and participant never meet face-to-face (as is likely online), it becomes more difficult to negotiate terms of consent and to gain a signature. Although prospective participants can be asked to tick a box on an online form to indicate consent, the researcher is not around to ensure that he or she reads the preamble (Lally et al., 2012) and, as discussed in Chapter 4, in large-scale online surveys it is often impossible for respondents to withdraw their data after they have completed the questionnaire as such surveys are usually anonymous. Moreover, it is possible for participants to conceal and/or misrepresent important demographic information, which might lead to potentially vulnerable populations being recruited without appropriate consent from their parents or guardians (Kanuka and

---

*This vaccine prevents infection from viruses associated with the development of cervical cancer and other less common cancers. It is recommended for young women up to the age of 26.

Anderson, 2007). Furthermore, if parental consent is deemed necessary, it may be impossible for the researcher to be certain that the relevant information has been passed on by the child or young person, and that the parental consent is genuine (Schuck et al., 2010). Education researchers have also expressed concern that by encouraging young people to interact with them in online spaces, for the purposes of research, they may unwittingly be clouding general guidelines for internet safety, which advise avoiding contact with strangers (Schuck et al., 2010).

Presenting information to potential research participants

If informed consent is to be sought, it is important that potential respondents are given appropriate information about the research project in which they are being asked to take part. Researchers typically suggest this information should include: the identity of the researchers and their institution(s); the source of funding for the research; an explanation of how and why respondents have been selected to take part; whether confidentiality and/or anonymity is promised, and the steps that will be taken to ensure this; how data will be reported (with brief details about the analytic framework, if known); and contact details for at least one of the researchers involved (Thorne, 1980; Iphofen, 2011). The use of a form to document consent is often required by university ethics committees and recommended by research texts. However, as Gallagher et al. (2010) argue, this can sometimes have the effect of focusing the researcher's attention on informed consent as a product, rather than a process. In some cases, however, particularly those involving young children, participation and engagement can be taken to imply consent. Furthermore, for some cultural groups, oral consent can also be deemed sufficient (Bridges, 2009). The Australian guidelines (NHMRC, ARC and AVCC, 2007, p.19) recognize that written consent is not always appropriate, stating that '[c]onsent may be expressed orally, in writing or by some other means (for example, return of a survey, or conduct implying consent), depending on: (a) the nature, complexity and level of risk of the research; and (b) the participant's personal and cultural circumstances'.

A number of education researchers who have conducted research with children in schools and other settings have discussed the way in which information can be provided in a 'child-friendly' manner. Suggestions typically include providing information packages to take home, discussing the research with children in classrooms, and giving them plenty of opportunities to ask questions (Danby and Farrell, 2004). Although it is important that the information provided is appropriate to students' level of competence, this is sometimes difficult in schools because of the way in which students are organized by age rather than educational competence, and the fact that researchers are often given access to a particular year group, rather than students who have reached a specific level of competence (David et al., 2001). It is also important to recognize that the way in which information is presented to potential respondents is not neutral. Indeed, the formality of some initial consent procedures may alienate some groups, particularly those who are vulnerable, do not wish their details to be recorded formally and/or fear the researcher is a representative of 'officialdom' (Miller and Bell, 2012). In other cases, the content of material used to introduce research can frame the study in particular, and often unanticipated, ways. This is illustrated well in David et al.'s (2001) account of the various approaches they used to inform their potential respondents about their research on children's understandings of parental involvement in education. For example, they argue that the information sheets that were handed out to students, in advance of asking for participants, gave the impression of situating the research within particular discourses – despite the researchers' attempts to be as neutral as possible. They note, for example, that the information sheets were 'sprinkled with question marks' (p.353). This, they argue, could be read as

> a sign or symbol of the questioning nature of liberal education and our liberal approach to children and their right to a voice. It can also be read as signalling that children and young people could and should be questioning and challenging dominant received ideas about parental involvement in education. (p.353).

Furthermore, David et al. (2001) argue that, although their aim was to situate the research outside dominant education discourses, their decision to introduce the project by talking to whole classes and standing at the front of the class assuming a quasi-teacher role had the effect of blurring the boundaries between education and information-giving. They suggest that this framed their study as closely aligned to dominant discourses of education, and may have affected participants' understandings of the nature of the research project. This alignment may also have made it more difficult for students to decline to participate.

Limited disclosure

A frequent dilemma, when providing initial information about a research project, is the extent to which one should be explicit about the aims and objectives of the study. It is a common practice to offer only 'partial truths' when negotiating access (Hammersley and Traianou, 2012b). For example, Riddell (1989) describes how, when negotiating access for her research on subject choices and how these were mediated by messages about femininity and masculinity transmitted by schools, parents and peer groups, she chose not to be explicit about the purpose of her study. She notes that, despite the important grounding of the project within feminist perspectives, 'since the headmaster clearly had a view of educational research as neutral and objective, it would have been catastrophic to introduce myself as a feminist' (p.82). Similarly, Kelly's (1989) framing of her own project as one about 'equal opportunities' rather than feminism was largely due to her knowledge that the teachers with whom she would be working tended to have a negative view of feminism. Furthermore, in her initial contact with the school, she emphasized her focus on children's behaviour and attitudes, even though she was equally interested in those of the teachers, believing that the teachers would be unlikely to cooperate if they thought they were seen as part of the problem. Her approach, she acknowledges, 'did not conform to the high ideals of informed consent' (p.108). Although the research conducted by Riddell and Kelly was conducted in the 1980s and the focus of feminist research has changed considerably over the intervening period, the broader point – about offering only 'partial truths' to help secure access – often remains relevant for those conducting critical research.

Many researchers would argue, nevertheless, that this type of 'incomplete disclosure' can sometimes be justified if it can be demonstrated that participants should not be told too much in order to accomplish the goals of the research. Hammersley and Traianou (2012b), for example, argue that if a researcher is interested in the questions asked by students in classrooms, being explicit about the focus of the research may encourage the students involved to ask more questions than they would normally. In such cases, where the focus of the research has been deliberately withheld at the start of the research, retrospective consent to use the data can be sought. There is less agreement among researchers, however, with respect to *covert* research – in which details of the research may never be revealed to those involved. While some argue that this level of deception can never be justified, research codes typically indicate that covert research may be justified in some particular situations. The British Educational Research Association's guidelines (BERA, 2011), for example, state that while securing voluntary informed consent should be the norm, researchers should avoid deception 'unless their research design specifically requires it to ensure that the appropriate data is collected or that the welfare of researchers is not put in jeopardy' (para. 14). In such cases, researchers are expected to obtain approval from their local REC, and disclose full details of their approach in subsequent reporting.

Options for reciprocity

Many education researchers believe that it is important to offer potential respondents something 'in return' for participating in a research project. This is sometimes motivated by an appreciation of the burden that being involved in research can impose on a particular institution and/or the individuals involved. In other cases, it can be part of an attempt to reduce the power inequalities within research relationships, and to avoid what Lather (1986) has termed 'rape research', in which 'the researcher gets what they want and then clears off, giving nothing or little in return and perhaps even causing damage' (Sikes, 2006, p.112). Sometimes it can also be part of a strategy to encourage participation, or a mark of cultural respect (Daley, 2002). Below, we explore three particular types of reciprocity: the offering of incentives; the provision of advice; and the invitation to become fully involved in the research project.

Offering incentives

Financial incentives are offered increasingly commonly in education research as a means of valuing the contribution of participants (and particularly the time they have given up to be involved) and, for some, an attempt to reduce the power differentials between the researchers and those being researched (Dockett et al., 2009). In some situations, it has been shown that financial compensation can broaden the range of participants prepared to take part in a particular piece of research, and thus the overall representativeness of the study (Cuskelly, 2005). In general, researchers try to ensure that the incentives offered are not so attractive that they cannot be refused. Nevertheless, there is some evidence that even relatively modest inducements can have an important bearing on decisions whether or not to participate and, in some cases, may undermine the principle of free choice, upon which informed consent is based (Farrugia, 2013). Drawing on her research on children with disabilities, Cuskelly (2005) argues that financial incentives offered to parents may increase the likelihood that children's wishes about participating in research are given less heed by their parents. It is also possible that inducements can have the opposite effect, and *discourage* participation, as Dockett et al. (2009) experienced when they offered financial compensation to families who took part in their research on transitions to school: 'In one site, staff from the partner organisation [that was facilitating recruitment of families for the research] explained that two potential participants had chosen not to attend a meeting because they were embarrassed to be regarded as in need of the vouchers' (p.361). They note that another participant refused the vouchers on offer, explaining that he did not expect to be paid for giving up his time for something that he believed would, either directly or indirectly, help his family.

Providing advice

Providing advice and/or information to respondents is often used as a means of increasing the reciprocal nature of the research – either instead of other incentives or alongside them. This is frequently underpinned by a feminist perspective that emphasizes the importance of the researcher sharing his or her own experiences and reciprocal mutual disclosure (Oakley, 1981; Duncombe and Jessop, 2012). Here, there are few concerns about the provision of advice and the sharing of experiences undermining the freely given nature of consent. Instead, however, other ethical issues are brought into play. In the research on transitions to primary school, discussed above, the research team provided relevant information when asked for it by the families involved in the study (Dockett et al., 2009). However, they remain sceptical that this did anything to negate the power they held within the research relationship. Moreover, they note that such requests presented ethical dilemmas for the researchers 'who were conscious of influencing the research itself, wary of setting up relationships of dependence from which they would have to withdraw, as well as judging whether or not they were capable of providing the help being sought' (p.360).

Inviting participants to become fully involved

Some researchers advocate full involvement of research participants in all stages of a project, from data collection through to analysis and dissemination (Alderson, 2001; Hill, 2006). From this perspective, research is conceived of as a shared enterprise, involving the exchange of ideas and understanding (Birch and Miller, 2012). For some, this is understood primarily as a means of achieving more equal research relationships (Lather, 1986). Others perceive it as more closely aligned to the concept of informed consent: that if we are properly to respect the freedom and autonomy of people, then they have the right, if they so wish, to participate on an equal footing with researchers (Hammersley and Traianou,

2012b). While some education researchers have taken significant steps to involve their respondents in their projects (e.g. Rogers and Ludhra, 2011), this approach is, again, not without its critics. Hammersley and Traianou (2012b), for example, characterize the ideal of equality within research relationships as both unrealistic and unjustifiable, arguing that it would be impossible for people to be equally involved in the governance of all the many activities that touch their lives. It has also been suggested that aiming to achieve equality with respondents can mask deeper forms of exploitation (Stacey, 1988), and that researchers should not assume that respondents welcome closer involvement in projects (Birch and Miller, 2012).

Conclusion

In this chapter, we have suggested that although informed consent can be defined in relatively simple terms, it is a complex and sometimes problematic concept. In particular, we have drawn attention to: the ways in which consent is linked to our understanding of competence; the significance of power relationships in educational institutions in affecting consent processes; some differences of approach by method; the implications of presenting information in particular ways; and options for establishing reciprocal relationships with research participants. On the basis of this analysis, we would agree with Gallagher et al. (2010, p.473) that informed consent can be seen as valuable 'only in as far as it is used reflexively, in a way which opens up – rather than closes down – a space for negotiation, questioning and dialogue'. Approaching the concept in this way, as part of a broader acceptance that ethics is about how to deal with ambivalence rather than attempting to eliminate it altogether (Edwards and Mauthner, 2012), will help to ensure that it does not induce a false sense of security nor a tick-box mentality.

CHAPTER 6

IDENTITY, POWER AND POSITIONALITY

> Jane, a white, mid-aged academic researcher, was conducting research in a diverse metropolitan secondary school. She saw Tunde, a young Black African male student, coming along the corridor. He was a student with whom she found it hard to establish a relationship, although she wanted to recruit him for her work. She greeted him and said how she liked his new hairstyle – cornrows. He replied, 'You are just saying that 'cos you want me to be in your project' as he walked past. How should Jane respond?

In this chapter, we explore some of the issues involved in negotiating ethics in practice. As we have already signalled in this book, we see ethics as a participatory process that needs constant negotiation and renegotiation. Now we want to concentrate on some of the complexities that come into play when issues of identity, power and positionality are being considered. We argue that ethically conducted research has to pay careful attention to all these factors. As we have already claimed in this book, 'Ethical practice is an ongoing interaction of values in shifting contexts and relationships rather than something delivered by a signed consent form or adherence to a static set of principles' (Hughes, 2005, p.231). In this dynamic process, a critical analysis of the identity of, and the positionalities and power relationships between the researcher and the researched, is part of the process of being ethical and being reflexive.

The relations between researcher and researched can throw up sometimes unexpected ethical tensions as the research is being undertaken. Ethical matters have to be continually negotiated in practice; at different moments and in different spaces, power relations may shift and change. Research relationships 'can be characterized as fluid, negotiable and unpredictable' (Barker and Smith, 2001, p.146) as we shall see. Different aspects of identities may become foregrounded at different times and may alter the dynamics of the research. Differences in roles, power and identity will be constantly reworked and renegotiated in the process of doing research. Positionality effects the research process – and thus, 'positions matter' (Hart, 2001, p.1).

The focus of this chapter is on the ethics of positionality. It considers power relationships between researchers and research participants, and debates about the extent to which 'matching' social characteristics can be important in establishing and maintaining rapport and trust. It explores the ways in which researchers present themselves during the course of a research project, and how they understand the position of those they are researching. The chapter then considers some of the ethical complexities of positionality that come into play when 'researching the margins'. Finally, we explore the ethical issues involved when research is conducted with one's own colleagues.

Power relationships between researchers and research participant

When researchers are starting to design their research projects, they will become involved in a process of submitting ethics approval documentation for the institution where they are studying (see Chapter 2). They will generally consult professional ethical guidelines. While most guidelines will locate their advice in a set of principles concerned with respect and beneficence, Macfarlane (2009) argues that, '[i]nvariably, codes and guidelines produced by these various parties tell researchers what they must *not* do' (p.3). Very often, in the advice provided to researchers about how to complete ethics approval documentation, rather than detailing fundamental principles for research, concerns will be expressed about issues of power and position that may make it harder for (some) researchers to obtain ethics approval, particularly practitioner-researchers. For example,

teachers researching in their own schools will have to be extremely careful to ensure that their students or colleagues participate voluntarily, giving their 'informed consent' and ensuring that the participants know that
they can withdraw if they so wish, without any 'harm' or repercussions to
their well-being. So far, so good.

However, power differentials are not always 'obvious' and may be
asymmetric in practice. In the case study at the start of this chapter,
in many contexts and 'readings', Jane could be regarded as the more
powerful person. In this particular instance, Tunde holds the power
to label and define what is going on in this short encounter – and
what is more, seems to have identified Jane's strategy, from his
perspective, as being somewhat manipulative. Power relations cannot always be read off from status in any straightforward way,
although there are obvious ethical issues where the researched are
positioned as 'vulnerable' as is frequently the case with research on/
with children.

Researching with children

Researching with children can be fraught with ethical concerns, before,
during and after the data has been collected. Working with children is
generally regarded as ethically more sensitive as well as more complex;
this is because children are frequently positioned as 'vulnerable' and
relatively powerless due to their social status and positioning in society.
As Greig et al. (2007, p.176) point out, 'researchers must be particularly
aware that age alone is not a foolproof indicator of a child's ability to
understand or give either consent or assent' (see Chapter 5 in this book).
In contrast, it has been argued that some overly protective ethical concerns only serve to infantilize children through particular versions of
'vulnerability' that signal their powerlessness and lack of knowledge/
experience. In contrast, it could be argued that Tunde was far more contextually powerful than Jane in our case study at the start of this chapter.

In the UK, the work of Alderson has radically addressed children's
capacities and capabilities to be consulted and to make decisions about
their medical treatment. She has consistently argued that children should
be regarded as competent and sophisticated decision-makers, and
treated as holders of human rights (Alderson, 1990, 1995). In terms
of children, the ethical issues are the same as with any participant: all
participants are free to participate or not; they should come to no harm
through their participation and they should be treated fairly and
respectfully in the research process. When it comes to matters of
data interpretation and dissemination, there is some potential for the

mis-representation of children's perceptions, values and behaviours by adult researchers, who may not always check back with their participants about their findings and conclusions. Thus, it could be that even where all the ethical preparations for access, participation and consent were carefully managed, differential power relations may sometimes result in unequal and disrespectful outcomes where children's views become sensationalized or trivialized in research publications or other reports of the research (although this is a problem with the representation of all research with all sorts of participants).

Barker and Smith (2001) conducted fieldwork with children who were members of various out-of-school clubs. They found that once they were in the research field, observing and recording the children's activities, power relationships were far more complicated than they had anticipated. John Barker's decision 'not to collude with practices that excluded girls' (he refused to play boys-only football) meant that 'some of the boys withdrew their support and consent for the research' (p.144). Researchers are not always situated in more powerful positions than children; 'positionality is never fixed but rather shifts' (p.144). In this case, the children were the final gatekeepers and controlled access and participation in a unequivocal manner.

So far, we have stressed some of the more 'common-place' ethical issues that are involved in researching with children – issues to do with access, consent and power – that will have to be dealt with by any researcher as they complete ethics approval application documents. But there are other sets of ethical issues that relate to working with children that are sometimes side-lined; issues that can reflect assumptions about competence. There are ethical issues that surround the methodological framework more generally, that might not always be given the same level of consideration. For example, Clark (2004) undertook some of the fieldwork in a project with children in a multi-agency childcare network. The children were aged from three to four, and the sample also included some of the under-two-year-olds in the nursery. Clark describes a range of approaches where children and adults collected data together. However, the point that we are interested in is what she says of her theoretical underpinnings: a need to regard children as 'beings not becomings' (Qvortrup et al., 1994, p.20); to take the stance that children, even very young children, have 'important perspectives to contribute about their lives in an early years institution' (Clark, 2004, p.142). This approach is based on an ethics of respect – an ethics where children are positioned as having 'assumed competency'. This recognition of competency includes being aware of children's capabilities when particular methods are being selected. As she says,

> At the time of undertaking the study one approach to gathering the views of young users was by the use of stickers with 'smiley' faces and 'sad' faces to express preferences. This shorthand may be useful on occasions but there is a limit to such a simplified approach. Children are not in charge of the questions but only, in a limited way, of the answers. (Clark, 2004, p.153)

Here what we want to highlight is that ethical considerations of positionality and power apply to questions of methods as well.

Researching 'up', 'down' and 'up and down' with adults

Power differentials between adults can also present a range of ethical tensions for the researcher. Although research relations are nearly always going to be marked by some issues of difference/identity (as will be discussed below), they will also nearly always be characterized by status-power differentials. It is one thing when these power differentials are present in a formal interview situation where a senior academic may be interviewing a junior teacher, for instance. In negotiating access and informed consent, the researcher will have to document their procedures for voluntary recruitment methods in their application for ethical permission to do this work. It could be argued that the interviewee controls the interview as they decide what to say and what not to say. However, the researcher retains ultimate control, for example in deciding when to finish the session and in what counts as data (Brinkman and Kvale, 2005).

When conducting interviews or collecting data 'upwards', there can be different ethical dilemmas that will need to be considered. As Cormode and Hughes (1999, p.299) have written: 'Researching the powerful presents very different methodological and ethical challenges from studying "down". The characteristics of those studied, the power relations between them and the researchers and the politics of the research process differ considerably between elite and non-elite research'.

Some of the ethical tensions that arise occur in the field. If a researcher is planning to observe an 'elite' group at work (e.g. an education committee meeting or a senior leadership meeting in a school) there may be major ethical concerns about privacy and confidentiality and therefore access may be difficult to negotiate. If a researcher is planning to interview a member of an elite group (e.g. a current education minister – if that were possible – or a leading advocate for a key policy about which the researcher is critical), then different sorts of ethical concerns come into play. Walford (2011) says that these ethical concerns may take several forms; one issue may be the 'degree to which the researcher should make clear his or her own views' (n.p.).

Walford suggests that 'it is best to not be too explicit' (n.p.). Another ethical issue may arise in relation to the management of anonymity for public figures who are not representatives of a wider population but stand for their own policies or actions. As Walford acknowledges, 'the fact that the named people are powerful can also lead to self-censorship' (n.p.) on the part of the researcher, and this censorship can be fuelled by the 'need to retain good relations for future research' (n.p.). Walford also highlights a fear of possible 'threats of libel which can lead to the researcher being ultra-careful about what is written where there is any doubt about interpretation' (n.p.). Power and ethics are tightly interconnected in 'upwards' research.

Different ethical-power issues arise in different research settings. For example, some time ago, Burgess (1989) edited a collection of research-ers' accounts of the ethical implications of their work. At this time, very little had been published that provided this detailed perspective. Burgess discussed his own work; he had undertaken fieldwork in Bishop McGregor school in 1972 as a postgraduate student. Ten years later he went back to the same school to undertake ethnographic research on teachers. He describes accessing regular meetings of the school governors and being able to attend a series of teaching-post appointments where he took down in his notebook 'almost verbatim statements of what was said' (1989b, p.63). The chair of governors repeatedly asked for his opinions about the candidates and their suitability for appointment, and although Burgess explained his ethical situation, on one occasion the chair said 'I'm not worried about your moral position,' in an attempt to elicit a response. On another occasion, the head of the teachers' union approached him to enquire about how he had obtained access and what he was going to do with some data; another teacher wrote to him to ask for the return of his 'tape' (interview). Burgess describes a complicated set of different power relations between himself and the chair of governors (arguably the most important management role in the school), the head teacher and other teachers in the school where issues of trust, loyalty, disclosure and confi-dentiality were played out in various ways and at different times. Different interactions between different stakeholders within the same research set-ting were producing complicated and shifting sets of ethical questions of power/access/confidentiality for this researcher and would be predictable in any complex case study like this (Burgess, 1989).

More recently, Mansaray (2012) undertook a study of relations between different groups of Teaching Assistants (TAs) in two London primary schools. (TAs offer support to teachers and help children with their edu-cational and social development, inside the classroom and in other set-tings like playgrounds and dining areas. While they do not need formal qualifications to do this work, sometimes graduates apply for these posts to 'try out' teaching as a career). Mansaray had worked in one of these schools as a TA himself before registering for a PhD. One of the ethical tensions that he charted was between himself and some of the TAs with whom he had previously been a colleague. Returning as a researcher had irrevocably tipped the balance of power between himself and some of his former colleagues. He knew more about their perspectives as he had worked alongside them and, from what he says in his research, some of them were concerned that his different status-power position might cause them some difficulties. They told him that they were concerned that he might not respect their past confidentialities about in-school issues and about certain key personalities (teachers) in the school with whom he now shared a similar status. He had been an 'insider' and was now an 'insider-outsider' – or perhaps an 'in-betweener'. His status had changed and so had his perceived power relations – at least for some of the TAs.

In these examples, we have purposively selected published research where adult researchers are researching other adults who are sometimes more powerful/less powerful than the researchers. We have done this to stress the way that power differentials are not just located in powerful/ powerless or powerful/vulnerable sets of relations; power relations are immanent in all research settings, in different approaches such as case studies and ethnographies as well as in micro settings such as interviews and small group observations. As Foucault (1998, p.94) wrote, 'power is not something that is acquired, seized or shared ... power is exercised from innumerable points, in the interplay of nonegalitarian and mobile relations'.

In this brief review of some of the relations of power that require a need for ethical reflexivity, we want to emphasize two points. First, power relations are often structured in ways that would not be unexpected. Thus, national governments may wield more power than trade unions – but not in all settings! In schools, for example, generally teachers seem to hold more power than the children; the head teacher holds more power than a 'beginning' teacher, although here too context is crucial. However, power can also be understood as more diffuse and more complex than status differentials might imply. Foucault challenges the idea that power is wielded by people through what he calls 'sovereign' acts of domination or coercion. 'Power is everywhere' and 'comes from everywhere' (Foucault 1998, p.63) and this interpretation incorporates a sense of slippage and reversals and alternative possibilities in power relations. Different patterns of power and positioning can sometimes produce unexpected and somewhat contradictory outcomes, and this possibility may not always be appreciated by ethical committees or by researchers starting out on their work. For example, who is more powerful in our case study at the start of this chapter, Jane or Tunde? Power relations are not fixed and immutable; 'both researchers and researched are positioned simultaneously by a number of "fields of power", including gender, age, class, ethnicity, "race", sexuality and so on' (Barker and Smith, 2001, p.142) and these positionings can overlap and intersect, as we shall see.

Matching, rapport and gaining trust

In our case study at the start of this chapter we provided signals that located some of the positional, identity and power issues in play between the researcher and the (potential) participant. Jane, is a white, female academic and she is older than the Black, male school student. Already we have a constellation of complex identifications in play and as Griffiths (1998, p.138) points out, 'all these categories are themselves heterogeneous'. We might think that Jane is middle class because of her occupational status, but we know nothing about her background or many other aspects of her identity that might be critical in her research. We do not know what she is researching. If she were researching gender, or sexualities in schooling, or class-related issues, or issues of attainment, would knowing more about her give us more or less reassurance that she was well placed or better placed than someone else (as some sort of insider) to do this work? Would it concern us that Jane's experiences might position her 'outside' what she is researching? Would this make her more/less susceptible to allegations of bias, of distortion? What sort of ethical issues would she have to navigate in these different possible scenarios?

While these sorts of questions help reveal and document the complexity involved in identity-positionality matters, they also signal the potential significance of researchers' identifications for the ways they collect, analyse and represent their data. (Perhaps too, their lived identity may inform some of their reasons for doing the research, such as for purposes of advocacy.) But, as we have already suggested, reflecting on Jane and Tunde, positions and identities are always contingent, situated, contextual – they cannot simply be read off. The ethical issue that we want to consider in this part of the chapter centres on the ways in which the identifications of the researcher and the participant can/do shape the research process and perhaps the findings too because of 'insider' and 'outsider' (as well as 'in-betweener') positionality and identity. These complexities are illuminated in the following extract by Walkerdine:

> I went into the home of a white working-class family to conduct some research. Where and who was I: the working-class child of my fantasies, or the middle-class researcher who was part of an attempt to tell a truth about 'The Working Class'? (Walkerdine, 1990, pp.157–8, cited in Griffiths, 1998, p.138).

In Walkerdine's reflections about the research she is involved in, she raises some questions about power, her own shifting identities, and data collection. One of the key questions about positions in research is about the impact of the researcher's identity-biography on the data they collect. Many of the accounts of qualitative research frequently discuss the various ways in which position/identity can affect the capacity to gain entry and access participants. However, there are other ethical issues that need to be considered in the connections (or not) between the identity-biography of the researcher and the researched. Here we will explore the problematic matter of 'doing rapport' (Duncombe and Jessop, 2002) and some of the ethical dilemmas involved in 'researching one's own' (Daley, 2001). Personal biographical details do influence data collection; they 'can not only hinder or facilitate their initial access to data but also their ability to see and notice the nuances of behavioural patterns' (Hart, 2001, p.2).

Feminist researchers raised these sorts of concerns some time ago, arguing that women were often best placed to conduct research with women because gendered experiences shaped social relations and informed knowledge (Stanley and Wise, 1993). Therefore women would be better placed to understand the lives and social worlds of other women. This 'matching' argument has also been applied to research with other 'minorities' such as ethnic, racial, linguistic and religious groups. The suggestion has been that researchers who share some experiences and perspectives with those whom they are researching with are better placed to do this research. But this isn't always as straightforward as it seems, as we see in Walkerdine's extract (above) – even if it were possible to 'match' biography-experience-identity profiles, there would always be significant points of difference.

We start with the first point and its ethical correlates – that some form of 'matching' facilitates better access to a research community and perhaps leads to the collection of richer data. In a project designed to explore the decision making of school students in London who were in the process of moving to post-compulsory provision (Ball et al., 2000), the research team quickly noticed that the young women in the study were responsive, open and keen to participate in the interviews. In contrast, as team members started interviewing the young males, they appeared to be diffident, monosyllabic and 'hard to warm up', even though they had all consented to participate in interviews. Two of the research team (both white women in their fifties) conducted all the interviews with the young people. Initially, the two women researchers thought that the diffidence they were seeing might be related to their age-gendered differences. One younger male (white undergraduate) was recruited from the university where the research was based and was trained to do interviewing. He had the same difficulties in getting some of the male students to talk a great deal. After some reflection, the team realized that the lack of response was more to do with the subject-matter of the interview and the young males' uncertainties and anxieties about transition; the identity positions of the interviewers were irrelevant. Indeed, and further into the project, it seemed that with some of the young people, being much older was an asset as the researchers were seen as non-threatening. Frequently the young people had to explain things to the researchers – about their music and fashion – and this meant that the power/knowledge balance was far more fluid. However, to what degree could it be seen as manipulative to try to ensure that a 'matched' interviewer was in place to 'extract' more data? Is this an ethical action or merely a pragmatic response to a research dilemma?

In relation to the ethical dimensions involved in forms of 'insider' research where the researcher–researched do share some biographical-identity aspects, it could be argued that the (usually more powerful) researcher is drawing on their position to enhance their access or to produce a form of 'rapport' in order to 'extract' the data (better and richer and more authentic data) that they are after. To what degree are they 'using' their identity to smooth access? Is this acceptable? To what degree are they 'faking friendship' for their own ends? Is this ethical? For example, in our case study at the start of this chapter, we see Jane trying to establish connections with a younger person whom she would like to 'recruit' for her research – is her naïve attempt a form of insincerity, or even manipulation? Or is she just trying to greet a student in the corridor?

Evidently, it will be better for interview studies and qualitative research more generally if the researcher and the researched have a good working relationship. Where researchers and the researched are 'insiders' in the same culture, and where there is a 'minimal distance' between them, there are potentially greater opportunities for reciprocity, support and intimacy (Oakley, 1981). However, there is simultaneously perhaps greater opportunity for exploitation. 'The greater the intimacy, the apparent mutuality of the researcher/researched relationship, the greater is the danger' (Stacey, 1988, p.21, cited in Duncombe and Jessop, 2002, p.107).

Duncombe and Jessop (2002, p.120) have raised concerns about ethical problems where interviewers try to build 'false friendships' in order to 'encourage or persuade interviewees to explore and disclose experiences and emotions which – on reflection – they may have preferred to keep to themselves or even "not to know"'. They argue that in some cases, the need to be a 'good interviewer' as part of developing marketable skills (e.g. to obtain employment as a researcher) sometimes produces what they call the 'commodification of rapport'. However, in terms of the 'false friendship' theme, or the 'I am just like you' approach in conducting research, there are often unavoidable dilemmas.

For example, as an older woman, one of us (Maguire) frequently interviews other older people who work in educational settings. The fact of her own visible age and the fact that she works in education signals that she may share some experiences with the people she interviews. This would be evident even if she were not to refer to these biographical details. However, because of her autobiographical identity, she is fascinated by the experiences of older teachers specifically in relation to their age and occupation. This biographical similarity, or matching, would also be the case for other education researchers: for example, teachers researching the impact of performance management on colleagues in their own schools; teacher-parents researching the impact of parenting with other teacher-parents. For busy teacher-researchers, studying for part-time degrees while they are working full-time in school, there may be little alternative to do anything other than 'insider' research of this kind. In these examples, biography-occupation matching are facts of life – although they may also be research assets. However, even where there are evident 'matches', there can be many complex instances of difference too.

Griffiths recounts a story told by one of her colleagues who was part of a research team. One of the researchers suggested that each team member introduce themselves. She then started off by saying she was an 'Anglo-Saxon, heterosexual, working-class woman'. 'Some other members of the team were dismayed to find themselves under pressure to reveal aspects of their personal and medical histories or their sexuality – or to lie about them – when they had already gone to some lengths to conceal them, at least in professional settings' (Griffiths, 1998, p.137).

As Iphofen (2009, p.59) states, 'To some extent exploitation of the subject is inevitable. People, opportunities, situations and meaningful spaces are all exploited' to capture rich data sets. As he points out, 'even survey interviewers are trained to accomplish rapport in order to maintain response rates'. For example, in collecting data (e.g. through an interview), a stance of care, respect and sensitivity to nuances of emotional changes are what makes for a 'good' interview as well as an ethical interview: 'qualitative social research is "people work" and is therefore also "emotional" work' (Lee-Treweek and Linkogle, 2000, p.128). Establishing and maintaining rapport is a central part of the research endeavour. Iphofen qualifies this stance by explaining that the rapport that is being established is one of 'formal informality': 'In all likelihood the relationship would not have existed without the need for one party to secure a research goal' (Iphofen, 2009, p.59). However, Duncombe and Jessop (2002, p.121) argue that 'interviewers need to worry about all these things' but also remember that 'interviewees are not totally power-less, and that they can withhold their participation – as long as interview-ers do not "do rapport" too convincingly'.

Researching one's own

'Researching one's own' may involve different sorts of issues and pres-sures. Song and Parker (1995), writing of the 'dynamics of disclosure' in interviewing, argue that more attention needs to be paid to how research-ers may be perceived by interviewees and that researchers may 'want to respond to positionings of themselves'. As Daley (2001, p.43) says, 'researching one's own as an outsider/insider is fluid and … multi-layered'.

Daley had worked as a deputy head teacher in a London school and, for her PhD, interviewed 30 experienced teachers with leadership posi-tions in secondary schools who shared her African-Caribbean heritage. She had started with certain expectations that, 'As an African Caribbean myself who worked as a senior manager for over five years … access to the proposed subjects would be easier and the narratives that I would be able to elicit would be rich' (Daley, 2001, p.36). What happened in practice was that 'my position as a researcher would mean that some of these friends and colleagues would see me differently' (p.39). She com-mented that in 'virtually every case' male leaders commented on the fact of her working towards a doctorate. One even asked if she had been any good as a manager – the inference being that she was doing research because she was not a good school leader. 'He ended the interview by extolling me to get back into schools as quickly as possible'. In other cases, she inferred that some of her participants were envious of her position as a researcher. Overall, she recognized the way in which she could be positioned as an 'insider' – or an 'outsider' in ways that were assigned by her participants 'according to their own perceptions'. She was also concerned that 'as a black woman researching black people I felt that I may be perceived as "riding on the backs of others" to attain an additional qualification. Without these interviews, ultimately I wouldn't have a thesis!' (p.42).

Researching the margins – identity, power and positionality

In this chapter we are concentrating on some of the main ethical issues that are foregrounded when we explore the role of identity, power and positionality in data collection. In what we have already said, it is evident that structural/material differences such as class, race/ethnic and gender differences will be in play when the researcher is in the field collecting qualitative data, either through observations, interviews, focus groups and other methods. Other identity differences will also be present in the researcher–researched relationship: issues of age, sexuality, dis/ability and faith, for example. As May (2001, p.21) puts it, 'both the researcher and those people in the research carry with them a history, a sense of themselves and the importance of their experiences'. These experiences and differences will be complex, shaped by contextual and biographical factors, and interwoven with dimensions of multiple identities, intersectionalities and inequalities. In some cases, one category may dominate (e.g. matters related to social class); in other cases, identity categories will be fluid and will overlap and intersect and be contextually mediated. 'As social institutions change so does the environment within which specific sets of social inequalities are negotiated and struggled over' (Walby et al., 2012, p.231). What we want to address directly are the ethical complexities that can arise where potential research participants are 'members of so-called marginalized or minority communities and therefore have less apparent agency than other groups, reflecting wider sociocultural attitudes of difference and othering (Corrigan and Watson, 2007) as well as links between feelings of shame and resilience (van Vliet, 2008)' (Cook et al., 2013, p.140).

Activist groups within different 'disempowered' groups such as 'women, people with disabilities, gays and lesbians and Indigenous people in societies dominated by white former colonialists' (Bridges, 2001, p.371) frequently advocate a 'nothing about us without us' approach towards research that turns its gaze towards these constituencies. In the past, much social research that intended to illuminate aspects of different experiences was regularly undertaken by white men holding (or aspiring to hold) middle-class occupational positions in universities. One particular rupture in claims for legitimacy about who could do research with minority-ethnic groups was precipitated by the publication of Ladner's key text, *The Death of White Sociology*, which was first published in 1973 and then re-issued almost unchanged in 1998. Ladner argued that mainstream white sociologists had not understood the experiences of Black communities and that Black people and Black culture were positioned against white middle-class values and assumptions and therefore were perceived as 'deficit'. After the Civil Rights Movement in the USA and the spread of second-wave feminism in the same period, more women and members of minority ethnic groups started to move into education – into positions in schools and colleges – and started to 'research their own'. For some time, it was argued that 'insiders' were best placed to 'research their own': a de-legitimation of the outsider position (Minh-Ha, 1989; Davidson, 1998). Constantine-Simms (1995, p.15) put this point succinctly: 'Can a white researcher carrying out research on the Black community collect meaningful data on matters related to the Black educational experience, without resorting to the use of stereotypical paradigms as a premise of academic research on race?'

This view had some merits; it also had some limits. For instance, it could be seen as confining minority researchers to their own communities. It could also mean that complexities of intersectionality could make 'matching' or decisions of insider/outsider extremely difficult to resolve. This debate about who can/cannot do research with the 'other' continues to be part of the ethical questioning about positionality (Hoong Sin, 2007).

For these sorts of reasons, some researchers who work with participants who are different from themselves may employ researchers with a similar biography to the 'researched', who perhaps share the same faith, or speak the same community language. Ryan has undertaken a range of studies involving matters of difference (a study about Polish children in London primary schools, and a study involving Muslim young people in north London) and, on various occasions, she has had to involve different 'insiders' in order to facilitate data collection (Ryan et al., 2011). (There are also some related ethical issues here about who gets employed, on what sorts of contracts, and what happens to their career and progression.) In terms of power relations, there are ethical issues in terms of what representations of the 'researched' get selected in or out of any publications as well as who makes decisions about these questions.

There are also complex ethical issues related to what Cook et al. (2013, p.140) call 'naming, shaming and framing'. 'Naming' any group or community is a political process that can inadvertently maintain patterns of marginalization and exclusion. For example, naming groups as 'Travellers' or 'Gypsies' may exoticize these communities in ways that may contribute towards 'fixing' a set of assumptions and stereotypes while simultaneously framing and positioning the research. Naming and positioning may frame individual experiences in ways that can potentially emancipate as well as 'shame' participants. Cook et al. argue that research participants who identify as having a disability may be empowered through a form of 'naming and framing' that leads to a growth in confidence and perhaps too, through 'being supported in a more holistic way' (2013, p.143). The 'shame' may attach to being singled out, patronized or embarrassed. As Cook et al. (p.140) suggest, researchers need to 're-imagine' those research participants who may be in groups that are socially and culturally marginalized in more 'enabling and transformative ways', although this may be extremely hard to bring off (but see Cleary, 2013 for more discussion of this point).

Many Indigenous populations have been 'poked, prodded, measured and photographed ... and they have been bothered, queried and harried by every foreign expert under the sun' (Willis and Saunders, 2007, p.96). Willis and Saunders have conducted a great deal of research with Indigenous Australian communities. They believe that research teams made up of non-Indigenous and Indigenous researchers who use Indigenous 'reference groups in the development of data-collection methods, styles and techniques of analysis' as well as in 'checking the appropriateness of the interpretation of results' can produce a more socially just and ethically reflexive set of findings (p.96). (One develop-ment in Australia has been the publication of a set of principles and guidelines to support working with the communities often referred to as 'Indigenous' – a shorthand term that is not always acceptable: HRC, 2003). Willis and Saunders also discuss the need to frame the usefulness of research like this; is it relevant to the participating group *now*. They argue that knowing that an intrusive project will benefit people in the longer run, 'or that simply allows their story to be told is insufficient' (p.98). They are not arguing that research should not be done; they are claiming that 'the point of the research should be clear in terms that are comprehensible in local economies of knowledge as well as in academic circles' (p.98) – a point that could be usefully applied to all research with so-called marginalized communities and constituencies.

And what of class?

Turning now to social class and difficult differences, we have already highlighted some of the identity/position complexities in this area. Social class has been a consistent feature of education research and is in the ascendancy once more. Thus, the class position of the researcher may well play a part in her or his capacity to access participants and in build-ing and maintaining good research relations in the field. In a paper on class matters in interview studies, Mellor et al. (2013, p.1) preface their work by arguing exactly this point; that 'there remains an unspoken expectation that class matching, particularly when investigating working-class groups and practices, is desirable as it engenders empathy on the part of the interviewer which allows for openness on the part of the participant'. Their paper reviews many of the arguments that we have already detailed in this chapter; issues related to power, positionality and situatedness and the problematic of 'matching'. As they say, based on their field experiences where they contrasted the experiences of working-class and middle-class undergraduates, identities are not a unitary pheno- menon and 'power relations in qualitative research are multidirectional' (p.7), as we have shown in this chapter. One key point that may fre- quently be forgotten in all the 'matching'/ 'rapport' discussions that they highlight is that not all their student participants considered 'their class background and current class position to be an important identity cate- gory' (p.15). As they conclude, 'we *all* inhabit positions which work to both shut down and open up discussions, regardless of the participant we are interviewing' (p.10). This is as true for social class identity and position as it is for other difficult differences.

Researching with/on colleagues – more ethical conundrums

We now turn to explore briefly the ethical issues that are involved when we research on and with our colleagues. In the example that we consid- ered (above) where Burgess spent some time collecting data about teachers in one secondary school, he charted many ethical tensions. He was asked about his views of prospective teachers, and he was asked about aspects of his data set. For educationalists working in their own settings, there may be pressures from senior colleagues to reveal 'who said what' or to remove findings that might be critical of the institution. In a small primary school, it may be extremely difficult to 'disguise' some participants without changing aspects of their identity (e.g. their ethnicity or gender) but in so-doing, the impact of the work may be reduced. Frequently, the institution, which may be supporting the individual in some part, may want the researcher to make a short presentation of their work to their colleagues – and this can present the researcher with more ethical dilemmas in terms of what to say, or not say. There can be other ethical dilemmas involved with collecting data in one's own setting; it may be that the researcher is exploring a topic for which they have some responsibility and towards which they have a professional allegiance. This may make it difficult for respondents to be critical; they know the position of the researcher. This may also make it more difficult for the researcher to be reflexive about the way in which their position may shape their perceptions and approach to data collection (and analysis):

> We must consider the way in which our representational practices may serve to depict subjectivity in particular ways. The interpretation of interviews may involve legitimate, unavoidable and unacknowledged processes of projection onto participants, and when we present research accounts we may question our claims about representation in both the literal and political senses of the word. (Alldred and Gillies, 2002, p.158)

At the end of the project, the researcher may intend to continue working in their school or institution; thus, they may be constrained in what they report or write because of trying to ensure that they do as little harm as possible to their personal relationships with their friends/colleagues when these people become research participants.

Conclusion

In this chapter we have concentrated on some of the ethical complexities that come into play when identity, power and positionality are being critically considered. If there is any conclusion to be drawn from all of the cases we have documented and the arguments we have rehearsed in this chapter, it is that the ethical researcher needs to consistently ask themselves questions about how to conduct their research in a morally good way (Iphofen, 2009, p.180). 'Codes of ethics may reflect good intentions … practice can often depend on making fine-grained individual choices which represent the "least bad" course of action rather than any ideal' (Macfarlane, 2009, p.32). When it comes to ethical matters of positionality, power, and identity, there is what Iphofen (2009, p.184) calls a 'fundamental irony' that attaches to 'human life and to researching it': 'We behave at all times as if we were all the same and understand each other and, at other times, all so different that we could never understand each other. The truth is, of course, somewhere in between'.

CHAPTER 7

DATA ANALYSIS

Sevati was doing some research for her master's degree in Education Management based on a small number of interviews with head teachers about their views on leadership. She was talking about her data and her conclusions with her tutor Alex. 'I only did six interviews with head teachers,' she said, 'and one was no good, so I decided to drop it from my data set.' 'What do you mean, no good?' asked Alex. 'Well, what one of them said didn't really match with my literature review, and they didn't think there was such a thing as leadership anyway, so I have decided not to include it in my findings section.' Is it justifiable for Sevati to exclude this interview? What ethical issues are involved in decisions to include or exclude data?

This chapter explores some of the key ethical issues that are involved in data analysis. Kromrey (1993, p.24) says that data analysis 'serves a small but critical function in empirical research – that of separating information in the data from noise'. In ethical terms, this process requires that data be honestly and transparently analysed and managed as all research needs to be a 'trustworthy source of knowledge' (Ruane, 2005, p.27). This is because research findings can be persuasive and are frequently cited in support of, as well as in criticizing, a wide range of social policies. This requirement for an ethical approach towards data analysis can become complicated by the fact that 'both policy-makers and the public desire simple conclusions that appeal to the "common-sense" and make for positive headlines' (Black, 2012, p. xviii).

Ruane (2005, p.27) points out that statistics are frequently used as '"facts" beyond question'. In consequence, the public are deluged with evidence and data that they are sometimes only partly able to assess or critically evaluate, particularly if they have little training in basic statistics and if contradictory data are less widely reported. To take an example, Brown (2012, p.106) points out that many politicians cite international studies (such as the Programme for International Student Assessment, or PISA) as 'evidence that traditional teaching methods work best'. She adds that, while this method may be widely used by the Pacific Rim countries that lead in the tables, many countries at the bottom also use these methods – a fact that is less frequently circulated in the popular media.

Thus, care needs to be taken in the way in which data are managed and represented; for instance, different analyses of the same statistical evidence can produce quite different sets of findings and outcomes in practice. Whether research findings are statistically derived or are products of other approaches, the choices made by researchers may be more influenced by the story they want to tell rather than a more accurate version of what their findings suggest, and this may result in some distortion of the data. In our example above, Sevati seems to want to discard a discrepant case that she thinks will not 'fit' with her account of leadership and which may 'weaken' her account. Is this an ethical response, and if not, why not?

This chapter starts with a review of some of the advice that is given in ethical guidelines to education researchers about data analysis. Then the chapter considers some of the ethical dilemmas that occur in analysing data collected in quantitative research. Ethical slippages such as concealment and exaggeration are examined. The chapter then looks at some of the ethical issues that occur in the analysis of qualitative data sets as well as the complex matter of partisanship in personal ethics and in frameworks for analysis. The chapter turns to the question of whether participants should and can be involved in this process. The chapter concludes that an ethical stance towards data analysis reduces any temptation to produce findings that 'have been overly sliced, trimmed and cooked' (Kromrey, 1993, p.27).

Ethical guidelines and data analysis

We start by exploring the advice that is given by two national educational research associations about the ethics of data analysis and management; the first from the Australian Association for Research in Education (AARE), and the second from the British Educational Research Association (BERA). We have selected these two as indicative exemplars produced by and for generic education researchers; there are many others from different national settings and from different disciplines such as psychological bodies and social science research associations. However, these two bodies offer support for experienced and less-experienced education researchers, 'as a guide to the ethical conduct of research, and as a starting point for further thought, not as a set of laws' (AARE, 1993, n.p.). The AARE has published a general statement that deals with the analysis and reporting of research. The statement highlights the need to avoid exaggeration or misrepresentation of data. It details a need for honesty and rigour in data analysis and data reporting. In what it says about aspects such as intentional misrepresentation and the need to report details that 'might bear upon interpretations of findings', there are clear ethical statements that relate directly to data analysis:

> Reports of research should draw attention to the limitations of the results, both in reliability and in applicability. Researchers should avoid and if necessary act to correct misuse of research and misunderstanding of its scope and limitations. They should not exaggerate the significance of their results, nor misrepresent the practical or policy implications. This is particularly important where the results are for widespread public consumption. Nevertheless, researchers should not shun public controversy.

> Researchers must not fabricate, falsify or intentionally misrepresent evidence, data, findings or conclusions. They should report their findings fully without omission of significant data, disclosing details of their theories, methods and research designs which might bear upon interpretations of their findings. They should report research conceptions, procedures, results and analyses in sufficient detail to allow knowledgeable, trained researchers to understand and interpret them. (AARE, 1993, n.p.)

This Australian advice is reflected in the British Educational Research Association's ethical code (BERA, 2011). The BERA code contains a list of examples that specifically relate to data analysis and management. In the extract below there is a list of behaviours to be avoided, such as 'sensationalizing' or exaggerating findings or distorting findings through selective analysis. In our example at the start of this chapter, Sevati suggests that selective analysis will strengthen her argument. Her approach is not consistent with what BERA advocates as being an ethical approach towards data analysis. That is, researchers need to 'communicate the extent to which their data collection and analysis techniques, and the inferences to be drawn from their findings, are reliable, valid and generalizable' (BERA, 2011, p.9). The BERA code argues that all researchers have an ethical responsibility, not only to the research community, but also to the general public to ensure that their work is trustworthy:

> Researchers must therefore not bring research into disrepute by, for example:
>
> - Falsifying research evidence or findings;
> - 'Sensationalizing' findings in a manner that sacrifices intellectual capital for maximum public exposure;
> - Distorting findings by selectively publishing some aspects and not others …
>
> (Edited extract from BERA Code of Ethics, 2011, p.10)

Many research associations and academic disciplines publish their own ethical guidelines to support research that is grounded in principles that protect participants and minimize harm. Particularly in the social sciences, attention is paid to respect for and relations with participants as we have detailed throughout this book. However, when it comes to ethics and data analysis, generally the advice and support is less well covered and there are gaps and omissions in the accounts – although see the example below from the University of Pittsburg (see also Shamhoo and Resnick, 2009):

> Research integrity requires not only that reported conclusions are based on accurately recorded data or observations but that all relevant observations are reported. It is considered a breach of research integrity to fail to report data that contradict or merely fail to support the reported conclusions, including the purposeful withholding of information about confounding factors. If some data should be disregarded for a stated reason, confirmed by an approved statistical test for neglecting outliers, the reason should be stated in the published accounts. A large background of negative results must be reported. Any intentional or reckless disregard for the truth in reporting observations may be considered to be an act of research misconduct. (Office of Research Integrity, 2011, n.p.)

While there are some guidelines and recommendations for best practice in managing and analysing data, these topics are less likely to feature in the work of the ethical committees that universities have set up to review research proposals. In some part, this is because social scientists will be detailing their research design and the initial ways in which their relations with their proposed participants are respectful, inclusive, voluntary and beneficial, rather than anticipating how they will analyse their data sets, other than in the most general ways. As Sterba (2006, p.309) claims, 'Transgressions in data analysis and reporting are commonly only briefly mentioned in ethics texts or not discussed at all' and are frequently regarded as methodological weakness rather than an ethical matter. However, given the requirement for research to be trustworthy, 'the issue of how to ensure quality in data analysis in both qualitative and quantitative (and mixed analysis) is an ethical one' (Farrimond, 2013, p.69).

Quantitative research and ethical data analysis

One of the main ethical problems in dealing with quantitative research findings is that depending on the way the analysis is conducted, the findings can be quite differently represented and differently interpreted. Gelman (2011, p.53) says that, 'As a statistician, I think the key point is to recognize that different analyses can give different perspectives on a data set … openness should be the norm.' A useful example of the impact of different analyses is provided by Ruane (2005). She argues that when researchers report averages, they may report the mean (a mathematically derived average), or they may report the median (a middle point), or even the mode (a frequency-based conclusion). These different analyses may result in different accounts and different responses in practice. She illustrates this with a practical example where a researcher has to report on the average annual salary of a group of workers. If a minority of workers earn extremely high salaries while the majority earn significantly lower pay, then the median, mean and mode will not all tell the same story. As Ruane (2005, p.28) says, 'reporting the mean salary would give an inflated picture of just how much a typical member of the group is actually earning'. Reporting data analysed in this way could have practical consequences that might not be ethical and indeed, analysing the data in this way, without revealing alternative analyses, could be considered in itself as being highly unethical. Researchers also need to be open about any weaknesses in the process of data collection that produced the data set.

Equally worrying is the tendency for some researchers and policymakers to look for evidence that backs the case they wish to make, rather than dealing with more complex and perhaps less expedient findings. This can sometimes mean that dubious sources and extremely unreliable data sets are used for political ends. For example, in 2013, Michael Gove, the UK Secretary of State for Education, was pressing for a content-driven history curriculum in schools. He wrote a report in a national newspaper, the *Daily Mail*, where he claimed that 'Survey after survey has revealed disturbing historical ignorance, with one teenager in five believing Winston Churchill was a fictional character while 58 per cent think Sherlock Holmes was real' (23 March, 2013).

Janet Downs, a retired teacher, followed up this report by checking the source for these claims of 'survey after survey' through applying for more clarification, under the UK's Freedom of Information legislation, from the Department of Education. Eventually it was revealed that the 'surveys' were conducted by Premier Inns (a chain of motels) in which the children who responded to the in-house survey were arguably making fun of the questions by pretending not to know the correct answers. (For a more detailed account, see Brown, 2013.) Although this case may be more of an example of poor research or, indeed, of the mis-reporting of poor research for political ends, it illustrates the care needed for ethical analysis and representation of statistical results.

As we have already argued, contemporary society is marked by a focus on empirical data. We live in the so-called 'information age'. Many organizations exist solely to collate and circulate data, measure social phenomena and, in consequence, influence policy and practice. In the educational world, the widespread usage of the PISA data set testifies to the international pressure of statistics and the attempt to measure achievement (Breakspear, 2012). The media is complicit in presenting and spinning more and more 'evidence' from surveys, research findings, international and national think tanks. Some of the work is presented in partisan ways to accent certain policies or to sideline controversies: 'An enormous quantity of human information is currently being developed and used. Because there is so much human information, the potential for its misuse poses significant risks' (Bradley and Schaefer, 1998, p.9).

The risk of misuse has been particularly evident in the area of human intelligence and its measurement; itself a highly complex and contested arena. One extreme example is the controversy that still surrounds the work of Sir Cyril Burt, the pre-eminent educational psychologist of his time in the UK. His work on IQ and heredity had been used directly in education policy to promote the virtue of different types of schooling for different 'types' of children whose capabilities were considered to be measurable. The result was a tripartite system of secondary education where children were 'selected' for a more or less academic education on the basis of a national test, the 11+ (Cave, 1967). (However, it is only fair to point out that Burt did eventually rebut this use of his work and campaigned against the use of the 11+. Burt's work was also controversially applied in the USA to account for 'black-white IQ discrepancies' in relation to intelligence and heredity, rather than racism and socio-economic oppression (Hattie, 1991, p.259).)

In the 1970s, Burt was accused of fraudulent behaviour in the management and analysis of his earlier research on heredity. He was accused of fabricating data to fit his hypotheses and of manipulating his correlational findings. He was also accused of inventing co-workers whose names were attributed to some of his work. Hattie (1991) believes that the case is far more complex than is often appreciated. For instance, and drawing on Joynson's (1989) defence of Burt's research, Hattie argues that some of the data that was allegedly fabricated actually weakened Burt's arguments and so was unlikely to have been falsified. However, for the purposes of this chapter, the point that arises from the Burt case is the need to be scrupulous and honest in our data analysis: 'Be honest; never manipulate data; be precise; be fair with regard to priority; be without bias with regard to data and ideas of your rival; do not make compromises in trying to solve a problem' (Mohr, 1979, p. 45, cited in Hattie, 1991, p.272).

It can be very tempting for some researchers to want to magnify some of their findings. For this reason, it may be that some ethical weaknesses can slip into the way that data sets are analysed (both quantitative and qualitative). In any case, it is impossible to be entirely objective – an issue we explore in the section on value positions later on in this chapter.

Ethical slippage in data analysis

At the start of this chapter we cited the case of a teacher-researcher, Sevati, who wanted to match her findings with what she had found in her readings of the literature. She did not seem to appreciate that a discrepant finding was perhaps more useful in progressing understandings about her topic. Rather than collapsing her argument, her unexpected data may have lent an edge to her research work, although she did not appreciate this immediately. In Sevati's case, she did at least initiate a conversation about this matter with her supervisor. She was involved in ethical discussions about her data analysis and was not planning to discard her unusual interview without discussing this matter with her more experienced supervisor.

Writers in the field of research ethics are aware of the temptations to 'over-egg' data as well as sideline some of the 'less convenient' findings that may disrupt any claims. Macfarlane (2009, p.99) highlights what he calls the related issues of concealment and exaggeration that can bedevil analysis: 'Concealment and exaggeration are twin vices that can occur where a researcher cannot resist emphasizing some results or masking others, perhaps confirming his or her theoretical stance, at the expense of other observations that may contradict cherished opinions or hypotheses' (p.99).

Concealment can take place in many different ways – and sometimes by mistake, rather than any deliberate attempts to mislead. For the lone researcher, like Sevati, it might simply be that certain data sets get ignored or set aside if they are seen to weaken the hypothesis or argument. Where students are attempting to hold on to a central argument, it can sometimes be disconcerting to have to deal with limits and counter-evidence. For other researchers, there may be a temptation to 'data trim', which is what Burt was accused of doing, among other things: that is, 'altering or discarding data that appear to be anomalous' (Kromrey, 1993, p.25).

In analysing and presenting findings, selection does have to take place, particularly where there is a large data set: 'Choosing what to omit is rarely an easy decision' (Macfarlane, 2009, p.99). Macfarlane contends that 'outright data falsification is far less common among researchers than deliberate omissions or oversights' (p.100). However, Farrimond (2013, p.69) argues that it can be very tempting for a researcher to include a 'juicy quote', which may not represent the position of the majority of the interviewees. It may also be very tempting not to cite a contradictory piece of evidence. It can be particularly hard for students coming towards the completion of their dissertations or thesis if they discover, at a fairly late stage, that they now need to re-jig their claims and calculations in the light of some new findings or a paper that they have only just uncovered. However, if they decide not to do this, the selective reporting that ensues can seriously erode the usefulness of their research findings as well as the reputation and quality of education research.

Data trimming can occur in qualitative as well as quantitative data sets. Starting with quantitative data, particularly where a researcher is testing for statistical significance, outlier data points might sometimes be omitted 'if doing so swayed the significance level in the direction of their stated hypotheses' (Sterba, 2006, p.307). As Macfarlane (2009, p.102) says, researchers can be 'tempted to exaggerate the extent to which a pattern may be emerging in results'. It is sometimes believed through using larger samples, and deploying complex statistical analyses, that these approaches allow researchers to make broader claims about the veracity and power of their findings.

However, larger samples by themselves do not necessarily enhance reliability or significance. Macfarlane (2009) is quite clear on this matter.

He argues that 'sometimes a technique can be deployed for inflating the probability by using a sample size that is unnecessarily large. This can result in a weak effect being statistically enhanced' (p.103). He adds that the use of the word 'significant' can also be mis-used and can lead to unethical and misleading claims about research findings: 'In a specialized statistical sense the use of the word "significant" implies that the chance of something happening at random is, at most, just 1 in 20 (Rugg and Petre, 2004)' (Macfarlane, 2009, p.103). This is an important matter; one that deserves to be carefully considered in all analytical work where this term is being deployed. The term carries within itself a sense of 'proof' and sometimes is used to close down alternative debates.

There is another ethical dilemma that attends to research and its significance (or insignificance). In some research, it can be sometimes difficult to argue for some form of practical action without the existence of statistically significant data sets. However, doing nothing until proof is formally established in statistical terms may itself not be ethical. For example, in 1983, it was claimed that there was evidence of childhood leukaemia clusters around Sellafield, a nuclear power station in the UK (see Connor, 1999). This controversial finding caused great public anxiety amid concerns about alleged 'cover-ups' and eventually prompted a government-funded investigation. In high-risk contexts like this, some health researchers would argue that statistical proof should be subordinated to maintaining health and well-being. It is sometimes claimed that where a reasonable body of evidence exists, a lower threshold of evidence is acceptable. The problem is, what constitutes a reasonable amount of evidence?

More recently, there has been a revival of the discussion that surrounds the term 'significance'. Higgs (2013) has provided a useful summary of the debates in this area and argues that, in consequence of the sorts of difficulties that are involved, research students and researchers need to take a more nuanced approach towards claims of significance. It is worth quoting her main arguments on the ethics involved in data analysis in some detail. First, she argues for simplicity and directness in the analysis and reporting of data:

> For example, if we mean that the two-sided p-value is less than 0.05, then let us say just that. Let the reader judge whether that result is to be deemed significant by our modern scale and by their knowledge of the science. If, instead, we mean the result is in fact practically important, let's say as much and clearly communicate our justification for doing so. If we believe our research is important, let us convince our critics through our choice of other words. (Higgs, 2013, n.p.)

Higgs recognizes that not all readers are empowered to engage critically with the mathematics involved in statistical analysis. However, she believes that the methods being deployed for analysis and the basis for any claims do need to be provided in any related publications in order to assure transparency, honesty and social responsibility in research. Indeed, these matters of transparency and social responsibility were exactly what Janet Downs set out to address in respect of data being cited by Michael Gove (see above). 'For readers with the background necessary to successfully critique results, we should provide the information they need to make their own informed opinions, based on sound reasoning and justification' (Higgs, 2013, n.p.).

Finally, Higgs makes a powerful claim for the relative value of statistical analysis and the need for this approach being tempered with an appreciation of what is, and what is not possible: 'Statistical inference is an art, uncomfortably dependent on practitioners and their backgrounds. It should not be construed as a way to objectivize inference or a straightforward means to classify results as significant or not' (2013, n.p.).

So far, we have concentrated on some of the more well-known and well-reported ethical aspects that need consideration in quantitative data analysis. However, there are other matters that can lead to forms of concealment or deception: 'researchers who rely on quantitative techniques may be charged with using charts, tables and figures to similar ends' (Macfarlane, 2009, p.106). In our experience as educational tutors, research students sometimes seem to think that if they pepper their work with tables and diagrams, it lends an authoritative appearance, a scientific gloss that supports their claims from their analyses of their data. However, analysing and reporting findings in percentages without citing the size of the data set can be misleading. The different layouts of axes in graphs can also produce charts and tables that are visually impressive – but sometimes visually misleading (see Tufte, 1983 for further discussion). These ethical concerns may be as much to do with reporting as with analysis – although the desire to 'show' a powerful argument can lead to these unethical forms of distortion and exaggeration of data.

Ethics of data analysis in qualitative research

Turning now to the ethics of data analysis in qualitative work, it is likely that many more education researchers, particularly those embarking on postgraduate studies, will be undertaking this type of research. While some of the ethical problems are the same in qualitative and quantitative data analysis (e.g. the need for rigour and honesty), there are also some distinctive ethical demands in qualitative research projects. Some problems can occur where the data set is large. In funded projects, it is not uncommon to collect over one hundred in-depth extended interviews. In unfunded projects, such as doctoral research, while it would be rare to undertake quite so many interviews, it would be usual to have conducted between 20 or 30 in-depth conversations. With a large body of data, one of the obvious problems relates to how to avoid what Kvale calls the 1,000-page question: 'How shall I find a method to analyse the 1,000 pages of interview transcripts I have collected?' (1996, p.176). Miles and Huberman (1994) distinguish three processes in the analysis, all of which may be susceptible to some 'minor shadings and distortions' (Kromrey, 1993, p.24).

Miles and Huberman (1994) argue that analysis starts with attempts to reduce the data when the researcher begins the process of selecting and sorting the findings. In the first stage, the researcher will be interested in exploring various concepts, and emergent themes will start to be documented and followed up across the data set. At this point, decisions are starting to be made about what will be included or sidelined. Then, in the next stage, the researcher digs deeper to try to seek participants' meanings through constructing summaries and initial code maps. Miles and Huberman's (1994) third stage involves comparing, contrasting and identifying patterns in the data set. In each of these stages, there is the potential for some exaggerations or distortions of data. However, as Miles and Huberman (1994, p.110) argue, there should be an ingrained corrective: 'The meanings emerging from the data have to be tested for their plausibility, their sturdiness, their "confirmability" – that is, their validity'.

Sometimes, the 'testing' for rigour can be managed through additional forms of data analysis. One such approach is to subject transcripts to frequency counts of key words. This practice can indicate the influence of a key concept, the widespread use of a particular strategy or the dominance of a particular perspective through detailing its occurrence. For example, in a recent project on policy enactment in secondary schools, Ball et al. (2012) argued that raising standards, assessment and testing were policies that drove much of what was going on. This policy dominance meant that schools put raising standards before any other policy. Teachers who were interviewed and talked about this phenomenon frequently started their narratives by saying 'obviously' and then describing what their school was doing and had to do. Counting and charting the frequency of 'obviously' lent validity to the claims that were made because of this approach to data analysis (Ball et al., 2012, pp.78–9).

As we have already stated in this chapter, from our readings of many texts on research ethics, there does seem to be a gap in relation to data analysis, or at the very least, this area is often skimmed over when discussing qualitative approaches to research. One core research text that does address ethics in qualitative data analysis is Schutt's (2013) frequently revised work on research methods and methodology. Schutt (2013, p.353) claims that 'the qualitative data analyst is never far from ethical issues and dilemmas'. He makes a number of important points about this process where ethical matters intersect with data analysis. First, he considers privacy, confidentiality and anonymity and he claims that these all need to be considered during the analysis. 'It can be easy for participants in the study to identify each other in a qualitative description, even if outsiders cannot' (p.354) and thus, during the analytical process, researchers have an ethical responsibility to check their emergent work to 'gauge the extent' to which confidentiality has been maintained.

Schutt's second point relates to what he calls 'advocacy and intervention'. His case is that sometimes, in the process of analysis, the researcher finds that something damaging has taken place, some form of wrongful behaviour. If this occurs, what is the role of the data analyst? He highlights the sorts of ethical tensions that can come into play: 'maintaining what is called guilty knowledge may force the researcher to suppress some parts of the analysis so as not to disclose the wrongful behaviour, but presenting "what really happened" in a report may prevent ongoing access and violate understandings with participants' (p.354).

Schutt (2013, p.354) asserts that 'real analyses have real consequences' and so the researcher has an ethical responsibility to maintain professional integrity, accuracy and rigour in working to elucidate their conclusions during the process of data analysis. For example, if a researcher were investigating the ways in which schools were trying to boost the attainment scores of their students and they found a small example that they thought was unprofessional (e.g. teachers encouraging their students to hire them as private tutors), then the researcher might want to discuss this matter with the teachers and think carefully about how to manage this finding in their final analysis.

One more ethical issue that Schutt raises relates to the question of who owns and controls the data set. This can be complex where a funding organization maintains control and vetting authority over the data set and any conclusions stemming from the analysis. This is a common occurrence in government-sponsored research, as discussed in Chapter 4 where we stressed the importance of negotiating intellectual property rights at the start of a project, if possible.

Schutt's fifth point relates to the use and misuse of results – a matter that we have already discussed in this chapter. However, he adds some more ethical concerns that come into play in doing data analysis: for example, he highlights the fact that some Indigenous communities will have their own codes for working with outsider researchers; these may involve the community or its elders reviewing the research and being active participants in any critical discussions of the analysis that is being conducted.

We have argued in this chapter that we live in the 'information age'; we also live in an increasingly visual age where the power of the image is recognized, celebrated and critiqued (Ball and Smith, 1992; Emmison, 2004). It is therefore not surprising that many researchers now draw on images and visual sets of data: photographs, video materials, internet ethnography. As with the cases that we have already explored, many of the same issues apply to the ethical analysis of visual data sets. They can be trimmed, cropped and edited in order to tell different versions of stories. In a society where a visual image is often taken at face value, as 'true' (even in an age where technologies such as Photoshop are readily available), visual data can have powerful consequences in practice. As Ball and Smith (1992, p.18) assert, 'the sense viewers make of them [photographs] depends upon cultural assumptions, personal knowledge, and the context in which the picture is presented'. One way in which these sorts of problems can be addressed is in detailed annotation of the visual data, describing what has been done and why, in order to ensure rigour in what is being represented:

> It is important to leave out assumptions and only look at what the source data actually shows. If you have to make some basic assumptions, and if these assumptions aren't obviously visible in the finished product, you need to make them known with annotations. Because the data analysis happens behind closed doors, so to speak – a viewer can't see what exactly it is that you did – this is the stage where the viewer needs to trust the presenter to have done their job well. (Skau, 2012, n.p.)

Ethics, findings and value positions

One of the most difficult and complicated ethical issues that comes into play in the data analysis process relates to the values and value positions of the researcher. We all have beliefs and values that shape the way in which we see the social world. The issue then becomes one of ensuring that the data are analysed and managed in a rigorous way; this might involve attempts to corroborate claims across the data set and perhaps 'test' these out by trying to seek alternative explanations. It may also involve searching the data set for disconfirming evidence or discrepant cases – such as Sevati's story at the start of this chapter.

The fundamental dilemma is that, in many cases, a sole researcher will be working in an area where they have some personal investment; for example, they may undertake research about their own communities or about a disenfranchised group to whom they have some allegiances. For these sorts of reasons, it is common-place to argue that all researchers should make their value positions clear in their work. However, because of holding certain commitments, it may sometimes be tempting for some researchers to want to 'find' what they think should be in their data sets. This process is far more complicated than merely being seen as an attempt at deception. As Macfarlane (2009, p.102) says, 'It is important to understand that concealment or exaggeration is often far from deliberate since our assumptions about what is important to "look for" in a data set can be shaped by our values or attitudes'.

Critical alignments between what the researcher thinks is important, perhaps their own positionality and identity, as well as their socio-political commitments, will often draw them towards certain research questions, rather than others. Thus, where the qualitative researcher is interpreting evidence and attempting to develop a thick rich description of the social world, the data analysis will need to be constructed out of a range of illustrative examples all managed in a rigorous manner to ensure accuracy and authenticity.

In this chapter, we have argued that political expediency sometimes leads policymakers and politicians to seek out evidence that supports their views. One of the difficulties with education research is that it can be relatively easy to 'skew' a data set, or to be selective in what is being reported, in order to support a particular perspective or advocate one approach over another. This can be particularly demanding in research settings where there are strong beliefs and contradictory findings. One useful example of this tension in education research can be illustrated if we consider the arguments that continue to typify debates about whether students should be grouped by 'ability' or grouped in other ways. To demonstrate this long-standing dilemma in education research, policy and practice, Baines (2012) compared some 'highly controlled' studies into ability grouping with other 'naturalistic' studies.

In controlled research studies, the findings strongly suggest that ability grouping has very little impact on learning, although naturalistic studies indicate that ability grouping has different impacts on 'achievement and progress for different ability groups' (Baines, 2012, p.50). Baines explains that findings, such as ability grouping, negatively influencing friendships and self-esteem, will be more evident in naturalistic studies. His central argument is that the evidence about ability grouping is well established and clear: there is no research basis for grouping children according to ability. However, the 'common sense' views of politicians, swayed by their concerns with parental beliefs and values displace the evidence base that exists – at least in classroom practice: 'To the extent that social research explores topics that are inherently unstable, and embedded within wider political and ideological debates, social researchers have to be especially skilled in managing the value content of their work' (Ransome, 2013, p.170).

Ransome (2013, p.70) argues that the researcher always has a stake in their research process and, for ethical reasons, needs to ensure that they 'apply rigorous techniques of systematic investigation'. Where the researcher is undertaking evaluative research, the task can also involve coming to a judgement about the analysis of findings. As he says, 'research produces data, evaluation produces opinion' (p.96). The normative response is that the researcher must work carefully in their analysis to ensure that they take an objective approach towards their accurately recorded data. As Hammersley (2003, p.124) has written, 'the fact that people have background assumptions, preferences, interests, etc. does not automatically mean that their accounts are biased'. The problem is that, in the real world, it can be very hard to divorce analysis from values.

Overall what we are concerned with is that there can be a danger that personal beliefs, values and attachments may lead us to search for what we think should be in our data. Thus, we can get involved in a form of analysis where we look to justify our claims rather than subjecting them to scrutiny:

> Consequently, much like tunnel-visioned parents who can see no fault with their offspring, we convince ourselves that the empirical data would speak in favour of our theories if only we could analyse them 'properly'. From this perspective, our research efforts become directed towards supporting our theories rather than testing them. (Kromrey, 1993, p.26)

Frameworks of analysis and partisanship

One adjunct to this discussion about ethics and values in research is that it may be the framework for analysis that contains sets of value assumptions. For example, critical race theory (CRT) is based on an explicit assumption that racism is deeply embedded in and shapes the everyday, common experiences of all people of colour in settings where white dominance is in the ascendancy. CRT holds that even in so-called liberal societies, only the most deliberate and blatant forms of racism and discrimination ever get addressed. This is because racism works to maintain white advantage, what Gillborn (2008) calls 'white supremacy'. In the same way, feminists argue that recognition of, and challenges to, the exclusion of women, their perspectives, their voices 'have ushered in important shifts in thinking for researchers and the consumers of research' (Marshall and Young, 2006, p.68). 'With feminist framing, research requires redefinitions and question shifting, an activist values stance ... gender research designs must often transgress boundaries ... present[ing] uncomfortable challenges to dominant practices' (p.74). In reference to much research with Indigenous peoples, Battiste (2008, p.504) writes of how Eurocentric colonizers 'believe they have the authority to impose their tutelage over Indigenous peoples and to remove from those peoples the right to speak for themselves' (Battiste, 2008, p.504). In these instances, the dominant group will have spoken about the 'other' using an analytical framework devised by their own constituencies' experiences, often taking their own norms and values to be in the ascendancy, sidelining any alternative world views such as those offered by CRT, feminism and Indigenous perspectives.

In 1998, Tooley, with Darby, published a critique of education research in the UK that was sponsored by the UK's Office for Standards in Education (Ofsted). The study was based on calls from some senior researchers (Hargreaves, 1996), the educational press and the Department for Education and Employment to explore some of the alleged problems with education research. Hargreaves (1996, p.7) had claimed that there was a lot of what he regarded as 'Frankly second-rate educational research which does not make a serious contribution to fundamental theory or knowledge; which is irrelevant to practice ... and which clutters up academic journals that virtually nobody reads' (cited in Tooley, with Darby, 1998, p.7).

Tooley and Darby (1998) explored a number of matters such as relevance to practice, good practice in education research, and the issue of partisanship in research. Their study was based on a review of a 'snapshot' of 264 British articles in some major educational journals – and in the report the authors state that it was 'not intended that generalisations about educational research can be drawn from this work' (p.27). They did, however, claim that 'one of the most striking themes which emerged from our scrutiny was how partisan much of the educational research seemed to be' (p.28) and added that 'some of the areas which exhibited the most dramatic evidence of partisanship were research in gender and sexuality, and race and ethnicity' (p.33).

They illustrated their arguments by discussing specific slices of data and the researchers' analysis and presentation of this data as evidence of racism and/or sexism. Tooley and Darby (1998) seemed to be suggesting that the alleged partisanship they identified stemmed from an over-reading of the data and they provided examples where they argued that this had happened. They also reported examples from papers that they claimed avoided this problem; where researchers 'did not feel the need to reinterpret … [data] in the light of their own ideological perspectives' (p.40). They added that in some cases they believed that some of these 'less partisan' researchers may well have been sympathetic to certain political views. Indeed, this sympathy 'is likely to have been one of the motivations for doing this research' (p.40). However, in their examples of what they identified as non-partisanship, they claimed that the researchers 'looked coolly at the evidence and … report on what the evidence shows, not on what they wanted to find' (p.41).

In this chapter, we cannot deal in sufficient detail with all the points raised by Tooley and Darby (1998) (but see Oancea (2005) for some critical comments). For our purposes, the debate about partisanship and ethics in data analysis raises questions about interpretation and rigour in handling data. At the same time, there are other aspects to consider. First, as Ransome (2013, p.74) says, 'The idea of theory-free or "pure" data is just as silly as the idea of data-free or "pure" theory'. Second, as Ladner (1987, p.74) argues, 'why should anyone think it good to be "objective" (indifferent, disinterested, dispassionate, value neutral)? (cited in Marshall and Young, 2006, p.72). The ethics of any claims about partisanship can be dealt with, to some extent, through explicitly detailing the analysis, documenting any data editing and a requirement that 'the boundaries of inference should be clearly delineated' (Kromrey, 1993, p.25).

Conclusion

This chapter has considered how ethical issues are raised in, and by, the process of doing data analysis. Here we have explored issues such as data trimming and slicing, concealment, exaggeration as well as selective reporting; in other words, cooking, trimming and fabricating data. We have also argued that the data analysis stage of research deserves more explicit consideration in guidelines, training and the conduct of research. Social science researchers may be better at anticipating ethical issues related to working with their participants and these matters may frame their application for ethics approval. The sorts of ethical issues that emerge during the process of doing the research, and more specifically in doing data analysis, may not have been anticipated at the start. As White and Fitzgerald (2010, p.284) have suggested, one way forward may be the 'appointment of resident ethicists or ethics ombudsmen and women' who can offer support and advice with the 'unanticipated ethical concerns' that arise during research, and during the data analysis process.

Farrimond (2013, p.69) argues that 'doing data analysis with integrity may also include involving the participants themselves in the analysis'. She maintains that getting participants to check their own interview transcripts or what she calls 'member checking' where 'participants check back on their own data to see if they agree with the interpretation' (pp.69–70) can help in this process. She also suggests that participants can review articles and papers before they are presented or published; in addition, she discusses the co-production of papers with participants. However, education researchers have different views about the extent to which research participants should be involved in this stage of the research process and much will depend on context, setting, the research questions themselves, the samples, the time available as well as the views of the researcher or research team.

Overall though, in relation to data analysis, there needs to be clear evidence in reporting all research that a systematic approach has been taken towards coding and analysis – and sometimes this can be aided by the use of specific software (e.g. NVivo) and on other occasions through dialoguing and discussing data analysis in research groups or teams in order to 'increase the number of perspectives that are taken account of in the analysis' (Tully et al., 2009, p.124). Perhaps this was what Sevati was attempting to do in the case study with which we started this chapter.

In sum then, we would agree with what Kromrey says about the need for enhanced awareness, and we hope that this chapter has made a contribution towards ethical reflexivity so that data analysis does become more centrally located in an ethically informed perspective. At the very least then, 'As a beginning, the development of an awareness of the subtlety of ethical issues in data analysis will lead to improved practice' (Kromrey, 1993, p.26)

CHAPTER 8

DISSEMINATION

Sam's doctorate is about race relations and education. She has just started conducting fieldwork in one school: visiting the school on three separate days, observing three teachers in their classrooms, and writing down snatches of conversation she overheard in the staff room. Based on these experiences, she describes the school as 'racist' in her field notes. Sam has the opportunity to present at a national conference next month. She's excited that she has some interesting data to report on. What might she need to consider as she writes up her perceptions of this school?

The scrutiny of university Research Ethics Committees (RECs) tends to focus on the preparation for and carrying out of data collection: the selection of participants, consent procedures, and the activities participants are asked to engage with. This may lead to the impression that the reporting and dissemination of research are ethically unproblematic, beyond the common principle of confidentiality (see Chapter 3 as well as later in this chapter). In this chapter, in contrast, we suggest that the dissemination of research findings through various kinds of reporting poses its own ethical challenges. The case study at the start of the chapter illustrates one set of ethical challenges that may arise, namely in relation to the representation of research participants in reporting. In addition, ethical dilemmas may occur in relation to sponsors of research and to the researchers as authors. We will address each of these in turn, following this introductory section, with the majority of attention being devoted to the ethical commitment to participants in the reporting phase of research.

A closer look at research ethics guidelines does demonstrate reference to reporting (see BERA, 2000, 2011; BSA, 2002; NHMRC, ARC and UA, 2007; APA, 2010). After all, as much as fieldwork and data collection may be at the heart of our research, our findings count for nothing if we do not make them public in some way – whether through a dissertation, scholarly papers or presentations. This is recognized first in relation to the notion of academic freedom. The widely accepted assertion is that scholars have a fundamental right to conduct research and publish their findings, limited only by the overarching principles of harm prevention, respect and justice – or as Hammersley and Traianou (2012a) argue, by the importance of the contribution to knowledge that the research makes. Second, this places the onus on researchers 'to ensure that their findings are accurate and properly reported' (NHMRC, ARC and UA, 2007, para 4.5). Research using qualitative methods and working in critical or post-structuralist paradigms tends to acknowledge explicitly that achieving 'accuracy' in reporting is complicated because research design, analysis and writing all require the researcher's interpretation. Although quantitative research is sometimes assumed to be more neutral or value-free, we argue that 'accurate' reporting poses challenges for such investigations as well.

The reporting and dissemination stage of research is not independent of choices made earlier in the research project. Choices about accepting funding from certain sources raise expectations about types of reports for specific audiences at specific times. Particular research approaches, such as visual methods or participatory action research, have implications for reporting. Conceptual frameworks affect both the kinds of data generated and the meanings researchers draw from data through their analysis, which has flow-on effects on decisions about publication of findings. In this chapter we make some of these connections explicit, but we also suggest the chapter needs to be read in the context of the entire book.

Ethical commitment to research participants in reporting

In this section we review several ethical dilemmas in relation to participants that may arise during the reporting stage, including researchers being (or being seen to be) judgemental, questions about whose voice is being represented, and limits to confidentiality.

Being judgemental

In the case study at the start of this chapter Sam describes the school as racist in her field notes based on three visits, with her data including 'snatches of conversation she overheard in the staff-room'. The focus of Sam's research is 'race relations and education'. Would it be reasonable for Sam to repeat her field note assessment of the school as racist in the conference presentation (and any other publications flowing from her research)? To help Sam make this decision, we need some more information. For example, had Sam disclosed the focus of her research, and the use of indirect data (such as overheard conversations) to the school and teachers before commencing her fieldwork? If not, she simply cannot use any of her early material as data, and needs to ensure that she obtains proper informed consent first (see Chapter 5). The exception would be if her REC had allowed her to adopt limited disclosure for her data collection (see also Chapter 5). This is quite uncommon, and if it is permitted usually requires the researcher later to make full disclosure both to participants and in reporting. For example, the BERA guidelines advise:

> Decisions to use non-disclosure or subterfuge in research must be the subject of full deliberation and subsequent disclosure in reporting. [...] if it is possible to do so, researchers must seek consent on a post-hoc basis in cases where it was not desirable to seek it before undertaking the research. (BERA, 2011, p.6)

It is possible, however, that Sam had fully disclosed her research topic and obtained informed consent from all staff. Would that mean she can, perhaps even should, report her findings? Howe and Moses (1999, in Henderson, 2008, p.213) discuss a situation where a school was found to be racist and sexist and ask: 'Shouldn't such findings be reported in the interests of those who are being oppressed, at the site in question and elsewhere?' Assuming Sam has sufficient evidence, the next question then is: Who would be the audience for Sam's reporting about the school? Sam will need to consider how the interests of those being oppressed are served by different kinds of reporting. The Australian Association for Research in Education (AARE, 1993, n.p.) suggests the option of reporting evidence of problems to an 'appropriate authority'. In some cases, such as concerns about a child's safety, alerting authorities is legally mandatory in many countries (see also Chapter 3).

In cases such as Sam's, is it enough to report (to the organization, an authority or in publications) negative or critical findings? Luke (2002, in Henderson, 2008, p.214) argues that researchers also need to contribute to developing suggestions 'of what educationally is to be done'. If the issue is at the core of the researcher's scholarly interest, as it is with Sam, then an ethical stance could be to work collaboratively with participants and other practitioners to tackle the issue and make improvements. In our experience this may not be possible straightaway but rather is likely to be a long-term goal for a new researcher like Sam, requiring building up both her expertise and her relationships with practitioners.

Even when research does not uncover clearly illegal or unethical activities, it may implicitly or explicitly have an evaluative dimension. Much research in education is sparked by wondering whether or how something works. The researchers' duty to report their findings accurately means critique is inevitable in such projects, since no human activity is flawless. Choices about where to publish such findings and how to phrase them enable researchers also to meet their ethical duty to prevent harm and demonstrate respect. In research that draws on critical and post-structuralist paradigms, critique may be of central importance in order for research to support social transformation or to 'trouble' taken-for-granted conceptions or practices. The onus is on the researchers to ensure that consent by participants for such research is genuinely 'informed' (see Chapter 5) so that participants should not be surprised that publications from the research include critique. This may be more complicated, however, than it sounds, as the next section demonstrates.

Being perceived to be judgemental by participants

While some researchers intentionally are critical about their research sites and participants in their publications, others may not mean to be critical, but are perceived in that way by others. This happened to Michael Reiss, following the publication of his book *Understanding Science Lessons* (Reiss, 2000, cited in Reiss, 2005), based on his five-year research at one school. Reiss's frank reflection on what happened not only offers insights into why participants may feel hurt by a publication, but also may help others avoid such an unwanted outcome. The main sources of data for Reiss' book were interviews with all 21 students in a single mixed-ability class and observations in their science classes over five years. This was supplemented with observations in the school, conversations with teachers, and an analysis of students' exercise books. Since the research was conducted over five years, Reiss got to know both students and staff quite well. The book was published at the end of the school year and Reiss sent copies to the students, to the school for the staff in the science department, and to individual teachers who were no longer at the same school. Reiss received various, mostly neutral or positive, responses, but the focus here is on a joint letter sent to him by the teaching staff who were still at the same school. In the letter (included in Reiss, 2005, pp.132–4) staff state that the presentation of the research in the book 'caused us some disquiet', including concerns about 'verbatim reporting of comments about individual pupils' and perceived bias. As Reiss (2005, p.131) sums it up, these teachers seemed to feel that 'I came to their school, contributed nothing to it, and then told tales about them for my benefit and at their expense'.

After getting over his initial shock, and 'defensive self-righteousness' (p.127), Reiss proceeded to analyse what went wrong. Without reproducing his entire argument, several specific points are of particular interest for this chapter. At a general level, Reiss (2005) argues that abiding by ethical guidelines (which he did) is not sufficient and suggests an overarching adherence to 'respect for persons' is necessary. While Reiss had followed research ethics protocols for informed consent and confidentiality, the letter-writers were hurt by the book and felt there had been 'a real breach of trust' (Reiss, 2005, p.133). Following her research in an Australian primary school, Malin (2000, p.3) attempted to avoid similarly hurting her teacher-participant by not giving her a copy of the report, so that 'she would remain oblivious of my critique and thus protected'. Arguably this could backfire, with participants potentially feeling even more upset if they come across a publication themselves.

The response by the teachers in Reiss's case seemed due to their different interpretation of the official research ethics information Reiss had given them during the project, for example considering certain conversations to be off-the-record. Although Reiss felt that, if anything, he had under-used potential quotations from teachers, he concludes that

> [t]here clearly were genuine fears [...] about the consequences the book's publication might have for their careers and for the perception of their capabilities by others. It seems that there was more hostility to the book from the teachers who remained at the school than among those who had left. [...] I failed to think through the loyalty some (probably the great majority) of the teachers clearly had to the school, and I failed to appreciate sufficiently the collegiate nature of a good school department. Criticism of the school or a colleague, even if muted or indirect, could therefore cause real anger or distress in someone for whom all (or the great majority) of the references in the book were very positive ones. (2005, p.130)

Although we concur with Herring's argument (1996, cited in Bruckman, 2002, p.225) that there is no requirement that the methods and findings from research always please the research participants, we also recommend that the kinds of fears and loyalties Reiss identifies need to be taken seriously. Wollcott (2005, p.129) argues that '[b]est intentions notwithstanding, I think we must concede that the person who stands to gain the most from any research is the researcher'. An ethical response would be to supplement scholarly publications with dissemination of more practical resources or reporting in order to benefit the community that participants were drawn from. In addition, a 'respect for persons' approach suggests the importance of treating informed consent as an ongoing process rather than a one-off form to be signed (see Chapter 5). Reiss (2005, p.128) also proposes a 'right of reply', through presenting interim findings or draft writings to participants.

This final suggestion is common practice in participatory and democratic approaches to research. Our assessment is that, depending on the specific research project, this may prevent some ethical challenges and/or create others. For example, Barnes et al. (2003) reflect on their experience of sharing early findings with staff in a project about 'Aftercare', a service for young people leaving local authority care in the UK:

> Before the meeting [with Aftercare Project workers] K and I went through the focus groups' tapes and agreed what we thought were the main points to feed back to the project . . . [At the meeting] we got half-way through the list and K looked at me. I knew what she meant. They looked so miserable that we had to stop. And I'd thought we had reported lots of positive things. (Excerpt from field-notes: Barnes et al., 2003, p.157)

Although the researchers had put together what they saw as 'a reasonable balance of positive and negative issues' the workers were shocked (Barnes et al., 2003, p.157). Everyday wisdom suggests that people tend to hear criticism more loudly than praise, and this may be particularly the case with feedback on professional performance. On the other hand, a collaborative approach by researchers can be appreciated by participants. Te Riele (one of the authors for this book) experienced this on a research project that used 'stories' as both a tool for interim dissemination and a product from the research. During feedback sessions, over several cycles of data collection, school executive staff discussed the current draft story with researchers, made modifications, and negotiated how it could be circulated. The final co-constructed stories demonstrated that staff were 'consistently self-critical and willing to share the breadth of their experiences with others' (Hayes, 2006, p.211).

Whose voice is represented?

The previous section has highlighted that the researcher's duty to report findings accurately is not straightforward, because the 'truth' we tell may be different from the 'truth' others hear (see also the discussion of the impact of power relationships in Chapter 6). As Reiss (2005, p.128) points out, 'We are all more sensitive now to the notion that there is no one definitive reading of a text, and that power relationships are of central importance in both the construction and reading of texts'. This extends beyond the researchers and participants to the audience of research publications and leads to a further set of ethical dilemmas in relation to the representation of various voices in our publications. Dissemination, whether through traditional scholarly writings or innovative performance/visual means, inevitably requires the author to make decisions about what to include, how to sequence material, and what style to adopt. The intersections of reflexivity, positionality and truth can make it difficult to produce publications that are both 'truthful' and ethical (Clemens, 2013). All researchers face the difficult task of transforming the complexity of research data into coherent stories, although they differ in the extent to which they write themselves into a story.

Regardless of research paradigm, researchers aim for what they variously term 'accuracy', 'validity', 'credibility' or 'trustworthiness' in how they represent their findings.

A particular challenge is posed by research that draws on creative arts for dissemination, fictionalizing to a lesser or greater extent the research findings. White and Belliveau (2010, p.85) used theatre as a tool for 'performatively representing and disseminating research findings'. Their script was informed by their data from research on professional interactions in schools, but the exact dialogue of characters and their 'inner voices' was purposefully fictionalized in order to focus attention on specific findings. They ask themselves 'Can a work of fiction contain certain "truths" that approximate the reality of a particular research context?' (p.94). A (partial) answer is provided through audience response. Dissemination through performance enabled the researchers to actively involve the audience in interpreting and discussing the play (i.e. the dissemination of research findings), gaining immediate feedback on the authenticity of the representation. Although the play was explicitly introduced as a work of fiction aimed at informing reflection, these interactions demonstrated that it resonated with audiences. This answer is partial, however, because the manner in which research publications are received by an audience is only one way of measuring 'validity' or 'trustworthiness'. A research account may have 'truth' even when audiences feel it does not accurately represent their voice (see Reiss's experience earlier in this chapter). Some of the most important research is that which reveals findings that run counter to our intuition or taken-for-granted assumptions.

Researchers who work with marginalized groups, especially if drawing on critical or democratic traditions, are faced with juggling purposes of publication that include scholarship, advocacy and empowerment. Their concern may be not just to 'avoid harm' (non-maleficence) but to 'do good' (beneficence). The AARE (1993) *Code of Ethics* states that at the very least the communication of research results should avoid reinforcing public prejudice about socially disadvantaged groups. In relation to their research on young people, Walsh et al. (2013) point to the tension between publicly recognizing and promoting youth agency while also documenting young people's marginalization and exclusion (Walsh et al., 2013). A high-profile annual publication by their non-government organization is *How Young People Are Faring* (FYA, 2010), which 'provides a national point-in-time stock-take on how well young people are making the transition from school to work, further study or training' (Walsh et al., 2013, p.45). The report is based largely on quantitative research and relies on available statistical data sources, which means certain aspects of these transitions are made visible (e.g. gender differences) while others remain invisible because they are not included in the measures. The method also tends to highlight social inequalities, prompting Walsh et al. (2013, p.47) to ask: 'Is research that amplifies the structural exclusion of young people entirely beneficial to the young people whose exclusion is being described, or does it reinforce the deficit discourses that already abound in relation to marginalised youth?' The researchers were concerned that their report, which receives much media and policy attention, could reinforce simplistic or limited normative notions of successful transitions. To address this, the organization decided in 2010 to include qualitative vignettes of purposely selected young people with diverse transition experiences. Interviewing these young people, the authors found that they frequently were much more optimistic about their agency than seemed warranted based on the statistical data, for example in relation to the labour market opportunities for a 24-year-old male without post-school qualifications. This highlights the difference between statistical probability and the possibilities that young people may perceive in their own lives. As a positive, including this in publications can help to counter stereotyped, deficit discourses. As a negative, it can reinforce meritocratic beliefs and work to absolve governments from the harsh realities that many young people face due to systemic inequalities rather than personal failings.

Youth participatory researchers may also find that young people actively conform to stereotypes in their portrayal of themselves. Using participatory film-making with young people, Blum-Ross (2013) found that rather than embracing the opportunity to 'voice a counter-discourse to mainstream media portrayals that almost exclusively represent young people in terms of deviance' (p.60), young people instead 'choose to replicate, rather than resist, these mainstream representations' (p.62). Blum-Ross concludes that the products participants themselves create are not necessarily more 'authentic' than researcher-led publications. Dissemination of such products requires care by the researcher, with particular consideration of the 'digital afterlife' of audio/visual products that identify young people (Blum-Ross, 2013). The latter also entails considering whether informed consent is perpetual (see Chapter 5).

Limits to confidentiality

Confidentiality is commonly seen as one of the key ethical tools for protecting participants in research. It requires attention from researchers during the course of the study, for example through secure storage of data and avoiding disclosing comments from one participant to another. Our point in this chapter, however, is that considerations about confidentiality are most prominent in the reporting stage when findings are made public. Some publishers of academic books and journals have requirements in relation to confidentiality. For example, the delivery checklist SAGE provided us for this book states: 'If you are including case studies in your manuscript please ensure participants' real names are not used and cannot be identified' (SAGE, 2013).

One of the concerns of the teachers in the study by Reiss (discussed above) was that they considered themselves to be too easily recognizable for a 'local audience' (Reiss, 2005, p.133). The distinction between insider and outsider confidentiality is not always made in research ethics guidelines, although such a distinction may make 'common sense' to participants. The British Sociological Association (BSA, 2002, p.5) does suggest that if research participants have characteristics that make them easily recognizable, they 'may need to be reminded that it can be difficult to disguise their identity without introducing an unacceptably large measure of distortion into the data'. For her doctoral research with itinerant families and school staff in a small regional community, Henderson (2008) realized that she could not fully keep her promise of confidentiality because participants could be identifiable to other participants. This created a particular tension when families revealed information to her, based on trust, that the teachers of their children did not know. As she explains:

On the one hand, the information provided understandings about how particular families dealt with aspects of their itinerant lifestyles and was therefore very useful information to my research. On the other hand, my use of those insights meant that I would have been 'telling the world' information that families had deliberately kept from the community in which they were temporarily living. (Henderson, 2008, p.216)

Henderson's solution was to discuss this dilemma with the families, and be guided by their preferences. In some cases families wanted her to use the information, as an indirect way of informing teachers about their lives. In others, the information was profoundly de-identified and only used publicly after a reasonable amount of time had passed. In this way Henderson applied the limitation to the right of academic freedom that is created by the overarching principles of harm prevention and respect (e.g. see NHMRC, ARC and UA, 2007; BERA, 2011). A further limit to confidentiality comes from the lack of control that researchers have over the actions of participants following publication. Reiss (2005) mentions that most of his participants accurately identified their own pseudonym in the book and this is likely to be the case for many publications based on qualitative research. There may be peer pressure to 'tell me your pseudonym if I tell you mine' or a 'detective game' to work out the real identity behind other pseudonyms (see Bruckman, 2002, p.220).

The potential for insiders to be able to identify sites and individuals is most problematic when the research findings reflect negatively on participants. One of the ethical dilemmas for Sam (in our initial case study) is that, even if she uses pseudonyms, the identity of the teachers she quotes may well be identifiable for those who know them, including their principal and students' parents. Bruckman (2002, p.225) suggests that a helpful Research Ethics Committee (REC) 'might give serious consideration to the idea that the revelation might be justified, even if it does substantial real harm to the subject'. It is also possible, however, that an 'innocent' teacher is wrongly identified by readers as making the racist comments quoted in the publication. Sam, with the help of her supervisor and REC, would need to weigh up carefully the risk of potential harm to all these teachers' careers and lives versus the beneficial contribution the research aims to make. Moreover, researchers also have a responsibility to the community of researchers not to 'bring research into disrepute' (BERA, 2011, p.10). There is a risk that a person or organization may never wish to take part in research again if they feel they have been misrepresented and were not properly de-identified.

Finally, visual methods pose considerable challenges in relation to confidentiality. Pope et al. (2010) examine the experience of conducting visual research on a school regatta event. Using examples of photographs taken and insights into the judgement of Pope (the researcher-photographer) and his two co-authors (who both had extensive experience in research ethics) they illustrate the grey areas in the use of photographs, where even three informed researchers do not always agree. The core issue for Pope et al. (2010) is the potential risk of harm that may result from publication of specific images. Harper (2005, cited in Pope et al., 2010, p.302) refers to the concept of researchers' 'webs of obligation and moral regard'. This requires decisions to be made based on the context and implications of each photograph by the researcher, and trust in the researcher by the REC, rather than an across-the-board approach.

Addressing all the specific complexities of visual research is beyond the scope of this book, but in relation to limitations to confidentiality in reporting and dissemination, two further issues are worth mentioning. First, commonly used practices to reduce potential identification in photographs of people may not themselves be ethical. The use of black bars across the eyes and of pixilation or blurring may carry implications of perpetrators or victims of crime, even though that is not the topic of the research. Moreover, advances in technology such as 'reverse image' searching mean that a disguised image may become identifiable if similar undisguised images of the same person are publicly available through the Internet (Media Watch, 2012). Second, promising confidentiality in itself may not always be ethical when participants themselves produce images. BERA (2011, p.7) points to 'participants' rights to be identified with any publication of their original works or other inputs, if they so wish'. Moreover, participants may want 'to be included in the project – their images, their faces, their friends and family' (Wood and Kidman, 2013, p.153). In participatory visual research a priori restrictions on the images that participants are permitted to take and that can be included in public dissemination may be disrespectful and run counter to the democratic nature of such research approaches.

Ethical commitment to sponsors and authors

Throughout this book, the emphasis has been on considering research participants. This reflects the similar emphasis in guidelines and codes for research ethics. Reporting, however, may also raise ethical dilemmas in relation to sponsors of research and for the researchers as they individually or collectively author publications. These will be briefly addressed in this part of the chapter.

Responsibilities to sponsors of research

For many academics the most prestigious research funding is through the relevant national agency, such as the Economic and Social Research Council (ESRC) in the UK, the Australian Research Council (ARC), or the Netherlands Organization for Scientific Research (Nederlandse Organisatie voor Wetenschappelijk Onderzoek, NWO). These organizations tend to be relatively hands-off, permitting scholars to proceed with their research once a grant has been made with little interference apart from requests for progress reports and for inclusion in the acknowledgements of any publications. Such grants, however, are increasingly competitive and as a consequence academics are turning to government and industry as sponsors of contract or commissioned research. For research students, sponsors may include their own employer (who may pay their fees) or industry partners of research projects that include a postgraduate scholarship. The potential for ethical conflict between researchers and sponsors is well-recognized in codes of research ethics (AARE, 1993; BSA, 2002; NHMRC, ARC and UA, 2007; BERA, 2011). They highlight issues of academic freedom and warn researchers to avoid contractual agreements with sponsors that restrict the right to publish findings as well as avoiding pressures to censor or modify their findings in order to reach conclusions that are more palatable to the sponsor.

An example of a dilemma faced by an experienced research team comes from Grant (2003). Responding to a tender by a government education department, the team entered into a contract to research, analyse and document what the department called 'exemplary practices' in literacy and numeracy education in primary schools. Although the department did not set out to influence what the researchers should report, by mandating *how* they should report their findings (through a 'profile'), the department imposed restrictions that also influenced the content. The researchers ended up excluding practices that did not suit the profile format, found it difficult to provide sufficient context for practices, and were concerned that the profile should not be seen as a simple step-by-step framework for action. The main suggestion made by Grant (2003) for others facing similar challenges is to make clear to readers the boundaries set by sponsors and the way the researcher worked within those boundaries. This is perhaps not so different from the common academic practice of acknowledging the limitations of one's research methods, but may require particularly careful attention in publications for a policy or practice audience.

The most crucial ethical challenge for sponsored research is that it may pose a dangerous restriction on academic freedom. The risk is that government and industry sponsors' emphasis on practically useful outcomes ends up 'stifling intellectual work' (Macfarlane, 2009, p.76) and limits the creativity required for new understandings and discoveries. As highlighted by the experience of Grant described above, control of the form of reporting is a contributing factor to this risk. In addition, the policy predilection for 'evidence-based practice' favours research that draws on positivist assumptions and experimental methods (Biesta, 2007; see also Chapter 4). De Vries (1990, in Biesta, 2007, pp.18–20) distinguishes between the technical and cultural roles of research. While sponsors who ask for evidence-based practice emphasize the technical role (focusing on providing means for given ends), researchers usually have some freedom to include discussions in their reporting that reflect the cultural role, for example by questioning the range of possible ends or discussing limitations to the transferability of evidence to other sites. For Biesta (2007), this is not only possible (even when not preferred by sponsors) but essential for protecting the contribution research makes to democracy.

For research students, the expectation by sponsors for timely reporting may become problematic (Marsh and Burnell, 2007). Even with the support of supervisors, it can be difficult for students to know how much time a project will take. A research degree lacks the short deadlines of regular assignments that characterize undergraduate study. Without intending to, inevitably some students end up taking more than the expected time to complete their degree. Although universities also prefer on-time completion, this issue becomes critical when a contract has been signed with an external sponsor that includes a deadline for a final report. While it may be possible to separate the writing of the report for the sponsor (sometimes by the supervisor; see Marsh and Burnell, 2007, p.75) from the writing of the thesis, this is not an ideal solution.

Researchers as authors

Several research ethics guidelines point out that credit for authorship on publications should reflect the substantive contributions made by researchers to generating the publication (AARE, 1993; NHMRC, ARC and UA, 2007; APA, 2010; BERA, 2011). It is suggested that researchers should come to an agreement about authorship early into the project, rather than leaving this until the end. The BERA *Charter for Research Staff in Education* (2012, p.8) includes consideration of the order of authors, opportunities for a range of outputs, and acknowledgements after the project has been completed. Conflict may occur over the right to authorship between junior and senior researchers, for example when a doctoral student wishes to publish from their project. Various guidelines make explicit that seniority or status ought not be taken into consideration, so that, for example, 'Mere possession of an institutional position, such as department chair, does not justify authorship credit' (APA, 2010, p.11). BERA offers the following advice:

> The authorship of publications is considered to comprise a list of everyone who has made a substantive and identifiable contribution to their generation. Examples of substantive contributions include: contributing generative ideas, conceptual schema or analytic categories; writing first drafts or substantial portions; significant rewriting or editing; contributing significantly to relevant literature reviewing; and contributing to data collection, to its analysis and to judgements and interpretations made in relation to it. (2011, p.10)

The conventions over authorship by supervisors of research students vary between sub-disciplines in education. The American Psychological Association (APA, 2010) recommends that supervisors normally would not be named as the principal author on a publication resulting from the research student's project, while the Australian Association for Research in Education (AARE, 1993) goes further, stating that supervisors cannot assume an automatic right to being named as co-author at all. Marsh and Burnell (2007) also point to issues around intellectual property in research teams that include research students. The Committee on Publication Ethics (whose members are journal editors from a variety of fields, although dominated by the sciences) maintains an extensive database of anonymised cases of publication-related dilemmas (COPE, 2013). Some of these illustrate disputes over the order of authorship, conflicts between research students and supervisors over authorship, and questions over the distinction between contributions that warrant co-authorship or merely acknowledgement. The cases demonstrate that even when journals have explicit statements regarding authorship, the potential for dilemmas remains.

Authorship has become a particularly thorny issue due to increasing pressures to publish for academic tenure and promotion. The invocation to 'publish or perish' is reinforced by policy strategies for measuring research performance. Although the specific details vary between countries, performance metrics tend to include the quantity of publications and a simplified measure of quality, for example based on journal rankings or citations. Jennings and El-adaway highlight the ethical concerns such accountabilities create:

> The effect of these facile measurements of research contributions is a sort of careerism when research turns from a vocation or hobby to a form of artificial counting, in which scholarship may fall short of the standard of meaningful contribution to the field but does qualify for the measures used for career advancement. (2012, p.39)

The audit culture of research has been extensively critiqued both for its assumptions and consequences. In relation to consequences for reporting, unethical practices by researchers include:

- 'salami slicing' to create multiple low-quality publications rather than fewer high-quality ones
- excessive citation of one's own and one's friends' publications
- excluding contributors as co-authors to gain the prestige associated with single-authored publications
- including co-authors undeservedly, for example to help boost the career of a research student; within an alliance of colleagues; or as self-preservation by including a senior academic as co-author (see Jennings and El-adaway, 2012).

Such practices are unethical and damaging, Jennings and El-adaway (2012) argue, because the quality of publications is in part assessed through the status of its authors (i.e. perceived quality may be artificially enhanced) and because publications contribute to building a track record that in turn enhances a researcher's potential for obtaining competitive research grants. The audit culture was partly caused by a public erosion of trust in academic scholarship and, perversely, has led to some practices that exacerbate rather than mitigate that problem.

A separate concern to do with authorship is raised by Viete and Phan (2007). They demonstrate how new (doctoral or early career) researchers who are from a different language background may feel silenced in their writing by dominant academic writing conventions, particularly in using English as a hegemonic global language. As a postgraduate research student from Vietnam at an Australian university, Phan worked with her supervisor Viete to create a space for her own writerly identity in her publications, aiming to find a balance between compliance with expected conventions and fostering acceptance of greater diversity in writing style. Phan argues: 'In my writing I affirm my legitimate right not to be colonised by norms that alienate my writing from myself' (Viete and Phan, 2007, p.46). Phan's scholarly discipline is what is known as TESOL in Australia: Teaching of English to Speakers of Other Languages. The resulting synergy between her personal experience as a researcher from a different language background and her research topic facilitated both her reflection and her scope for experimenting with including her 'Vietnamese self' in her English academic writing. Although likely to be more difficult in other fields of education research, we encourage supervisors and non-English speaking research students to explore their options for such experimentation as an ethical approach to writing.

Feeling silenced in one's own publications is a particularly pertinent issue for novice writers and writers from different language backgrounds, but it also can affect other researchers. Barnes et al. (2003, p.158) refer to 'the gatekeeping practices of journal editors and their associated reviewers' and argue that these limit the potential for challenges to rigid conventions. Reviewers may reject non-traditional papers, despite guidelines by journals and associations for avoiding bias based on one's preferred paradigm or methodology. Siegelman (1991) highlights the impact of the reviewer's personality, describing some as 'assassins' and 'demoters' who tend to reject most papers and others as 'zealots' and 'pushovers' who too easily accept papers that fit their own field of research. Ethical examining of dissertations and reviewing of journal articles is an important contribution we can all make to support the ethical reporting of research.

Conclusion

We have demonstrated in this chapter that ethical considerations extend to the reporting and dissemination stage of research. In relation to researchers' commitment to their participants, we have highlighted challenges in relation to the judgements researchers (appear to) make, to complexities around 'voice', and to limitations to confidentiality in publications. In the second part of the chapter, we examined ethical challenges that researchers experience due to tensions with the sponsors of research or linked to the authorship of publications. The discussions regarding participants indicate that Sam, the protagonist of the case study at the start of our chapter, needs to address several fundamental concerns: ensuring that she has sound evidence as a basis for her findings; checking that she has the right to use overheard conversations as data; weighing up who may benefit from or be harmed by her reporting; and considering how different ways of reporting may enhance or threaten confidentiality. We conclude that resolving this dilemma requires Sam to explore in some depth her own fundamental ethical stance (see Chapter 2).

Within critical research traditions, it is customary to ask in whose interest the practices are that are the topic of investigation. In any paradigm, however, education researchers apply critical thinking to the analysis of their data. Taking these conventions a step further, we argue that all researchers would benefit from applying the same scrutiny to the reporting of their research as to data analysis. Ideally, this would not be a solitary endeavour but involve frank discussion with RECs, advisors and peers and it may even contribution to broader debates through publication about ethical challenges. Such critical reflection, both while preparing research publications and throughout their dissemination, enables researchers to carry their ethical commitment through to the end – which usually is well beyond the formal completion of their project.

CHAPTER 9

CONCLUSIONS

Lauren had completed her PhD, which was an ethnographic investigation of the professional identity of a group of women lecturers working in a Christian teacher education institution. Two years later, Lauren was still using her data set in order to write articles and papers for possible publication. One of her key participants, Aysi, had talked passionately about her work and her commitment. She also talked (on tape) about how her sexuality meant that she sometimes felt she had to 'keep my head down and not take risks' in her workplace. Lauren had given Aysi assurances that she would not use this personal information as Aysi was concerned that other colleagues might read the PhD and would be able to identify her from other parts of her interview. Lauren now wants to use this information in a paper on the complexities and exclusions that some academics experience in relation to their identities in their workplace. What should she do?

In writing this book, and this last chapter, we have come up against some conflicting sets of values and ethical issues of our own. To what extent, if at all, should this book concentrate on helping education researchers to produce acceptable ethical documentation, to be compliant, in order to be able to proceed to data collection? Should this book be more concerned with the wider questions and debates that characterize research ethics? Can both of these projects usefully be combined in one text? In the final analysis, is it better that some students undertaking dissertations decide *not* to do empirical research because of reading this book and come to the conclusion that to do so is not in the interests of the 'subjects'/ 'objects' of their concern? Is Lauren's proposed paper really in Aysi's interests, or is it more related to Lauren's career? And does it matter?

This book has been written for different constituencies of researchers from a range of disciplinary backgrounds and different settings, albeit with an educational focus to their work. We have tried to speak to the new researcher as well as, we hope, adding to the knowledge and expertise of the more experienced social science researcher. If there is a central *motif* that runs through our discussion it is that relying solely on principles and roles derived from a formal research ethics framework can displace our own responsibilities for making decisions and for thinking and acting ethically as part of the research process. Whatever the circumstances, or the setting and the type of research that is being undertaken, ethical issues are situated and fluid and need to be engaged with reflexively before, during, as well as after the project, as we have illustrated above in the case of Lauren and Aysi. 'Ethical practice is an ongoing interaction of values in shifting contexts and relationships rather than something delivered by a signed consent form or adherence to a static set of principles' (Hughes, 2005, p.231).

This final chapter is divided into three sections. First, we draw together the main arguments that have been rehearsed in this book. Then we turn to consider some of the gaps, shortcomings and dilemmas in our work. Finally, we make some recommendations for further developments in what we see as the most important part of doing good research – the ethical core that shapes everything else.

An overview of the key arguments

In this book, we started by exploring the justifications for taking ethical considerations seriously in all work with human subjects. 'History has taught us the danger of allowing ethical considerations to be the sole responsibility of individual researchers' (Ruane, 2005, p.28). Thus, many professional associations from a wide-ranging set of disciplines and subject areas now publish their own ethical standards and guidelines.

Generally, these guidelines assert the need for researchers to approach any participants with respect and treat them with dignity. They also stress the wider obligations of research to the scientific community and to society at large, as we have argued in this book. All research needs to be evaluated in terms of any benefits and costs, and the potential risk it may pose to possible participants as well as any steps needed to manage any emergent risks. Matters such as informed consent, working with so-called 'vulnerable' groups and issues of anonymity are all part of a basic set of ethical questions that need careful attention. With Ruane (2005, p.29), we strongly assert that 'good research demands that ethical concerns occupy a central place in the entire ethical process'.

We have argued that doing social science research involves more than 'following instructions or applying rules' (Hammersley and Traianou, 2012a, p.7). The researcher has to be reflexive and sensitive to ethical dilemmas and questions that might arise, for things change and unforeseen events can throw up new ethical questions. Such questions are not always straightforward; they sometimes contain 'grey areas' (Burgess, 1989b). However, Scott and Fonseca (2010) warn that there may be pressure for researchers to sculpt their documentation to ensure that they can do their fieldwork and get started quickly. This may be a particular problem for undergraduate and master's students, who necessarily have limited time in which to undertake their empirical research. They may concentrate on filling in the form rather than extending their own research persona through taking on the language and praxis of ethical research (Bridges, 2009). If students get the impression from their supervisors that ethics is a 'necessary evil' that has to be got out of the way as quickly as possible, this may preclude the generation of the sort of ethical reflexivity that we are calling for in this book.

Getting started

In many nation states, going through the process of completing ethics approval documentation and obtaining institutional consent to undertake research is a necessary step forward in the process of conducting ethical research, but it is not the only step. As Bridges (2009) says, ethical codes still need to be interpreted and applied in a manner that may include virtues such as open-mindedness, humility and real concern for the well-being of others. For instance, if Lauren were to approach Aysi to start to discuss the possibility of using some of what she had said, but had embargoed, how might she do this? Should she even consider doing this? These are the sorts of ethical questions that can arise long after ethical consent has been granted and even after the original fieldwork has been completed.

One dilemma is that ethical committees may focus on the preparation for data collection – such as matters of the sample construction and issues of informed consent. However, as any researcher starts to think about the topic and the focus of their proposed research, they will need to explore questions of whose interests are being served by their work, as well as matters of power, cultural sensitivities, respect and harm prevention, before approaching the ethics committee. As we have said, it may be that the researcher will decide that what they had been thinking of doing is not ethically justifiable or indeed practically possible. If this happens, it can only be a good outcome.

Making decisions about the topic and focus of any research is the starting point but, as we have argued throughout this book, the choice of topic is a political act; many of the questions that education researchers focus on are deeply ideological in nature. For example, research exploring matters of underachievement and socio-economic status, child poverty or the impact of a new policy development will inevitably involve value positions being taken and judgements being made. To some extent, scholarship and rigour in approach and analysis will off-set any concerns about issues of bias or distortion. More directly, we would argue that it is not unethical to adopt an overt political position (indeed, it may be unethical not to do so in some cases); nevertheless, we would need to make our own positions clear. Right at the start then, ethical matters are woven into the sets of related decisions that will need to be considered. Who will be asked to participate? Where will the work be done? How will the data be collected and analysed? What methods will be used?

While the independence of the researcher to choose their own topic is generally thought of as important, a variety of pressures can sometimes be brought to bear on this choice-making. This pressure may occur because institutions are funding their staff to undertake postgraduate courses, or those who commission research may have a particular 'take' on the social world. It may even be the case that the researcher may feel pressured into not asking certain questions in the belief that to do so might threaten the beliefs or values of a particular group. However, Sikes (2010) argues that researchers must not avoid difficult areas to research because, as she says, 'invisibility' allows problems to go unchallenged. Obtaining ethics approval to tackle 'difficult' areas may take more time to explain and justify to Research Ethics Committees (RECs); but this discussion is part of the process of a more reflexive and sensitized approach towards good research practice.

Social relations and ethical matters

Essentially, social science research is concerned with an exploration of some aspect of the lives of human beings, drawing directly on their perceptions and experiences, and as such, will always be interpolated by different sets of ethical concerns. The ethical issues of social relations emerge in all dimensions of the social science research process. Working with other people who may be co-researchers, participants, gatekeepers – the full range of stakeholders in the enterprise of doing good research – inevitably involves a complex set of social relationships. In working to prevent harm in a sensitive, informed and reflexive manner, many ethical decisions will have to be made along the way.

One of the major stages in the research process where these matters will possibly be more overt may occur in the negotiation around issues of 'informed consent', as we have previously discussed. The socially embedded nature of decision making means that, in northern hemisphere cultural settings, notions of 'informed consent' often assume a liberal, individualistic perspective. However, social institutions, like schools and colleges, can have an impact on processes of decision making and children may feel they have to take part in a school-based research project. In these settings, survey-based methods may carry some connotations of being a form of 'test', with the implicit assumption that all have to take part. Hierarchical relationships with teachers may make it harder for children and school students to decline to participate. However, even in the most formal school relations, there is some evidence that students may say 'yes' to participation but contribute nothing to discussions or to other forms of data collection – what Morrow (2005) calls 'informed dissent'.

While there are myriad sets of ethical issues that will relate to the social relations involved in all social science research, we want to highlight one other aspect that is less frequently dealt with in the published literature: that is, those social relations that exist within research teams. Generally, in a funded project, there will be a principal investigator who, perhaps with a co-applicant, has written the research design and proposal. If the project goes ahead, a research officer may be employed to carry out aspects of the work. These people will be dependent to some extent on the 'good will' of the more senior members of the project team; for opportunities to extend their career or for further employment. Social relations in research teams may be such that research officers may feel less able to challenge views or develop their own ideas. In cases where the officer is recruited for their 'match' with the participants, they may feel used, and perhaps even abused, if an ethics of care is not extended to themselves and their own well-being.

The ethics of access

Trying to gain access to a research setting and then gaining access to potential participants is a multi-stepped process that is laced with ethical concerns as well as potential conflicts. For example, it may well be the case that a head teacher or principal is keen to welcome a research team into their school and grants permission for the work to go ahead. However, while key gatekeepers, such as head teachers, may well be thinking about the interests of their institution as a whole and believe that the research is in the school's best interests, there may be tensions where individual members of the school community do not want to participate but feel pressured to do so by the school management. Equally, a gatekeeper may turn down a request for their organization to become involved in a study and not allow individual members their own say about whether they want to participate or not. In some cases, it may be that less powerful individuals may feel almost compelled to become participants because a powerful other, acting as gatekeeper, has allowed the researcher to join their group. For instance, a teacher may grant a researcher access to a parents' group in the school without clearing this with all the parents beforehand, who then feel compelled to go along with the teacher's wishes.

There can be ethical concerns where a researcher is involved in a longitudinal study and has to renegotiate access on a number of occasions over an extended period of time (Miller and Bell, 2012). It may be harder for participants to withdraw later on because they feel obligated towards the researcher or even responsible for the researcher's success. In some educational settings, teachers may grant access to teacher-researchers to help them on their academic pathway while they are doing a master's degree. However, the teachers may not want to continue participating in the study if the teacher-researcher then proceeds to doctoral-level study, but may feel obligated to their colleague and less able to withdraw.

This raises a related and equally important ethical issue. When researchers complete their ethical documentation, they have to assert the way in which they will manage any refusals to participate or withdrawal from the project. There will usually be a set phrase or statement that will need to be included in the documentation stating that the person will not be harmed or excluded in any way if they decide not to participate or to withdraw. Researchers will need actively to ensure that any non-participants or early withdrawers are not harmed in any way; the researcher will need to ascertain that this really *is* the case in practice and perhaps will need to recheck at a later stage in the research process.

As we have already discussed in this book, there are a wide range of ethical issues that centre on the matter of access. One of the most contentious issues in education research relates to accessing child participants. While parental consent is demanded by ethics committees for any child participant, this approach has been criticized for being essentially adult-centred and as reinforcing normative views of children as dependent (Albon and Rosen, 2014). However, it is not always clear who should be providing such consent for groups such as looked-after children, for instance.

There are also complicated ethical questions about how to explain the research study when access is being negotiated. How much information should be provided to potential participants when negotiating access, and how should it be framed? If it is framed too formally, this may put off some potential participants: for example, those who do not wish there to be a formal record of their involvement. 'Partial truths' are sometimes provided about a research project, in the belief that some groups would not participate if they knew the true focus. It is debatable as to whether this somewhat covert approach is dishonest or sometimes justified. If the latter, then retrospective consent should usually be sought, once the research is complete. There is a similar debate about whether covert research is ever justified. The BERA guidelines suggest that it is permissible in certain circumstances (where the welfare of researchers would be at risk and/or data could not otherwise be collected). Iphofen (2011, p.81) says that perhaps the real question is not whether deception is wrong, but whether harm could be done to participants, the researcher(s), as well as more widely, if a form of deception were to be practiced in negotiating access. In some research work, such as some forms of observation or in immersive fieldwork, incomplete or restricted disclosure may be essential to the research design.

Collecting data in an ethical way

In this book, we have discussed a wide range of issues related to the collection of data in an ethical manner. Here we want to stress two central matters that need consideration in this part of the research process. First, there will be questions that centre on the methods being selected and deployed. There may be cases where the choice of research methods may well be affected by values-based decisions. Some researchers may see a need to adopt qualitative approaches; feminists may have a political commitment towards working collaboratively with participants. One common dilemma for many education practitioner-researchers may centre on the fact that they will frequently need to and want to conduct their research and collect their data in their own work settings (Mercer, 2007). Qualitative methods and practitioner-research may be regarded as harder to gain approval for from institutional ethical review boards. RECs will raise concerns about insider effects, possible coercion and distortion as well as other ethical tensions that may arise in the workplace. However, we believe that researchers should not let ethical concerns determine their choice of methods. Simultaneously, we would argue that that methodological choices do not prioritize collection of data over ethical considerations. Essentially, ethical considerations arise in respect of all methods, not just qualitative approaches (as is sometimes assumed). Where there is a research project, there are always going to be ethical considerations!

Second, and equally important, ethical issues are also raised by the design of research instruments – not just the choice of methods. For instance, it may be that in some cases, pressures are exerted on survey researchers from sponsors to include/exclude particular variables. It may also be the case that because of the design of a project there may be difficulty in being able to extract one individual's data from an online survey, if they wish to withdraw from a study.

Ethical issues of power and reciprocity

Taking an ethical approach in social science research is a process that needs constant negotiation and renegotiation. This is true of all of the dimensions involved in research such as planning, undertaking, analysing and completing research work but is *particularly* the case in respect of the power relations that are inherent in all research with human subjects. The challenge for the ethical researcher is to be able to frame his or her research approach in a way that takes seriously the fact that power relations can be asymmetrical in practice. As we have argued, positions cannot always be read off from roles or occupations. For instance, prospective participants such as school students can sometimes exercise power in ways that may be quite unpredictable. In consequence, we argue that what is needed is a reflexive stance towards power relations throughout the research work (and beyond), for these relations are not static. Perhaps some additional opportunities and provisions need to be put into place by the university that is supporting the research, so that team members have the possibility to discuss any unexpected ethical issues and any complexities in power relations that emerge as they move towards negotiating access and as the work proceeds.

The ethical researcher needs to be alert and sensitive to differences and nuances of power relationships and be aware that these relations shift at different times in the research process:

> A research project follows a developmental trajectory, though this is by no means a linear trajectory, as some stages are done parallel to others and some occur in the course of the development of research. Each stage has a different purpose that, to a certain degree, shapes the respective roles of the participants and the researcher. (Karnieli-Miller, et al., 2009, p.282)

At the start of any research, when the researcher is working to access participants, or respondents or co-researchers (and the terminology itself is imbued with different constructions of power relations), initially more power may lie with those being accessed to assent or refuse to participate. However, once they are 'in' the research, distinctions of class, race, gender and other social markers may assert themselves, sometimes unconsciously as well as more overtly, for both the researcher and the researched. It is the ethical responsibility of the researcher to ensure that they are sensitized to the need for mindfulness about the power relations that characterize their work. Overtly exploring power-relation dynamics, as the work is being initially conceived, constructed and then enacted, is a central ethical requirement in all social science research, but this requirement is not without its own dilemmas and tensions.

There are obvious power and positionality issues where the researched are positioned as 'vulnerable', as is frequently the case with research on/with children. However, there are counter-claims that some overly protective ethical concerns only serve to infantilize children (who tend to get the most attention in this area) through particular versions of 'vulnerability' that signal powerlessness and lack of knowledge or experience. Sometimes the relatively powerless are more able to assert control in the research setting; at other times, this will be less possible. Power relations in contexts where participants are constructed as 'vulnerable' are situated and context-bound and require ongoing reflection and examination in the process of doing the research. One consequence may be that researchers take a deliberate decision to exclude so-called 'vulnerable' groups, perhaps in an attempt to manage the process of obtaining ethical permission to proceed with their research. Students doing small-scale investigations for postgraduate degrees may be susceptible to the pressures of time; thus their study may sometimes result in a different kind of 'unrepresentative sample' (Iphofen, 2011, p121) where some more vulnerable participants may have been purposely excluded. One more point relates to the concept of 'vulnerability' itself. This is a social construction and its interpretation will shift and be differently understood in different times and in different places. Iphofen (2011) points out that everyone has the potential to become vulnerable and that ethics committees are no more or less able to 'anticipate vulnerability' than anyone else. 'What matters is that both researchers and reviewers anticipate the potential for its emergence and make available procedures for dealing with it' (Iphofen, 2011, p.107).

One of the most contentious issues of power in social science research relates to who can speak for whom and who is better placed to conduct research with excluded groups and communities (Hoong Sin, 2007). As we have already argued, Cook et al. (2013, p.140) suggest that researchers need to 're-imagine' research participants, who may be in groups that are socially and culturally marginalized, in 'enabling and transformative ways'. This reworking may lead to a more sophisticated approach towards relative understandings of power as well as the development of insights that shore up more respect for these constituencies. However, there is always a danger that the researcher may simply resort to deploying a rhetoric of empowerment and transformation, rather than the more complicated and demanding processes that would be entailed. For instance, if this point were really taken seriously, it could be that some research might have to be abandoned.

Another ethical matter that we want to return to in this final chapter relates to the ways in which we justify the need for work with those individuals and groups that are socially excluded. Frequently, social scientists argue that their research 'gives voice' to long-standing oppressions. Cook et al. (2013, p.98) believe that research work of this kind cannot simply be justified on the basis of 'giving voice' or telling an untold story. They believe that 'the point of the research should be clear in terms that are comprehensible in local economies of knowledge as well as in academic circles' (p.98). That is, it has to be recognized as valuable by the community who is being researched (with).

A further and related ethical matter, and perhaps a point that we have not addressed enough, relates to who does the work in these contexts of difference. It is common practice for researchers to employ 'insiders' in order to collect data with different groups and communities (Ryan et al., 2011). Sometimes this has meant that researchers are employed to undertake fieldwork within their own communities. They may be employed on casual contracts to do fieldwork; they may not participate in the analysis or writing, and thus, they may not get to progress their own careers – a form of internal exploitation and certainly a lack of duty of care. However, it must also be recognized that some researchers just want to help in the data collection and not participate in writing up; some research contracts are not large enough to employ a researcher to do more than some data collection. In cases like this, it would be unfair to 'blame' the principal investigator for a lack of duty of care. Nevertheless, our point is that an ethical stance extends beyond the actual research to include the employment of the research team and to practices in this occupational setting.

The attempt at 'matching' the social characteristics of researched and researcher raises additional questions about ethics, power and, more specifically, questions related to the possibility of manipulation. To what extent could it be seen as somewhat manipulative to try to ensure that the fieldwork is being undertaken by an 'insider' in an attempt to 'extract' more and better data? How can these concerns be considered, explored and possibly addressed? One of the difficulties in many of these sets of ethical questions is that there are no easy answers; the response that gets called up frequently just reverts to a call for the need for reflexiveness and sensitivity – a tactic that we have deployed in this book! While we would argue for these stances towards research work, there may be other steps that can be taken. For example, funded projects often set up steering groups in order to discuss emergent concerns as the project unfolds. One problem is that sometimes support groups may be set up to 'attract' and 'satisfy' funders; in practice, what may happen is that steering groups may deal with more practical ongoing matters and eschew any ethical debate, particularly if they see their role as supporting the progression of the work schedule. In contrast, Edwards and Weller (2013) provide a more positive view of advisory groups. After the death of one of their participants in a longitudinal study they were conducting with a cohort of young people, they consulted their advisory groups about some emergent ethical issues such as confidentiality and sharing data with his family because of the 'moral responsibility to his parents and siblings brought about by his death' (p.127). Through discussion and consultation the researchers were able to negotiate a way forwards. In some ways, with complex and highly sensitive ethical matters, perhaps the best that can be arrived at in making these 'fine-grained choices' is the 'least bad' decision (Macfarlane, 2009, p.32).

A final point that can be forgotten in the area of power relations is the sometimes complex matter of who owns the data and who controls what can and cannot be said, particularly after some time has lapsed and when the participants are removed from the research process (as in our example at the start of this chapter). Questions about who 'owns' the data as well as how long does 'informed consent' last for, are pertinent here:

> Even if the consent form signed by participants at the beginning of the process grants some approval to disseminate data, it is possible that

participants were not completely aware of the fact that their authorization amounts to a complete enunciation of knowledge ownership to others. In qualitative studies, this is especially true when unexpected data emerge from the study that were not included in the original goals of the study and were not specified in the consent form. (Karnieli-Miller et al., 2009, p.284)

The point made by Karnieli-Miller et al. (2009) about signing consent forms that then give a form of 'eternal' permission may need to be fully explained to prospective participants; even more importantly, in areas of sensitivity, it will be necessary (if possible) to reassure and re-obtain informed consent when some time has lapsed. It may also be necessary to explain what is involved in giving informed consent where the data set is to be archived when the project is completed (Mauthner, 2012).

Analysing data ethically

Turning now to data analysis, we have argued that this is another step in the research trajectory that does not always claim the ethical attention that it demands. The underlying principle is that data needs to be honestly and transparently analysed so that research is a 'trustworthy source of knowledge' (Ruane, 2005, p.27). One problem is that in many cases, if 'transgressions' occur in the data analysis stage, this may be regarded as a methodological problem rather than anything else (Sterba, 2006).

Researchers always have a stake in their research and may be tempted to claim greater significance for their work than is warranted (statistically or otherwise). It can be appealing to apply a statistical analysis that lends strength to arguments that the researcher wants to make. It can be equally tempting to exaggerate findings for the same sorts of reasons. For the qualitative researcher, the temptation to include a 'juicy bit of data' may sometimes override the requirement to accurately represent the key findings that have emerged from the analysis. Data may also be 'diced and sliced' in order to present a more powerful set of outcomes than may be warranted.

A normative response to ethical issues that arise in the process of analysing data is to argue that the researcher must ensure that they take an objective approach towards their accurately recorded and rigorously analysed data. The problem is that, in practice, where it does occur, ethical slippage in data analysis might not always be a consciously driven behaviour. Sometimes a researcher may be overtaken by their passion for their project; sometimes a researcher may want to use their more 'sensational' findings to draw attention to a lacuna in policy and practice for the very best of motives to effect social change.

In their research training, researchers will have been exposed to debates related to power and positionality, and to the ethics of access and informed consent; these concerns dominate many of the available ethics texts. To what extent will they have received any training in, or exposure to, the ethics related to analysis? We are not arguing that the processes of ethics approval need to be extended. In some ways, as we have argued at the start of this chapter, extensive ethical procedures in order to obtain ethics approval may indirectly lead to some researchers taking the view that they have 'done' ethics and that all they need do is collect their data. Paradoxically, a greater emphasis on ethics approval before the work is started may work to reduce ethical sensitivity and ethical reflexivity during and after the research project. Instead of more demands for compliance, we argue that the data analysis stage of research, and its ethical dimensions, deserves more explicit consideration in guidelines, training and the conduct of research.

Writing up and publishing

At an earlier point in this book, we argued that while fieldwork and data collection lie at the heart of our research work, we need to do something with our findings, making them public through our dissertations, published papers or presentations. In our reporting of our research findings, the main ethical issues that will arise are related to how we represent our participants in our texts as well as how we manage any conflicts that can arise in terms of who 'owns' the data that is being reported. As we have also said, these issues are related to choices and decisions that have been made earlier about methods and sponsorship and funding. For example, visual methods raise questions about representation, respect for persons and confidentiality as well as how participants' identities are concealed and how this can be managed effectively in using photography or filming techniques (Wood and Kidman, 2013). If a researcher is sponsored by their employer and does research in their own place of work, then it may be that the employer could seek to ensure that a favourable story is being told about their workplace. In terms of ethical dilemmas with sponsors of research, the potential for conflict is well recognized in the literature and in codes of ethics (AARE, 1993; BERA, 2011). Therefore it is crucial, when reporting back, to make clear to readers any boundaries set by sponsors and the ways in which the researcher worked within these constraints.

A researcher can be caught up in a critical tension between needing to report their findings accurately, in a rigorous and 'truthful' manner and in ensuring that they prevent harm, while respecting their participants (Henderson, 2008). This can sometimes mean that because of the way in which findings are reported, some participants may feel betrayed or, at the very least, that their confidences have either been misinterpreted or misreported (Barnes et al., 2003). The problem is that inevitably in social science research, some critique will be involved; either of the institutional setting or perhaps of some of the practices that have been observed. It might be argued that participants, who must be fully 'informed' about the research, need also to be made aware of the possibility that the project may involve critical commentary as part of this 'fullness'. There can also be a play-off between adhering to respect for persons as well as reporting accurately. As we have said, there are related difficulties because of the wider recognition that 'there is no one definitive reading of a text' (Reiss, 2005, p.128); 'truth' is a social construction that comes out of a critical interplay between position, power and reflexivity. The bottom line is that researchers aim for what they call 'accuracy, credibility or trustworthiness' in how they represent their findings – and this is not often a straightforward process. It is bedeviled with ethical concerns. In the final analysis, all researchers could benefit from thinking hard about how they report their research in their writing up, and in this way, carry forward their ethical reflexivity throughout and beyond the formal ending of their research project.

Gaps and possibilities

In this book, inevitably there are some things that we have not included. There are some matters that we could have and would have liked to write more about. One shortcoming is that we have only been able to draw on texts written in English. There are also some points and concerns that we did not have enough space for. Some of the areas that we have not fully addressed include a much deeper philosophical analysis of the social and moral values that underpin and 'regulate' the ethical relations of social research (Ransome, 2013). In particular, there is a need for more critical analysis of what is meant by 'vulnerability' and any ethical procedures that flow from this labelling and positioning. There is a need to ensure that paternalism and infantilization are avoided; simultaneously, there is a need to take seriously the impact and possible consequences of being part of a research project, and it coming to an end (exits and withdrawing are not always given as much consideration as access) for any intended participant.

In this book there are some research approaches that we have not dealt with in sufficient detail: for example, working with visual data from film and video; working with artefacts; and collecting data through social media such as Twitter and Facebook (Whiteman, 2012). There are also some research settings that have not had sufficient direct attention but that may provoke ethical concerns that we have been not been able to deal with fully enough. For example, working with communities or groups that are socially or culturally marginalized is highly complex and begs many difficult ethical questions – not least, about who should, can or ought to be doing this research work and who benefits from the research. There are 'inescapable structural power disparities inherent in the relationship between the Global North and Global South' (Jeanes and Kay, 2013, p.28) and matters of sensitivities and difference that need constant mindfulness and purposeful attention. Some 'parts' of education provision are more hidden from view and may be under-researched: for instance, substantive fields such as prison education, and education with disenfranchised groups such as refugees and asylum seekers. These hidden fields may also include the social relations and experiences of those in some of the 'Cinderella' parts of education; here we might want to include some parts of youth provision, home schooling, adult education, health education and education with and for elders and seniors. However, what we hope that we have achieved is to provide some sensitizing questions, exemplars and accounts of some central debates from practice and from the related literature that offer some transferability as well a touchstone for good ethically inflected research.

On becoming ethically responsible

One of the greatest challenges in doing research that is ethical and that sustains research integrity is that there are no easy answers, no simple lists or codes of behaviour to be followed so that the researcher can arrive at an ethical decision. This is because ethical decisions derive from moral views and values and some of these will shift and become refined or refuted over the passage of time. It may be useful for the 'good' researcher to stay with the ethical dilemmas and puzzles and resist any easy quest for certainty (Delandshere, 2004). Not only will values shift and deepen over time, so too will the thoughtfulness and awareness of the researcher to the complexity of some of the issues to be considered. Inevitably, in some cases, there will not be an 'obvious' ethical response; the researcher will have to pick their way through sets of possible actions and possible reactions in order to come to a decision about what is the right thing to do.

These questions are far wider than some of the base-line matters that ethical committees generally deal with. In some ways, ethics committees are merely an initial start, perhaps a form of fire-proofing, rather than an holistic approach towards ethical practice. 'A responsible researcher is one who understands and examines the ways in which the moral and the methodological principles of their work are interwoven' (Iphofen, 2011, p.4), and to this we would add, in a continual way across all the dimensions of the research process. As we argued in the first chapter, there is a need for researchers, and members of RECs, to develop habits of 'moral self-cultivation' (Cua, 1992, p.61). The mindfulness and reflexivity that this necessarily involves means that each researcher has to consider the 'rights, dignity and well-being' (p.180) of all those others involved in the research process: gatekeepers, participants, other research colleagues. But it is not enough merely to be mindful; what is needed is a capacity to articulate and be responsive to changing circumstances through visiting and revisiting a set of values and a moral code of conduct as the work progresses. It may be that more education and training will be needed to support and refine understandings and insights in ethical research practices, a process that is continued over the researcher's career. As different challenges arise, responsible researchers may need to ensure that they have forums or supportive and knowledgeable others with whom they can explore the sorts of ethical issues that will emerge.

One problem may be that some ethical issues are simply just not recognized by researchers, and our hope in writing this book is that we have opened up some new terrain for critical consideration. Our point is not to argue for a more detailed ethical approach at the committee stage in those settings where this is the conventional requirement; in many ways, this could be counterproductive and merely lead to a process of telling researchers 'what they must *not* do' (Macfarlane, 2009, p.3). A way forward may be to see the 'appointment of resident ethicists or ethics ombudsmen and women' (White and Fitzgerald, 2010, p.284) who can offer support and advice with the 'unanticipated ethical concerns' that arise before, during and after the research process. There is a need, in some cases, to resituate the work of ethics committees in the research process away from being regarded as a compliance exercise and instrumental activity into a more holistic form of 'moral compassing' (Halse, 2011).

In the final analysis, the responsibility for ethical conduct before, during and after the research must lie with the researcher. They have a responsibility to ensure that they strive to understand and apply ethical approaches and practices in their work in order to ensure, at the very least, that no harm is done to any participants and that they meet their ethical responsibilities towards the academic community and society in general. The researcher has a responsibility to keep abreast of debates in ethics so that they are able to bring an informed sensitivity to their ethical decision making. Sets of rules and codes can never cover every eventuality, which is why all researchers need to become ethically informed and ethically reflexive themselves. At the end of the day, even after seeking advice and considering various options, the researcher will have to make a decision to act. Any decisions will need to be justified in order to explain why certain steps are to be taken and others avoided. Ethical decision making is a deeply moral business and one that requires a moral perspective rooted in knowledge of the complexity involved, sensitivity towards participants and colleagues involved in the process as well as, fundamentally, an accountability towards and a respect for the dignity of the participants set within a duty of care and empathy. In what we have written here, we hope that we have helped to raise and address these sorts of questions.

REFERENCES

AARE (Australian Association for Research in Education) (1993) *Code of Ethics*. Available at www.aare.edu.au/pages/ethics.html.

Adley, P. and Dillon, F. (2012) *Bad Education: Debunking Myths in Education*. Open Maidenhead: University Press.

AERA (American Educational Research Association) (2011) 'Code of ethics', *Educational Researcher*, 40(3): 145–56. Available at www.aera.net/Portals/38/docs/About_AERA/CodeOfEthics(1).pdf.

Ahsan, M. (2009) 'The potential and challenges of rights-based research with children and young people: Experiences from Bangladesh', *Children's Geographies*, 7(4): 391–403.

AIATSIS (2012) *Guidelines for Ethical Research in Australian Indigenous Studies*. Available at www.aiatsis.gov.au/research/docs/ethics.pdf.

Akiko, T. (2005) 'Teachers' practices at a hospital school: A qualitative approach to analyzing the education of children who are hospitalized', *Japanese Journal of Educational Psychology*, 53(3): 427–38.

Albon, D. and Rosen, R. (2014) *Negotiating Adult–Child Relationships in Early Childhood Research*. London: Routledge.

Alderson, P. (1990) 'Consent to children's surgery and intensive medical treatment', *Journal of Law and Society*, 17(1): 52–65.

Alderson, P. (1995) *Listening to Children: Children, Ethics and Social Research*. London: Barnardos.

Alderson, P. (2001) 'Research by children', *International Journal of Social Research*, 4(2): 139–53.

Alexander, L. and Moore, M. (2012) 'Deontological ethics', in E. Zalta (ed.), *The Stanford Encyclopedia of Philosophy*. Available at http://plato.stanford.edu/archives/win2012/entries/ethics-deontological/.

Alldred, P. and Gillies, V. (2002) 'Eliciting research accounts: Re/producing modern subjects?', in M. Mauther, M. Birch, J. Jessop and T. Miller (eds), *Ethics in Qualitative Research*. London: Sage. pp.146–65.

Alldred, P. and Gillies, V. (2012) 'Eliciting research accounts: Re/producing modern subjects?', in T. Miller, M. Birch, M. Mauthner and J. Jessop (eds), *Ethics and Qualitative Research*, 2nd edn. London: Sage. pp.140–56.

Allen, R. (2013) 'Evidence-based practice: Why number-crunching tells us only part of the story', *IOE London Blog*. Available at http://ioelondonblog.wordpress.com/2013/03/14/evidence-based-practice-why-number-crunching-tells-only-part-of-the-story/.

ALRC (2008) For Your Information: Australian Privacy Law and Practice (ALRC Report 108). Available at www.alrc.gov.au/publications/report-108.

ANDS (2012) *Ethics, Consent & Data Sharing*. Available at www.ands.org.au/guides/ethics-working-level.pdf.

APA (2010) *Ethical Principles of Psychologists and Code of Conduct*. Available at www.apa.org/ethics/code/index.aspx.

ASADA (2013) *Investigations and Intelligence*. Available at www.asada.gov.au/rules_and_violations/investigations_intelligence.html.

Australian Institute of Family Studies (2013) *Mandatory Reporting of Child Abuse and Neglect*. Available at www.aifs.gov.au/cfca/pubs/factsheets/a141787/.

Baines, E. (2012) 'Grouping pupils by ability in schools', in P. Adey and J. Dillon (eds), *Bad Education: Debunking Myths in Education*. Maidenhead: McGraw Hill, Open University Press. pp.37–56.

Balen, R., Blyth, E., Calabretto, H., Fraser, C., Horrocks, C. and Manby, M. (2006) 'Involving children in health and social research: "Human becomings" or "active beings"?', *Childhood*, 13(1): 29–48.

Ball, J. (2005) 'Restorative research partnerships in Indigenous communities', in A. Farrell (ed.), *Ethical Research with Children*. Maidenhead: Open University Press. pp.81–96.

Ball, M.S. and Smith, G.W.H. (1992) *Analysing Visual Data*. London: Sage.

Ball, S. (1981) *Beachside Comprehensive*. Cambridge: Cambridge University Press.

Ball, S. (2013) *Foucault, Power and Education*. New York: Routledge.

Ball, S.J., Maguire, M. and Braun, A. (2012) *How Schools Do Policy: Policy Enactment in Secondary Schools*. London: Routledge.

Ball, S.J., Maguire, M. and Macrae, S. (2000) *Choice, Pathways and Transitions Post 16: New Economies in the Global City*. London: RoutledgeFalmer.

Barker, J. and Smith, F. (2001) 'Power, positionality and practicality: Carrying out fieldwork with children', *Ethics, Place and Environment: A Journal of Philosophy and Geography*, 4(2): 142–47.

Barnes, V., Clouder, D., Pritchard, J., Hughes, C. and Purkis, J. (2003) 'Deconstructing dissemination: Dissemination as qualitative research', *Qualitative Research*, 3(2): 147–64.

Battiste, M. (2008) 'Research ethics for protecting Indigenous knowledge and heritage: Institutional and researcher responsibilities', in N.K. Denzin, Y.S. Lincoln and L. Tuhiwai Smith (eds), *Handbook of Critical and Indigenous Methodologies*. Los Angeles: Sage. pp.497–510.

Battles, H. (2010) 'Exploring ethical and methodological issues in internet-based research with adolescents', *International Journal of Qualitative Methods*, 9(1): 27–39.

Becker, H. (1967) 'Whose side are we on?', *Social Problems*, 3: 239–47.

Becker, H., Geer, B., Hughes, E. and Strauss, A. (1976) *Boys in White: Student Culture in Medical School*. New Brunswick, NJ: Transaction.

Bélanger, N. and Connelly, C. (2007) 'Methodological considerations in child-centred research about social difference and children experiencing difficulties at school', *Ethnography and Education*, 2(1): 21–38.

Bell, L. and Nutt, L. (2012) 'Divided loyalties, divided expectations: Research ethics, professional and occupational responsibilities', in T. Miller, M. Birch, M. Mauthner and J. Jessop (eds), *Ethics and Qualitative Research*, 2nd edn. London: Sage. pp.76–93.

BERA (British Educational Research Association) (2000) *Good Practice in Educational Research Writing*. Available at www.bera.ac.uk/publications/ethical-guidelines/good-practice-educational-research-writing-2000.

BERA (British Educational Research Association) (2011) *Ethical Guidelines for Educational Research*. Available at www.bera.ac.uk/publications/ethical-guidelines.

BERA (British Educational Research Association) (2012) *Charter for Research Staff in Education*. Available at www.bera.ac.uk/publications/bera-charter-research-staff-education.

BERA (British Educational Research Association) (2013) *Why Educational Research Matters*. London: BERA.

BERA (British Educational Research Association) Working Group (2009) *Report of the BERA Working Group on BERA Ethical Guidelines and the Contemporary Requirements of Contract Research*. Unpublished report, version 3, 16 November.

Bergström, Y. (2010) 'The universal right to education: Freedom, equality and fraternity', *Studies in Philosophy and Education*, 29(2): 167–82.

Bessant, J. (2009) 'Aristotle meets youth work: A case for virtue ethics', *Journal of Youth Studies*, 12(4): 423–38.

Best, A. (2000) *Prom Night: Youth, Schools and Popular Culture*. London: Routledge.

Biesta, G. (2007) 'Why "what works" won't work: Evidence-based practice and the democratic deficit in educational research', *Educational Theory*, 57(1): 1–22.

Bigler, D. (2010) 'A child's world in the city: An ethnography of an East London adventure playground'. MA Dissertation, King's College London, University of London.

Birch, T. and Miller, M. (2012) 'Encouraging participation: Ethics and responsibilities', in T. Miller, M. Birch, M. Mauthner and J. Jessop (eds), *Ethics and Qualitative Research*, 2nd edn. London: Sage. pp.94–107.

Black, P. (2012) 'Foreword', in P. Adey and J. Dillon (eds), *Bad Education: Debunking Myths in Education*. Maidenhead: McGraw Hill, Open University Press. pp.xvii–xx.

Blum-Ross, A. (2013) 'Authentic representations? Ethical quandaries in participatory filmmaking with young people', in K. te Riele and R. Brooks (eds), *Negotiating Ethical Challenges in Youth Research*. New York: Routledge. pp.55–68.

Bochow, A. (2012) 'Let's talk about sex: Reflections on conversations about love and sexuality in Kumasi and Endwa, Ghana', *Culture, Health and Sexuality*, 14, S1, S15–S26.

Bolton, A. (1997) *Losing the Thread: Pupils' and Parents' Voices about Education for Sick Children*. London: National Association for the Education of Sick Children.

Bradley, W.J. and Schaefer, K.C. (1998) *The Uses and Misuses of Data and Models*. Thousand Oaks: Sage.

Brady, B. and O'Regan, C. (2009) 'Meeting the challenge of doing an RCT evaluation of youth mentoring in Ireland', *Journal of Mixed Methods Research*, 3(3): 265–80.

Breakspear, S. (2012) *The Policy Impact of PISA: An Exploration of the Normative Effects of International Benchmarking in School System Performance*. Paris: OECD Publishing. Available at http://www.oecd-ilibrary.org/education/the-policy-impact-of-pisa_5k9fdfqffr28-en.

Bridges, D. (2001) 'The ethics of outsider research', *Journal of Philosophy of Education*, 35(3): 371–86.

Bridges, D. (2009) 'Four issues for ethical code makers'. Paper presented at the British Educational Research Association Annual Conference, Manchester.

Brinkman, S. and Kvale, S. (2005) 'Confronting the ethics of qualitative research', *Journal of Constructivist Psychology*, 18: 157–81.

Brooks, R. (2005) *Friendship and Educational Choice: Peer Influence and Planning for the Future*. Basingstoke: Palgrave.

Brooks, R., McCormack, M. and Bhopal, K. (2013) 'Contemporary debates in the sociology of education: An introduction', in R. Brooks, M. McCormack, and K. Bhopal (eds), *Contemporary Debates in the Sociology of Education*. Basingstoke: Palgrave. pp.1–18.

Brown, J. (2013) 'Dumbing down, Minister? Michael Gove gets his educational facts from marketing surveys for Premier Inn and UKTV Gold', *The Independent*, 13 May. Available at www.independent.co.uk/news/uk/home-news/dumbing-down-minister-michael-gove-gets-his-educational-facts-from-marketing-surveys-for-premier-inn-and-uktv-gold-8614525.html.

Brown, M. (2012) 'Traditional versus progressive education', in P. Adey and J. Dillon (eds), *Bad Education: Debunking Myths in Education*. Maidenhead: McGraw Hill, Open University Press. pp.95–110.

Brown, P. (2010) 'Teacher research and university institutional review boards', *Journal of Early Childhood Teacher Education*, 31: 276–83.

Bruckman, A. (2002) 'Studying the amateur artist: A perspective on disguising data collected in human subjects research on the Internet', *Ethics and Information Technology*, 4(3): 217–31.

BSA (2002) *Statement of Ethical Practice*. Available at www.britsoc.co.uk/about/equality/statement-of-ethical-practice.aspx.

Burgess, R.G. (1989a) 'Ethics and educational research: An introduction', in R.G. Burgess (ed.), *The Ethics of Educational Research*. Lewes: Falmer Press. pp.1–9.

Burgess, R.G. (1989b) 'Grey areas: Ethical dilemmas in educational ethnography', in R.G. Burgess (ed.), *The Ethics of Educational Research*. Lewes: Falmer Press. pp.60–76.

Canadian Government (1985) *Privacy Act*. Available at http://laws-lois.justice.gc.ca/eng/acts/P%2D21/.

Carstens, L. (2004) 'Teachers' experience of teaching in a hospital school'. Magister Educationis research essay, Rand Afrikaans University, South Africa. Available at www.cerelepe.faced.ufba.br/arquivos/fotos/11/teacherssexperienceofteachinginahospitalschool.pdf.

Cassell, J. (1980) 'Ethical principles for conducting fieldwork', *American Anthropologist*, 82(1): 28–41.

Cave, E.D. (1967) 'The effects of the "eleven-plus" result on the subsequent careers of pupils', *British Journal of Educational Psychology*, 37(1): 41–6.

Chappell, T. (1998) 'Theories of ethics, overview', in R. Chadwick (ed.), *Encyclopedia of Applied Ethics*. San Diego, CA: Academic Press. pp.323–43.

Charlesworth, A. and Rusbridge, C. (2010) *Freedom of Information and Research Data: Questions and Answers*. Available at www.jisc.ac.uk/publications/programmerelated/2010/foiresearchdata.aspx.

Child Welfare Information Gateway (2012) *Major Federal Legislation Concerned With Child Protection, Child Welfare, and Adoption*. Available at www.childwelfare.gov/pubs/ otherpubs/majorfedlegis.pdf.

CIHR, NSERC and SSHRC (Canadian Institutes of Health Research, Natural Sciences and Engineering Research Council of Canada, and Social Sciences and Humanities

Research Council of Canada) (2010) *Tri-Council Policy Statement: Ethical Conduct for Research Involving Humans (TCPS 2)*. Available at http://ethics.gc.ca/eng/policy-politique/initiatives/tcps2-eptc2/Default/.

Clark, A. (2004) 'The mosaic approach and research with young children', in V. Lewis, M. Kellett, C. Robinson, S. Fraser and S. Ding (eds), *The Reality of Research with Children and Young People*. London: Sage. pp.142–62.

Cleary, L.M. (2013) *Doing Cross-cultural Research with Integrity*. London: Palgrave Macmillan.

Clemens, R. (2013) 'Something a little nearer to the truth: Ethical representations of African American and Latino male teenagers in ethnography'. Paper presented at the Annual Ethnography in Education Research Forum, Philadelphia, PA.

Coffey, A., Renold, E., Dicks, B., Soyinka, B. and Mason, B. (2006) 'Hypermedia ethnography in educational settings: Possibilities and challenges', *Ethnography and Education*, 1(1): 15–30.

Collins, F. (2012) 'Cyber-spatial mediations and educational mobilities: International students and the Internet', in R. Brooks, A. Fuller and J. Waters (eds), *Changing Spaces of Education: New Perspectives on the Nature of Learning*. London: Routledge. pp.244–60.

Connor, S. (1999) 'Science and history solve the mystery of the cancer clusters', *The Independent*, 14 August. Available at www.independent.co.uk/news/science-and-history-solve-the-mystery-of-the-cancer-clusters-1112520.html.

Connors, C. and Stalker, K. (2003) *The Views and Experiences of Disabled Children and their Siblings: A Positive Outlook*. London: Jessica Kingsley.

Constantine-Simms, D. (1995) 'The role of the Black researcher in educational research', in V. Showunmi and D. Constantine-Simms (eds), *Teachers for the Future*. Stoke on Trent: Trentham Books. pp.13–34.

Cook, J., Danaher, M., Danaher, G. and Danaher, P.A. (2013) 'Naming, framing, and sometimes shaming: Reimagining relationships with education research participants', in W. Midgley, P.A. Danaher and M. Baguley (eds), *The Role of Participants in Education Research: Ethics, Epistemologies, and Methods*. New York: Routledge. pp.140–56.

COPE (2013) *Cases*. Available at http://publicationethics.org/cases.

Cormode, L. and Hughes, A. (1999) 'Networks, cultures and elite research: The economic geographer as situated researcher', *Geoforum, 30*: 299–363.

Corrigan, P.W. and Watson, A.C. (2007) 'The public stigma of psychiatric disorder and the gender, ethnicity, and education of the perceiver', *Community Mental Health Journal,* 43(5): 439–58.

Crow, G., Wiles, R., Heath, S. and Charles, V. (2006) 'Research ethics and data quality: The implications of informed consent', *International Journal of Social Research Methodology*, 9(2): 83–95.

Cua, A. (1992) 'Competence, concern and the role of paradigmatic individuals (chun-tzu) in moral education', *Philosophy East and West*, 42(1): 49–68.

Cua, A. (2001) 'Confucian ethics', in L. Becker and C. Becker (eds), *Encyclopedia of Ethics*, 2nd edn. New York: Routledge. pp.287–95.

Cumming, J., Mawdsley, R. and De Waal, E. (2006) 'The "best interests of the child", parents' rights and educational decision-making for children: A comparative analysis of interpretations in the United States of America, South Africa and Australia', *Australia and New Zealand Journal of Law and Education*, 11(2): 43–71.

Cuskelly, M. (2005) 'Ethical inclusion of children with disabilities in research', in A. Farrell (ed.), *Ethical Research with Children*. Maidenhead: Open University Press. pp.97–111.

Dale, R. (2001) 'Shaping the sociology of education over half-a-century', in J. Demaine (ed.), *Sociology of Education Today*. Basingstoke: Palgrave. pp.5–29.

Dalen, K. and Jones, L. (2010) 'Ethical monitoring: Conducting research in a prison setting', *Research Ethics*, 6(1): 10–16.

Daley, D.M. (2001) 'Researching my own: The experience of an African-Caribbean researcher', in R. Hart (ed.), *Home and Away: Researching Familiar and Unfamiliar Sites*. London: King's College London. pp.36–43.

Daley, D.M. (2002) 'The experience of the African Caribbean manager in the British school system'. PhD thesis, King's College London, University of London.

Danby, S. and Farrell, A. (2004) 'Accounting for young children's competence in educational research: New perspectives on research ethics', *The Australian Educational Researcher*, 31(3): 35–39.

Danby, S. and Farrell, A. (2005) 'Opening the research conversation', in A. Farrell (ed.), *Ethical Research with Children*. Maidenhead: Open University Press. pp.49–67.

David, M., Edwards, R. and Alldred, P. (2001) 'Children and school-based research: "Informed consent" or "educated consent"?', *British Educational Research Journal*, 27(3): 347–65.

Davidson, D. (1998) 'The furious passage of the Black graduate student', in J.A. Ladner (ed.), *The Death of White Sociology*. Baltimore, MD: Black Classic Press. pp.23–61.

Del Monte, K. (2000) 'Partners in inquiry: Ethical challenges in team research', *International Social Science Review*, 75(3–4): 3–14.

Delandshere, G. (2004) 'The moral, social and political responsibility of educational researchers: Resisting the current quest for certainty', *International Journal of Educational Research*, 41: 237–56.

Denscombe, M. and Aubrook, L. (1992) '"It's just another piece of schoolwork": The ethics of questionnaire research on pupils in schools', *British Educational Research Journal*, 18(2): 113–31.

DePalma, R. (2010) 'Socially just research for social justice: Negotiating consent and safety in a participatory action research project', *International Journal of Research and Method in Education*, 33(3): 215–27.

Department for Education (DfE) (2013) *Department's Response to the Analytical Review*. Available at www.gov.uk/government/publications/department-for-education-analytical-review.

Derrida, J. (1995) *Points*. Stanford: Stanford University Press.

De Vries, G. (1990) *De Ontwikkeling van Wetenschap* [The Development of Science] Groningen: Wolters Noordhoff.

DHEW (Department of Health, Education and Welfare) (1979) *The Belmont Report: Ethical Principles and Guidelines of the Protection of Human Subjects of Research*. Washington, DC: Department of Health, Education and Welfare, National Commission for the Protection of Human Subjects of Biomedical and Behavioral Research. Available at www.hhs.gov/ohrp/humansubjects/guidance/belmont.html.

Dingwall, R. (2012) 'How did we ever get into this mess? The rise of ethical regulation in the social sciences', in J. van Loon and K. Love (eds), *Ethics in Social Research (Studies in Qualitative Methodology, Vol. 12)*. Bingley: Emerald Press. pp.3–26.

Dockett, S., Perry, B., Kearney, E., Hampshire, A., Mason, J. and Schmied, V. (2009) 'Researching with families: Ethical issues and situations', *Contemporary Issues in Early Childhood*, 10(4): 353–65.

Driscoll, J. (2013) 'Supporting care leavers to fulfil their educational aspirations: Resilience, relationships and resistance', *Children and Society*, 27(2): 139–49.

Duncombe, J. and Jessop, J. (2002) '"Doing rapport" and the ethics of "faking friendship"', in M. Mauther, M. Birch, J. Jessop and T. Miller (eds) *Ethics in Qualitative Research*. London: Sage. pp.107–22.

Duncombe, J. and Jessop, J. (2012) '"Doing rapport" and the ethics of "faking friendship"', in T. Miller, M. Birch, M. Mauthner and J. Jessop (eds), *Ethics and Qualitative Research*, 2nd edn. London: Sage. pp.108–21.

Edwards, R. and Mauthner, M. (2012) 'Ethics and feminist research: Theory and practice', in T. Miller, M. Birch, M. Mauthner and J. Jessop (eds), *Ethics and Qualitative Research*, 2nd edn. London: Sage. pp.14–28.

Edwards, R. and Weller, S. (2013) 'The death of a participant: Moral obligation, consent and care in qualitative longitudinal research', in K. te Riele and R. Brooks (eds.) *Negotiating Ethical Challenges in Youth Research*. London and New York: Routledge. pp.125–36.

Edwards, T. (2010) '"All the evidence shows …": Reasonable expectations of educational research', *Oxford Review of Education*, 26(3–4): 299–311.

Eglinton, K. (2013) 'Between the personal and the professional: Ethical challenges when using visual ethnography to understand young people's use of popular visual material culture', *Young*, 21(3): 253–71.

Ells, C. (2011) 'Communicating qualitative research designs to research ethics review boards', *The Qualitative Report*, 16(3): 881–91.

Emmison, M. (2004) 'The conceptualization and analysis of visual data', in D. Silverman (ed.), *Qualitative Research: Theory, Method and Practice*. London: Sage. pp.246–65.

Epstein, D. (1994) *Challenging Lesbian and Gay Inequalities in Education*. Milton Keynes: Open University Press.

ESF and ALLEA (2011) *The European Code of Conduct for Research Integrity*. Strasburg: European Science Foundation.

ESRC (2010) *Research Data Policy*. Available at www.esrc.ac.uk/_images/Research_Data_Policy_2010_tcm8–4595.pdf.

ESRC (2012) *Framework for Research Ethics*. Available at www.esrc.ac.uk/about-esrc/information/research-ethics.aspx.

Farrimond, H. (2013) *Doing Ethical Research*. Basingstoke: Palgrave Macmillan.

Farrugia, D. (2013) 'The possibility of symbolic violence in interviews with young people experiencing homelessness', in K. te Riele and R. Brooks (eds), *Negotiating Ethical Challenges in Youth Research*. New York: Routledge. pp.109–21.

Felzmann, H. (2009) 'Ethical issues in school-based research', *Research Ethics*, 5(3): 104–09.

First Nations Centre (2005) *Ownership, Control, Access and Possession (OCAP) or Self-Determination Applied to Research: A Critical Analysis of Contemporary First Nations Research and Some Options for First Nations Communities*. Available at www.naho.ca/documents/fnc/english/FNC_OCAPCriticalAnalysis.pdf.

Fisher, E. (2009) 'The moral consequences of studying the vulnerable: Court mandated reporting and beyond', *Narrative Inquiry*, 19(1): 18–34.

Foucault, M. (1980) *Power/Knowledge: Selected Interviews and Other Writings 1972–1977*. New York: Harvester Wheatsheaf.

Foucault, M. (1998) *The History of Sexuality: The Will to Knowledge*. London: Penguin.

Foucault, M. (2000) 'The subject and power', in P. Rabinow (ed), *Essential Works of Foucault 1954–1984, Volume 3: Michel Foucault – Power*. New York: New Press. pp.326–48.

Freakley, M. and Burgh, G. (2000) *Engaging with Ethics*. Katoomba: Social Science Press.

Furey, R. and Kay, J. (2010) 'Developing ethical guidelines for safeguarding children during social research', *Research Ethics*, 6(4): 120–27.

FYA (2010) *How Young People Are Faring*. Melbourne: Foundation for Young Australians.

Gallagher, M., Haywood, S., Jones, M. and Milne, S. (2010) 'Negotiating informed consent with children in school-based research: A critical review', *Children and Society*, 24: 471–82.

Garrett, J. (2004) *A Simple and Usable (Although Incomplete) Ethical Theory Based on the Ethics of W. D. Ross*. Available at http://people.wku.edu/jan.garrett/ethics/rossethc.htm.

Gelman, A. (2011) 'Ethics and statistics: Open data and open methods', *Chance,* 24(4): 51–53. Available at www.stat.columbia.edu/~gelman/research/published/ChanceEthics1.pdf.

Gibson, M. (1985) 'Collaborative educational ethnography: Problems and profits', *Anthropology and Education*, 16(2): 124–48.

Gillborn, D. (2008) *Racism and Education: Coincidence or Conspiracy?* London: Routledge.

Gillies, V. and Alldred, P. (2012) 'The ethics of intention: Research as a political tool', in T. Miller, M. Birch, M. Mauthner and J. Jessop (eds), *Ethics and Qualitative Research*, 2nd edn. London: Sage. pp.43–60.

Gilligan, C. (1982) *In a Different Voice: Psychological Theory and Women's Development*. Cambridge, MA: Harvard University Press.

Goldacre, B. (2013) *Building Evidence into Education*. London: Department for Education.

Graham, A., Powell, M.A., Fitzgerald, R., Taylor, N.J. and Moulat, B. (2012) *Draft Ethical Research Involving Children: International Charter and Guidelines*. Florence: UNICEF, Office for Research – Innocenti.

Graham, A., Powell, M., Taylor, N., Anderson, D. and Fitzgerald, R. (2013) *Ethical Research Involving Children*. Florence: UNICEF Office of Research – Innocenti. Available at http://childethics.com/wp-content/uploads/2013/10/ERIC-compendium-approved-digital-web.pdf.

Grant, P. (2003) '"Exemplary practice": so called? Dilemmas in reporting'. Paper presented at the NZARE/AARE Conference, Auckland. Available at http://publications.aare.edu.au/03pap/gra03537.pdf.

Greig, A., Taylor, J. and MacKay, T. (2007) *Doing Research with Children*, 2nd edn. London: Sage.

Griffiths, M. (1998) *Educational Research for Social Justice: Getting off the Fence*. Buckingham: Open University Press.

Gutting, G. (2013) 'Michel Foucault', in E. Zalta (ed), *The Stanford Encyclopedia of Philosophy*. Available at http://plato.stanford.edu/archives/sum2013/entries/foucault/.

Haggerty, K. (2004) 'Ethics creep: Governing social science research in the name of ethics', *Qualitative Sociology*, 27(4): 391–414.

Hallgarth, M. (1998) 'Consequentialism and deontology', in R. Chadwick (ed.), *Encyclopedia of Applied Ethics*. San Diego, CA: Academic Press. pp.602–13.

Halse, C. (2011) 'Confessions of an ethics committee chair', *Ethics and Education,* 6(3): 239–51.

Hamid, M.O. (2010) 'Fieldwork for language education research in rural Bangladesh: Ethical issues and dilemmas', *International Journal of Research and Method in Education*, 33(3): 259–71.

Hammersley, M. (1999) 'Reflections on the current state of educational research', *Research Intelligence (Newsletter of the British Educational Research Association)*, 70.

Hammersley, M. (2003) 'Recent radical criticism of interview studies: Any implications for the sociology of education?', *British Journal of Sociology of Education*, 24(1): 119–26.

Hammersley, M. and Traianou, A. (2012a) *Ethics and Educational Research.* Available at http://www.bera.ac.uk/resources/ethics-and-educational-research.

Hammersley, M. and Traianou, A. (2012b) *Ethics in Qualitative Research: Controversies and Contexts.* London: Sage.

Hargreaves, D. (1967) *Social Relations in a Secondary School.* London: Routledge.

Hargreaves, D. (1996) *Teaching as a Research-based Profession: Possibilities and Prospects.* Teacher Training Agency Annual Lecture. Mimeo.

Harold, B. (2004) '"Lifting the veil": Researching teachers' work in a Middle Eastern Sheikhocracy'. Paper presented at the AARE conference, Melbourne. Available at http://publications.aare.edu.au/04pap/har04291.pdf.

Harper, D. (2005) 'What's new visually?' In N.K. Denzin and Y. Lincoln (eds), *The Sage Handbook of Qualitative Research*, 3rd ed., Thousand Oaks, CA: Sage. pp.747–62.

Harris, G. (2001) 'Aristotelian ethics', in L. Becker and C. Becker (eds), *Encyclopedia of Ethics*, 2nd edn. New York: Routledge. pp.85–91.

Hart, R. (ed.) (2001) *Home and Away: Researching Familiar and Unfamiliar Sites.* London: King's College London.

Hattie, J. (1991) 'The Burt Controversy: An essay review of Hearnshaw's and Joynson's biographies of Sir Cyril Burt', *Alberta Journal of Educational Research*, 37(3): 259–75.

Hauge, M. (2013) 'Research with young people on female circumcision: Negotiating cultural sensitivity, law and transparency', in K. te Riele and R. Brooks (eds), *Negotiating Ethical Challenges in Youth Research.* New York: Routledge. pp.137–48.

Hayes, D. (2006) 'Telling stories: Sustaining improvement in schools operating under adverse conditions', *Improving Schools*, 9(3): 203–13.

Health Research Commonwealth of Australia (HRC) (2003) *Values and Ethics: Guidelines for Ethical Conduct in Aboriginal and Torres Strait Islander Health Research.* Available at www.nhmrc.gov.au/guidelines/publications/e52.

Heath, S., Brooks, R., Cleaver, E. and Ireland, E. (2009) *Researching Young People's Lives.* London: Sage.

Heath, S., Charles, V., Crow, G. and Wiles, R. (2007) 'Informed consent, gatekeepers and go-betweens: Negotiating consent in child- and youth-orientated institutions', *British Educational Research Journal*, 33(3): 403–17.

Henderson, R. (2008) 'Dangerous terrains: Negotiating ethical dilemmas', in R. Henderson and P. Danaher (eds), *Troubling Terrains: Tactics for Traversing and Transforming Contemporary Educational Research.* Teneriffe, Queensland: Post Pressed. pp.211–22.

Heptinstall, E. (2000) 'Gaining access to looked after children for research purposes: Lessons learned', *British Journal of Social Work*, 30(6): 867–72.

Herring, S. (1996) 'Linguistic and critical analysis of computer-mediated communication: Some ethical and scholarly considerations', *The Information Society*, 12(2): 153–68.

Hey, V. (1997) *The Company She Keeps: An Ethnography of Girls' Friendships.* Milton Keynes: Open University Press.

Higgs, M.D. (2013) 'Do we really need the s-word?', *American Scientist*, 101(1): 6–9. Available at www.americanscientist.org/issues/pub/2013/1/do-we-really-need-the-s-word/7.

Hill, M. (2006) 'Children's voices on ways of having a voice: Children and young people's perspectives on methods used in research and consultation', *Childhood*, 13(1): 69–89.

Hillyard, S.H. (2004) 'The case for partisan research: Erving Goffman and researching social inequalities', in B. Jeffrey and G. Walford (ed.), *Ethnographies of Educational and Cultural Conflicts: Strategies and Resolutions (Studies in Educational Ethnography, Vol.9)*, Bingley: Emerald Press. pp.9–24.

Hinton, D. (2013) 'Private conversations and public audiences: Exploring the ethical implications of using mobile telephones to research young people's lives', *Young*, 21(3): 237–51.

Hollway, W. and Jefferson. T. (2000) *Doing Qualitative Research Differently: Free Association, Narrative and the Interview Methods*. London: Sage.

Homan, R. (1991) *The Ethics of Social Research*. Harlow: Longman.

Hoong Sin, C. (2007) 'Ethnic-matching in qualitative research: Reversing the gaze on "white others" and "white" as "other"', *Qualitative Research*, 7(4): 477–99.

Howe, K. and Moses, M. (1999) 'Ethics in educational research', *Review of Research in Education*, 24(1): 21–59.

HSS (2007) *Protecting Personal Health Information in Research: Understanding the HIPAA Privacy Rule*. Available at http://privacyruleandresearch.nih.gov/pr_02.asp.

Hudson, C. (2004) 'Reducing inequalities in field relations: Who gets the power?', in B. Jeffrey and G. Walford (eds), *Ethnographies of Educational and Cultural Conflicts*. Amsterdam: Elsevier. pp.255–70.

Hughes, J. (2005) 'Ethical cleansing? The process of gaining "ethical approval" for a new research project exploring performance in place of war', *Research in Drama Education*, 10(2): 229–32.

Hursthouse, R. (2013) 'Virtue ethics', in E. Zalta (ed.), *The Stanford Encyclopedia of Philosophy*. Available at http://plato.stanford.edu/archives/fall2013/entries/ethics-virtue/.

Hutchby, I. and Moran-Ellis, J. (1998) *Children and Social Competence: Arenas of Action*. London: Routledge.

Hutchinson, D. and Styles, B. (2010) *A Guide to Running Randomised Control Trials for Educational Researchers*. Slough: National Foundation for Educational Research.

Iphofen, R. (2009) *Ethical Decision-making in Social Research: A Practical Guide*. Basingstoke: Palgrave Macmillan.

Iphofen, R. (2011) *Ethical Decision-making in Social Research: A Practical Guide*, new edition Basingstoke: Palgrave Macmillan.

Israel, M. and Hay, I. (2006) *Research Ethics for Social Scientists*. London: Sage.

James, N. (2013) 'Research on the "inside": The challenges of conducting research with young offenders', *Sociological Research Online*, 18(4): 14.

Jeanes, R. and Kay, T. (2013) 'Conducting research with young people in the global south', in K. te Riele and R. Brooks (eds), *Negotiating Ethical Challenges in Youth Research*. London: Routledge. pp.19–30.

Jennings, M. and El-adaway, I. (2012) 'Ethical issues in multiple-authored and mentor-supervised publications', *Journal of Professional Issues in Engineering Education and Practice*, 138(1): 37–47.

Joynson, R.B. (1989) *The Burt Affair*. London: Routledge.

Jubas, K. and Knutson, P. (2012) 'Seeing and be(liev)ing: How nursing and medical students understand representations of their professions', *Studies in the Education of Adults*, 44(1): 85–100.

Jubb, M. (2012) 'Freedom of information in the UK and its implications for research in the higher education sector', *International Journal of Digital Curation*, 7(1): 57–71.

Kanuka, H. and Anderson, T. (2007) 'Ethical issues in qualitative e-learning research', *International Journal of Qualitative Methods*, 6(2): 20–39.

Karnieli-Miller, O., Strier, R. and Pessach, L. (2009) 'Power relations in qualitative research', *Qualitative Health Research*, 19(2): 279–89.

Kelly, A. (1989) 'Education as indoctrination? The ethics of school-based action research', in R.G. Burgess (ed.), *The Ethics of Educational Research*. Lewes: Falmer Press. pp.100–113.

Kenyon, E. and Hawker, S. (1999) 'Once would be enough: Some reflections on the issue of safety for lone researchers', *International Journal of Social Research Methodology*, 2(4), 313–27.

Kraut, R. (2012) 'Aristotle's ethics', in E. Zalta (ed.), *The Stanford Encyclopedia of Philosophy*. Available at http://plato.stanford.edu/archives/win2012/entries/aristotle-ethics/.

Kromrey, J.D. (1993) 'Ethics and data analysis', *Educational Researcher*, 22(4): 24–27.

Kvale, S. (1996) *Interviews: An Introduction to Qualitative Research Interviewing*. Thousand Oaks, CA: Sage.

Ladner, J. (1987) 'Tomorrow's tomorrow: The Black woman', in S. Harding (ed.), *Feminism and Methodology*. Bloomington, IN: Indiana University Press. pp.74–83.

Ladner, J.A. (1998) *The Death of White Sociology*. Baltimore, MD: Black Classic Press.

Lalancette, H. and Campbell, S. (2012) 'Educational neuroscience: Neuroethical considerations', *International Journal of Environmental and Science Education*, 7(1): 37–52.

Lally, V., Shaples, M., Tracy, F., Bertram, N. and Masters, S. (2012) 'Researching the ethical dimensions of mobile, ubiquitous and immersive technology enhanced learning (MUITEL): A thematic review and dialogue', *Interactive Learning Environments*, 20(3): 217–38.

Lambert, M. (2008) 'Devil in the detail: Using a pupil questionnaire in an evaluation of out-of school classes for gifted and talented children', *Education 3–13*, 36(1): 69–78.

Lather, P. (1986) 'Research as praxis', *Harvard Educational Review*, 56(3): 257–77.

Lee-Treweek, G. and Linkogle, S. (eds) (2000) *Danger in the Field: Risk and Ethics in Social Research*. London: Routledge.

Lehmann, W. (2013) 'In a class of their own: How working-class students experience university', in R. Brooks, M. McCormack and K. Bhopal (eds), *Contemporary Debates in the Sociology of Education*. Basingstoke: Palgrave. pp.93–111.

Leonardo, Z. (2009) *Race, Whiteness and Education*. New York: Routledge.

Levinson, M. (2010) 'Accountability to research participants: Unresolved dilemmas and unravelling ethics', *Ethnography and Education*, 5(2): 193–207.

Luke, A. (2002) 'Curriculum, ethics, metanarrative: Teaching and learning beyond the nation', *Curriculum Perspectives*, 22(1): 49–55.

Luke, A. (2010) 'Documenting reproduction and inequality: Revisiting Jean Anyon's "Social Class and School Knowledge"', *Curriculum Inquiry*, 40(1): 167–82.

Luke, A. (2012) *What's Marx Got To Do With It? Inequality, Classroom Talk and Culture*. Presentation on 8 June to the Australian Sociological Association, Deakin University, Melbourne.

Macfarlane, B. (2009) *Researching with Integrity: The Ethics of Academic Enquiry*. New York: Routledge.

Malin, M. (2000) 'An undebated conundrum in the ethics of classroom research: The conflicting rights of researcher, teacher and student within an agenda of reform', *Critical Pedagogy Networker*, 13(1): 1–10.

Malone, S. (2003) 'Ethics at home: Informed consent in your own backyard', *Qualitative Studies in Education*, 16(6): 797–815.

Mama, A. (2007) 'Is it ethical to study Africa? Preliminary thoughts on scholarship and freedom', *African Studies Review*, 50(1): 1–26.

Manidis, M. and Scheeres, H. (2012) 'Towards understanding workplace learning through theorising practice: At work in hospital emergency departments', in P. Hager, A. Lee and A. Reich (eds), *Practice, Learning and Change: Practice-theory Perspectives on Professional Learning*. New York: Springer. pp.103–118.

Mansaray, A.A. (2012) 'The roles and positions of teaching assistants in two urban primary schools: An ethnographic study of educational work and urban social change'. PhD thesis, Institute of Education, University of London.

Mark, M., Eyssell, K. and Campbell, B. (1999) 'The ethics of data collection and analysis', *New Directions for Evaluation*, 82: 47–56.

Marsh, H. and Burnell, J. (2007) 'Intellectual properties: Yours, theirs and others', in C. Denholm and T. Evans (eds), *Supervising Doctorates Downunder: Keys to Effective Supervision in Australia and New Zealand*. Camberwell: ACER Press. pp.71–8.

Marshall, C. and Young, M.D. (2006) 'Gender and methodology', in C. Skelton, B. Francis and L. Smulyan (eds), *The Sage Book of Gender and Education*. London: Sage. pp.63–78.

Mathews, B. and Kenny, M. (2008) 'Mandatory reporting legislation in the USA, Canada and Australia: A cross-jurisdictional review of key features, differences and issues', *Child Maltreatment*, 13(1): 50–63.

Mauthner, M., Birch, M., Miller, T. and Jessop, J. (2012) 'Conclusion', in T. Miller, M. Birch, M. Mauthner and J. Jessop (eds), *Ethics and Qualitative Research*, 2nd edn. London: Sage. pp. 176–86.

Mauthner, N. (2012) '"Accounting for our part of the entangled webs we weave": Ethical and moral issues in digital data sharing', in T. Miller, M. Birch, M. Mauthner and J. Jessop (eds), *Ethics and Qualitative Research*, 2nd edn. London: Sage. pp.157–75.

May, T. (2001) *Social Research: Issues, Methods and Process*, 3rd edn. Maidenhead: Open University Press/McGraw Hill.

Mayer, D. (2006) 'Research funding in the US: Implications for teacher education research', *Teacher Education Quarterly*, 33(1): 5–18.

McCormack, M. (2011) 'Hierarchy without hegemony: Locating boys in an inclusive school setting', *Sociological Perspectives*, 54(1): 83–102.

McCormack, M. (2012) *The Declining Significance of Homophobia*. Oxford: Oxford University Press.

Media Watch (2012) 'Pixelating protects identity? Think again', 9 July. Available at www.abc.net.au/mediawatch/transcripts/s3542172.htm.

Mellor, J., Ingram, N., Abrahams, J. and Bleedell, P. (2013) 'Class matters in the interview setting? Positionality, situatedness and class', *British Educational Journal*, 40(1): 135–49.

Mercer, J. (2007) 'The challenges of insider research in educational institutions: Wielding a double-edged sword and resolving delicate dilemmas', *Oxford Review of Education*, 33(1): 1–17.

Miles, M.B. and Huberman, A.M. (1994) *Qualitative Data Analysis: An Expanded Sourcebook*. Thousand Oaks, CA: Sage.

Mill, J.S. (1863) *Utlitarianism*. London: Parker, Son, and Bourn.

Miller, T. and Bell, L. (2012) 'Consenting to what? Issues of access, gate-keeping and "informed" consent', in T.Miller, M. Birch, M. Mauther and J. Jessop, *Ethics in Qualitative Research*, 2nd edn. London: Sage. pp.61–75.

Miller, T., Birch, M., Mauthner, M. and Jessop, J. (eds) (2012) *Ethics and Qualitative Research*, 2nd edn. London: Sage.

Minh-Ha, T.T. (1989) *Woman, Native, Other*. Bloomington, IN: Indiana University Press.

Minniecon, D., Franks, N. and Heffernan, M. (2007) 'Indigenous research: Three researchers reflect on their experiences at the interface', *The Australian Journal of Indigenous Education*, 36S: 23–31.

Mohr, M. (1979) 'The ethics of science', *International Science Reviews*, 4(1): 45–53.

Morrow, V. (2005) 'Ethical issues in collaborative research with children', in A. Farrell (ed.), *Ethical Research with Children*. Maidenhead: Open University Press. pp.150–65.

Mutua, S. and Nicholls, S.C. (2013) 'Adolescent and disabled or adolescence disabled? Education and the construction of gendered identities among adolescents with intellectual disability', in R. Brooks, M. McCormack and K. Bhopal (eds), *Contemporary Debates in the Sociology of Education*. Basingstoke: Palgrave. pp.131–48.

National Research Ethics Service (2010) *Ethical Review of Student Research: Guidance for Students, Supervisors and Research Ethics Committees*. Available at www.nres.nhs.uk/applications/guidance/research-guidance/?1654606_entryid62=83668.

NHMRC (2003) *Values and Ethics: Guidelines for Ethical Conduct in Aboriginal and Torres Strait Islander Health Research*. Available at www.nhmrc.gov.au/_files_nhmrc/publications/attachments/e52.pdf.

NHMRC, ARC and AVCC (2007) *National Statement on Ethical Conduct in Human Research*. Canberra: National Health and Medical Research Council together with the Australian Research Council and the Australian Vice Chancellors' Committee.

NHMRC, ARC and UA (2007) *Australian Code for the Responsible Conduct of Research*. Available at www.nhmrc.gov.au/guidelines/publications/r39.

NHRPAC (2002a) *Recommendations on Confidentiality and Research Data Protections*. Available at www.hhs.gov/ohrp/archive/nhrpac/documents/nhrpac14.pdf.

NHRPAC (2002b) *Recommendations on Public Use Data Files*. Available at www.hhs.gov/ohrp/archive/nhrpac/documents/dataltr.pdf.

Nisselle, A., Green, J. and Scrimshaw, C. (2011) 'Transforming children's health spaces into learning places', *Health Education*, 111(2): 103–16.

Noddings, N. (1984) *Caring: A Feminine Approach to Ethics and Moral Education*. Berkeley, CA: University of California Press.

Nolen, A. and Putten, J. (2007) 'Action research in education: Addressing gaps in ethical principles and practices', *Educational Researcher*, 36(7): 401–407.

NOMS (2013) *National Offender Management Service: Research Applications*. Available at www.justice.gov.uk/publications/research-and-analysis/noms.

NSPCC (2010) *Child Abuse Reporting Requirements for Professionals*. Available at www.nspcc.org.uk/inform/research/questions/reporting_child_abuse_wda74908.html.

NSW DCS (2011) *Guidelines to Applying for Approval to Conduct Research*. Available at www.correctiveservices.nsw.gov.au/information/research-and-statistics/corrective-services-ethics-commitee.

NSW DEC (2012) *State Education Research Application Process SERAP: Guidelines for Approving Applications from External Agencies to Conduct Research in NSW Government Schools*. Available at www.det.nsw.edu.au/media/downloads/about-us/statistics-and-research/research-partnerships/research-guidelines.pdf.

O'Connor, H. and Goodwin, J. (2013) 'The ethical dilemmas of restudies in researching youth', *Young*, 21(3): 289–307.

O'Neill, J. (2010) 'One chairperson's experience of ethical review: Balancing principle, convention, relationship and risk in educational research', *International Journal of Research and Method in Education*, 33(3): 229–43.

Oakley, A. (1981) 'Interviewing women; a contradiction in terms', in H. Roberts (ed.), *Doing Feminist Research*. London: Routledge and Kegan Paul. pp.30–61.

Oakley, A. (2000) *Experiments in Knowing: Gender and Method in the Social Sciences*. Cambridge: Polity Press.

Oancea, A. (2005) 'Criticisms of educational research: Key topics and levels of analysis', *British Educational Research Journal*, 31(2): 157–84.

OECD (2007) *Principles and Guidelines for Access to Research Data from Public Funding*. Available at www.oecd.org/science/sci-tech/38500813.pdf.

Office of Research Integrity (2011) *Guidelines for Responsible Conduct of Research*. Pittsburgh, PA: Office of Research Integrity, University of Pittsburg. Available at www. provost.pitt.edu/documents/GUIDELINES%20FOR%20ETHICAL%20PRACTICES%20 IN%20RESEARCH-FINALrevised2-March%202011.pdf.

OHRP (2012) *International Compilation of Human Research Standards*. Rockville, MD: Office for Human Research Protection, US Department of Health and Human Services. Available at www.hhs.gov/ohrp/international/intlcompilation/intlcompilation.html.

Ong-Dean, C., Hofstetter, C. and Strick, B. (2011) 'Challenges and dilemmas in implementing random assignment in educational research', *American Journal of Education*, 32(1): 29–49.

Pascoe, V. and Radel, K. (2008) '"How hard can it be?": Negotiating our way through an ethical storm surge', *Studies in Learning, Evaluation, Innovation and Development*, 5(1): 13–23.

Pole, C., Mizen, P. and Bolton, A. (1999) 'Realising children's agency in research: Partners and participants?' *International Journal of Social Research Methodology*, 2(1): 39–54.

Pollard, A. (2007) 'The Identity and Learning programme: "Principled pragmatism" in a 12-year longitudinal ethnography', *Ethnography and Education*, 2(1): 1–19.

Pope, C., De Luca, R. and Tolich, M. (2010) 'How an exchange of perspectives led to tentative ethical guidelines for visual ethnography', *International Journal of Research and Method in Education*, 33(3): 301–315.

Powell, M.A., Fitzgerald, R., Taylor, N.J. and Graham, A. (2012) *International Literature Review: Ethical Issues in Undertaking Research with Children and Young People*. Available at http://epubs.scu.edu.au/cgi/viewcontent.cgi?article=1041&context=ccyp_pubs)

Pring, R. (2001) 'The virtues and vices of an educational researcher', *Journal of Philosophy of Education*, 35(3): 407–421.

Pūtaiora Writing Group (2010) *Te Ara Tika. Guidelines for Māori Research Ethics: A Framework for Researchers and Ethics Committee Members*. Auckland: Health Research Council of New Zealand. Available at www.hrc.govt.nz/news-and-publications/publications/maori.

Qvortrup, J., Bardy, M., Sgritta, G. and Wintersberger, H. (eds) (1994) *Childhood Matters*. Vienna: European Centre.

Raffe, D., Bundell, I. and Bibby, J. (1989) 'Ethics and tactics: Issues arising from an educational survey', in R.G. Burgess (ed.), *The Ethics of Educational Research*. Lewes: Falmer Press. pp.13–30.

Ransome, P. (2013) *Ethics and Values in Social Research*. Basingstoke: Palgrave Macmillan.

RCUK (2013) *Policies and Guidelines on Governance of Good Research Conduct*. Available at www.rcuk.ac.uk/documents/reviews/grc/RCUKPolicyandGuidelineson GovernanceofGoodResearchPracticeFebruary2013.pdf.

Read, B., Francis, B. and Skelton, C. (2011) 'Gender, popularity and notions of in/authenticity amongst 12-year-old to 13-year-old school girls', *British Journal of Sociology of Education*, 32(2): 169–83.

Reay, D. (2008) 'Class out of place: The white middle classes and intersectionalities of class and "race" in urban state schooling in England', in L. Weis (ed.), *The Way Class Works*. New York: Routledge. pp.87–99.

Reinharz, S. (1984) *On Becoming a Social Scientist*. New Brunswick, NJ: Transaction.

Reiss, M.J. (2000) *Understanding Science Lessons: Five Years of Science Teaching*. Buckingham: Open University Press.

Reiss, M. (2005) 'Managing endings in a longitudinal study respect for persons', *Research in Science Education*, 35(1): 123–35.

RESPECT Project (2004) *RESPECT Code of Practice for Socio-Economic Research*. Available at www.respectproject.org.

Rex, L. (2010) 'Respecting the struggle: Deciding what to research and why', *The Australian Educational Researcher*, 37(1): 1–19.

Richards, C. (2012) 'Playing under surveillance: Gender, performance and the conduct of the self in a primary school playground', *British Journal of Sociology of Education*, 33(3): 373–90.

Riddell, S. (1989) 'Exploiting the exploited? The ethics of feminist educational research', in R.G. Burgess (ed.), *The Ethics of Educational Research*. Lewes: Falmer Press. pp.77–99.

Robards, B. (2013) 'Friending participants: Managing the researcher–participant relationship on social network sites', *Young*, 21(3): 217–35.

Robinson, R. (2013) 'Michel Foucault: Ethics', in *The Internet Encyclopedia of Philosophy*. Available at http://www.iep.utm.edu/fouc-eth/.

Rogers, B. (2003) 'Educational research for professional practice: More than providing evidence for doing "x rather than y" or finding the "size of the effect of A on B"', *The Australian Educational Researcher*, 30(2): 65–87.

Rogers, C. and Ludhra, G. (2011) 'Research ethics: Participation, social difference and informed consent', in S. Bradford and F. Cullen (eds), *Research Methods for Youth Practitioners*. London: Routledge. pp.43–65.

Roose, R. and Bouverne-De Bie, M. (2007) 'Do children have rights or do their rights have to be realised? The united nations convention on the rights of the child as a frame of reference for pedagogical action', *Journal of Philosophy of Education*, 41(3): 431–43.

Rosenthal, R. (1994) 'Science and ethics in conducting, analysing and reporting psychological research', *Psychological Science*, 5(3): 127–34.

Ruane, J.M. (2005) *Essentials of Research Methods: A Guide to Social Science Research*. Malden, MA: Blackwell.

Rugg, G. and Petrie, M. (2004) *The Unwritten Rules of PhD Research*. Maidenhead: Open University Press.

Ruiz-Casares, M. (2013) 'Knowledge without harm? When follow-up services are not readily available', in K. te Riele and R. Brooks (eds), *Negotiating Ethical Challenges in Youth Research*. New York: Routledge.

Ryan, L., Kofman, E. and Aaron, P. (2011) 'Insiders and outsiders: Working with peer researchers in researching Muslim communities', *International Journal of Social Research Methodology*, 14(1): 49–60.

SAGE (2013) *Delivery Checklist* (via email communication).

Schrag, Z. (2011) 'The case against ethics review in the social sciences', *Research Ethics*, 7(4): 120–31.

Schuck, S., Aubusson, P. and Kearney, M. (2010) 'Web 2.0 in the classroom? Dilemmas and opportunities inherent in adolescent Web 2.0 engagement', *Contemporary Issues in Technology and Teacher Education*, 10(2): 234–46.

Schutt, R.K. (2013) *Investigating the Social World: The Process and Practice of Research*, 7th edn. Thousand Oaks, CA: Sage.

Scott, C.L. and Fonseca, L. (2010) 'Overstepping the mark: Ethics procedures, risky research and education researchers', *International Journal of Research and Method in Education*, 33(3): 287–300.

Setyowati, R. and Widiyanto (2009) 'Letters from the heart: A participatory approach to research with children', *Children's Geographies*, 7(4): 483–84.

Shamhoo, A. and Resnick, D. (2009) *Responsible Conduct of Research*, 2nd edn. New York: Oxford University Press.

Siegelman, S. (1991) 'Assassins and zealots: Variations in peer review', *Radiology*, 178(3): 637–42.

Sikes, P. (2006) 'On dodgy ground? Problematics and ethics in educational research', *International Journal of Research and Method in Education*, 29(1): 105–17.

Sikes, P. (2010) 'Teacher–student sexual relations: Key risks and ethical issues', *Ethnography and Education*, 5(2): 143–57.

Sikes, P. and Piper, H. (2010) 'Ethical research, academic freedom and the role of ethics committees and review procedures in educational research', *International Journal of Research and Method in Education*, 33(3): 205–213.

Singapore Statement on Research Integrity (2010) *Singapore Statement on Research Integrity: Principles and Responsibilities for Research Worldwide*. Available at www. singaporestatement.org/index.html.

Sinnott-Armstrong, W. (2012) 'Consequentialism', in E. Zalta (ed.), *The Stanford Encyclopedia of Philosophy*. Available at http://plato.stanford.edu/archives/win2012/ entries/consequentialism/.

Skau, D. (2012) *A Code of Ethics for Data Visualization Professionals*. Available at http:// blog.visual.ly/a-code-of-ethics-for-data-visualization-professionals/.

Small, R. (2001) 'Codes are not enough: What philosophy can contribute to the ethics of educational research', *Journal of Philosophy of Education*, 3(3): 387–406.

Smith, R. (2008) 'Proteus rising: Re-imagining educational research', *Journal of Philosophy of Education*, 42(S1): 183–98.

Snee, H. (2008) *Web 2.0 as Social Science Research Tool*. London: British Library.

Snee, H. (2010) 'Does travel broaden the mind? A critical review of learning through the gap year', *Lifelong Learning in Europe*, 15(3): 159–68.

Snee, H. (2013) 'Framing the other: Cosmopolitanism and the representation of difference in overseas gap year narratives', *British Journal of Sociology*, 64(1): 142–62.

Song, M. and Parker, D. (1995) 'Commonality and the dynamics of disclosure in in-depth interviewing', *Sociology,* 29: 241–56.

Social Research Association (SRA) (2003) *Ethical Guidelines*. Available at http://the-sra. org.uk/sra_resources/research-ethics/ethics-guidelines/.

Stacey, J. (1988) 'Can there be a feminist ethnography?', *Women's Studies International Forum*, 11(1): 21–27.

Stanley, L. and Wise, S. (1993) *Breaking Out Again: Feminist Ontology and Epistemology*. London: Routledge.

Sterba, S.K. (2006) 'Misconduct in the analysis and reporting of data: Bridging methodo-logical and ethical agendas for change', *Ethics and Behavior*, 16(4): 305–18.

Suaalii, T. and Mavoa, H. (2001) 'Who says yes? Collective and individual framing of Pacific children's consent to, and participation in, research in New Zealand', *Children's Issues*, 5: 39–42.

Taylor, Y. (2007) 'Brushed behind the bike sheds: Working class lesbians' experiences of school', *British Journal of Sociology of Education*, 21(1): 95–109.

te Riele, K. and Brooks, R. (2012) 'Making ethical deliberations public: Some provisional resources for youth research ethics', *Youth Studies Australia*, 31(3): 11–16.

te Riele, K. and Brooks, R. (eds) (2013) *Negotiating Ethical Challenges in Youth Research*. New York: Routledge.

Tetteh, P. (2013) 'Negotiating access and preventing risk in youth domestic labour research in Ghana', in K. te Riele and R. Brooks (eds), *Negotiating Ethical Challenges in Youth Research*. New York: Routledge. pp.71–83.

Thomas, G. (2013) 'Cash-rich, poetry-poor research will never merit Nobel notice', *Times Higher Education*, 14 November 2013.

Thomson, D. and Molloy, S. (2001) 'Assessing the best interests of the child', *The Australian Educational and Developmental Psychologist*, 18(2): 5–14.

Thorne, B. (1980) '"You still takin' notes?" Fieldwork and problems of informed consent', *Social Problems*, 27(3): 284–97.

Tong, R. and Williams, N. (2011) 'Feminist ethics', In E. Zalta (ed), *The Stanford Encyclopedia of Philosophy*. Available at http://plato.stanford.edu/archives/sum2011/entries/feminism-ethics/.

Tooley, J., with Darby, D. (1998) *Educational Research: A Critique. A Survey of Published Educational Research*. London: Office for Standards in Education.

Torgerson, C. (2001) 'The need for randomised control trials in education', *British Journal of Educational Studies*, 49(3): 316–28.

Torgerson, C. (2009) 'Randomised control trials in education research: A case study of an individually randomised pragmatic trial', *Education 3–13*, 37(4): 313–21.

Torrance, H. (1989) 'Ethics and politics in the study of assessment', in R.G. Burgess (ed.), *The Ethics of Educational Research*. Lewes: Falmer Press. pp.172–87.

Troyna, B. and Carrington, B. (1989) 'Whose side are we on? Ethical dilemmas in the study of 'race' and education', in R.G. Burgess (ed.), *The Ethics of Educational Research*. Lewes: Falmer Press. pp.188–204.

Tuck, E. (2011) *Urban Youth and School Pushout: Gateways, Get-aways, and the GED*. New York: Routledge.

Tufte, E.R. (1983) *The Visual Display of Quantitative Information*. Cheshire, CT: Graphics Press.

Tuhiwai Smith, L. (1999) *Decolonizing Methodologies: Research and Indigenous Peoples*. New York: Zed Books.

Tully, M.P., Vail, A., Roberts, S., Brabin, L. and McNamee, R. (2009) 'Methodological considerations in ethical review – 3: Sampling and data analysis', *Research Ethics*, 5(3): 121–24.

UK Government (1998) *Human Rights Act 1998*. London: The Stationery Office.

UK Government (2000) *Data Protection Act 1998*. Available at www.legislation.gov.uk/ukpga/1998/29/contents.

UN (1990) *Convention on the Rights of the Child*. Available at www.ohchr.org/en/professional-interest/pages/crc.aspx.

UNICEF (2005) *Fact Sheet: The Right to Participation*. Available at www.unicef.org/crc/files/Right-to-Participation.pdf.

UNICEF (2007) *Implementation Handbook for the Convention on the Rights of the Child*, fully revised 3rd edn. Available at www.unicef.org/crc/files/Implementation%20Handbook%203rd%20ed.pdf.

UNICEF (2013) *Convention on the Rights of the Child*. Available at www.unicef.org/crc/index_30160.html.

UUK (2012) *Concordat to Support Research Integrity*. London: Universities UK.

Van den Eynden, V. (2008) 'Sharing research data and confidentiality: Restrictions caused by deficient consent forms', *Research Ethics Review*, 4(1): 37–38.

Van Vliet (2008) 'Social welfare reforms in Europe: Challenges and strategies in Continental and Southern Europe' (La Documentation Française, Paris, 2006), *Journal of European Social Policy*, 18(1): 108–109.

Victorian DEECD (2013) *Conducting Research in Victorian Government Schools and Early Childhood Settings: Guidelines for Applicants*. Available at www.education.vic.gov.au/about/research/Pages/schoolresearch.aspx.

Viete, R. (2004) 'Ideology and the discourses of research: The ethics of ethics for cross-cultural research in education'. Paper presented at the AARE conference, Melbourne. Available at http://publications.aare.edu.au/04pap/vie041004.pdf.

Viete, R. and Phan, L.H. (2007) 'The growth of voice: Expanding possibilities for representing self in research writing', *English Teaching: Practice and Critique*, 6(2): 39–57.

Vojak, C. (2003) '*Mozert v. Hawkins*: A look at self-knowledge and the best interests of the child', *Educational Theory*, 53(4): 401–419.

Walby, S., Armstrong, J. and Strid, S. (2012) 'Intersectionality: Multiple inequalities in social theory', *Sociology*, 46(2): 224–41.

Walford, G. (2011) *Researching the Powerful*. Available at www.bera.ac.uk/system/files/Researching%20the%20Powerful.pdf.

Walkerdine, V. (1990) *Schoolgirl Fictions*. London: Verso.

Walkerdine, V., Lucey, H. and Melody, J. (2001) *Growing Up Girl: Psychosocial Explorations of Gender and Class*. Basingstoke: Palgrave.

Walsh, L., Black, R. and Berman, N. (2013) 'Walking the talk: Youth research in hard times', in K. te Riele and R. Brooks (eds), *Negotiating Ethical Challenges in Youth Research*. New York: Routledge. pp.43–54.

Wenar, L. (2011) 'Rights', in E. Zalta (ed), *The Stanford Encyclopedia of Philosophy*. Available at http://plato.stanford.edu/archives/fall2011/entries/rights/.

White, J. and Fitzgerald, T. (2010) 'Researcher tales and research ethics: The spaces in which we find ourselves', *International Journal of Research and Method in Education*, 33(3): 273–85.

White, V. and Belliveau, G. (2010) 'Whose story is it anyway? Exploring ethical dilemmas in performed research', *Performing Ethos*, 1(1): 85–95.

Whiteman, N. (2012) *Undoing Ethics: Rethinking Practice in Online Research*. New York, London: Springer.

Willis, J. and Saunders, M. (2007) 'Research in a post-colonial world: The example of Australian Aborigines', in M. Pitt and A. Smith (eds), *Researching the Margins*. London: Palgrave Macmillan. pp.96–114.

Willis, P. (1977) *Learning to Labour: How Working Class Kids Get Working Class Jobs*. Farnborough: Saxon House.

Wilson, J. (2011) 'Freedom of information and research data', *Research Ethics*, 7(3): 107–11.

Wollcott, H. (2005) *The Art of Fieldwork*. Walnut Creek, CA: AltaMira Press.

Wood, B. and Kidman, J. (2013) 'Negotiating the ethical borders of visual research with young people', in K. te Riele and R. Brooks (eds), *Negotiating Ethical Challenges in Youth Research*. New York: Routledge. pp.149–62.

Young, K. (2013) 'Researching young people's online spaces', in K. te Riele and R. Brooks (eds), *Negotiating Ethical Challenges in Youth Research*. New York: Routledge. pp. 163–76.

INDEX

Added to a page number 't' denotes a table.

Aboriginal peoples 12, 53
  see also Indigenous communities
academic freedom 38, 146, 147
access
  ethics of 157–8
  negotiation of 6, 96, 104
  to government-held information 57
  to research processes, in relation to
    Aboriginal people 53
accountability 168
accuracy 128, 136, 138, 141
action research 37, 48, 75, 91–2
action-oriented ethical theories *see*
  deontology; utilitarianism
actions 20, 22, 24, 25
activist groups 112
adult-child relationships 85, 87
adults, researching with 104–7
advice 98, 101
advisory groups 162
advocacy 48, 128, 142
age
  and ability to express oneself 48–9
  and ability to understand or consent 102

agency 53
agent-based ethical theory *see* virtue ethics
Ahsan, M. 48, 53
Alderson, P. 102
Alexander, L. 24
Alldred, P. 13
American Educational Research Association
  (AERA) 31, 81
American Psychological Association (APA) 148
American Secretary of Education 69
Andrew (case study) 29, 79–80, 87
annotation 129
anonymity 11, 12, 105, 128, 154
Anwar (case study) 18, 22, 23, 28, 40, 43
applicability 119
applications, for ethics reviews 37
archiving 77–8
Aristotle 24, 25
Article 3 (UNCRC) 46
Article 10 (HRA) 81–2
Article 12 (UNCRC) 37, 47–9
Article 28 (UNCRC) 46
Article 29 (UNCRC) 46
Article 36 (UNCRC) 49

assessment
  of legitimacy of investigating a topic 64–5
  of risk 27
assumed competency 103
assumptions 39, 65, 113, 129, 130, 131
attachments 131
Aubrook, L. 73
audit culture 149
Australia
  data destruction 78
  ethical approval 34, 87
  ethical guidelines and principles 27, 30,
    31–2, 40, 41–2, 60, 94, 114
  policy emphasis, commissioned research 63
  regulatory context 50, 51–2, 53–4, 55, 57
  research ethics literature 14
Australian Association for Research in
    Education (AARE) 32, 119, 137, 148
Australian Institute of Aboriginal and Torres
    Strait Islander Studies 41–2
Australian Research Council (ARC) 146
Australian Sports Anti-Doping Authority
    (ASADA) 56–7
authorship 34, 147–50
autonomy 13, 28, 41, 62, 85
averages 121

Baines, E. 130
Balen, R. 85, 88
Ball, J. 12, 78
Ball, M.S. 129
Ball, S. 21
Ball, S.J. 127
Barker, J. 103
Barnes, V. 140, 150
Battiste, M. 132
Battles, H. 93
Becker, H. 61
befriending role 56
Bélanger, N. 74
beliefs 64, 65, 131
Bell, L. 5
Belliveau, G. 141
Belmont Report (1979) 26–7, 28, 29, 30, 34
beneficence 24, 27, 28–9, 142
benefit assessment 27
benefit-maximization 22, 28
benefits 28–9
'best guess' compromises 11
'best interests of the child' 46–7
bias 62
Biesta, G. 147
Bigler, D. 90
biography-experience-identity 108, 109, 110
black bars 145

blog entries 93
Blum-Ross, A. 143
blurred images 9, 145
Bochow, A. 12, 76
body language 49
Brady, B. 70, 72
breach of confidentiality 56
breach of privacy 49
Bridges, D. 19, 33, 39, 43, 154
British Educational Research Association (BERA)
    7, 32–4, 81, 96, 119, 120, 145, 148
British Sociological Association (BSA) 32, 143
Brooks, R. 67
Brown, M. 118
Brown, P. 67
Bruckman, A. 140, 144
Building Evidence into Education 69
bureaucratisation 64
Burgess, R.G. 4, 86, 105, 115
Burnell, J. 148
Burt, C. 122–3

Campbell, S. 68
Canada 14, 27, 30, 34, 41, 53, 55, 67, 78
capacity to consent 81–3
care ethics 20–1
care-giver/receiver 20
case studies 3
categorical imperatives 23
'censor in advance' 72
Chappell, T. 23
Charter for Research Staff in Education
    (BERA) 148
child abuse, reporting 55
child-friendly information 49, 94
children
  and consent 28, 82, 83, 84, 85
  contribution to research design 74
  developmental approach 82
  RCTs and avoidance of harm 70
  relationships with adults 85, 87
  as research participants 48, 158
  researching with 102–4
    see also school-based research; youth
      participatory research
  respecting views of 47–9
  see also disabled children; looked-after
    children
children's rights 87
  see also United Nations Convention on the
    Rights of the Child
choice
  exercise of independent 48
  of method 8, 66–72, 158
  of topic 61–5, 155

Clark, A. 103
class (social) 114–15
co-authors 148
Code of Ethics (AARA) 31, 81, 142
code maps 127
coding 134
coercion 67, 106, 159
collaborative research 74–5, 140
colleagues, researching with 75, 115–16
colonial research practices 53
Committee on Publication Ethics 148
commodification of rapport 110
communitarianism 41, 83
community 21
community of practice 43
comparing data 127
compassion 21
competence
  and informed consent 80
  provision of research information 95
  see also assumed competency; Gillick
    competence
compliance (children's) 85
concealment 124, 126, 130
*Concordat to Support Research
    Integrity* (UUK) 32
conduct
  codes *see* ethical codes
  ethical 34, 167–8
  see also misconduct
confidentiality 105, 128
  compromised by research participants 9, 10
  legislation and regulation 54–8
  limits to 143–5
  promising 145
  right to 11, 54, 64
confirmability 127
conflict, right to authorship 148
Confucianism 25
Connelly, C. 74
consensus 21
consent 80
  age and ability to 102
  children and 28, 82, 83, 84, 85
  ethical dilemmas 89
  oral 94
  photography, Greece 55
  retrospective 96
  withdrawal of 103
  written 39, 40, 94
  see also capacity to consent; informed
    consent; parental consent
consent forms 36, 39, 94, 163
consequentialism 24
Constantine-Simms, D. 113

contextual specificity 3, 6
contract negotiation 64
contractual agreements 146
contractual rights 20
contrasting data 127
control
  of data/data sets 57, 128
  lack of, after publication 144
  over reporting 147
  of research 53, 74
control groups, in RCTs 70, 72
controlled research studies 130–1
Convention on the Rights of Persons with
    Disabilities 50
Cook, J. 113, 114, 161
cooperation 21
Cormode, L. 104
Council of Europe 55
courage 24, 25
court-ordered subpoenas 56, 57
Covenant on Civil and Political Rights 49–50
covert research 96
creative arts, in dissemination 141–2
creativity 147
credibility 141
credit (authorship) 147, 148
critical alignments 130
critical friends 25
critical race theory (CRT) 131–2
critical theorists 4, 63
critical thinking 151
critical work 63
criticality 62, 115, 138, 151
criticism 140
critique 138
cross-cultural principles 11
cross-cultural research 75
Crow, G. 81
cultural differences 13
cultural norms 12
cultural relevance 39–42
cultural role 147
culturally marginalized groups 166
Cuskelly, M. 83, 97

Dale, R. 65
Daley, D.M. 111
Danby, S. 49, 56, 82
Darby, D. 132, 133
data
  archiving 77–8
  control of 57
  deliberate omissions/oversights 124
  destruction 13, 78
  fabrication 123

data *cont.*
  falsification 124
  interpretation 71, 102–3, 116, 133
  over-reading 133
  ownership 13, 53, 128, 162–3
  protection 54–5
  publicly funded 57
  pure/theory-free 133
  quality 81, 88
  reduction 127
  representation 118, 122
  sharing 57, 58
  trimming 124
  use/misuse 122–3, 129
  see also qualitative data; visual data
data analysis 76, 117–34
  ethical 163–4
  ethical guidelines 119–21
  ethical slippage 123–6
  ethics, findings and value positions 129–31
  framework of analysis and partisanship
      131–3
  qualitative research 126–9
  quantitative research 121–3
  simplicity and directness in 125
  software 134
  team research 75
  transgressions in 121, 164
data collection
  ethical 158–9
  ethical committees 155
  ethical dilemmas 115
  permission for 13
  personal biographical details 108
  team research 75
data management plans 77
David, M. 95
The Death of White Sociology 112–13
deception 96, 126, 130
decision-making
  ethical 7, 11, 34, 168
  involvement of children in 82
  irresponsibilization 38
  situatedness 38
  social embeddedness 79–80, 83–8, 156
  teachers' status and authority 41
declining participation 6, 76, 80, 85, 86, 156
deductive logical reasoning 27
Deed of Agreement 52
deficit discourses 142
Del Monte, K. 75
Delandshere, G. 71
democratic research 54, 140
democratic values 33

Denscombe, M. 73
deontology 19, 20, 23–4, 26, 27, 29, 35
DePalma, R. 86, 91
Department of Corrective Services (DCS) 51, 52
Department for Education (UK) 69
Derrida, J. 38
developmental approach, to children 82
dialogue, with relevant communities 53
difference(s) 11–12, 112, 113, 161, 166
difficult areas of research 155
digital life 143
dignity 23, 49, 168
Dingwall, R. 36–7
disabled children 83
disclosure
  of abuse, reporting 56
  in interview research 111
  notices (ASADA) 56–7
  of personal information 54, 55
  power relations 105
  of research information 95–7
  see also non-disclosure
disempowered groups 112
disguised identity 143
disguised images 145
dissemination 9, 135–51
  ethical commitments
      to research participants 136–45
      to sponsors and authors 145–50
  misrepresentation 102–3
  scrutiny of 151
truthfulness 21
Dockett, S. 76, 85, 97
'doing rapport' 108
dominant narratives 65
Downs, J. 122, 126
Duncombe, J. 110, 111

Economic and Social Research Council (ESRC)
      57, 58, 77, 146
education, hidden parts 166
education research 5–7
  benefits and risks in 29
  consent *see* consent
  ethics *see* research ethics
  feminist 61
  legislation and regulation 50–8
  location of 65, 75–7, 84
  methods *see* research methods
  quality 32
  reciprocity 97–9
  in restricted settings 54
  stakeholders 22, 23
  UK critique of 132

education research *cont.*
  United Nations Convention on the Rights of
    the Child 45–50
education researchers
  as authors 147–50
  awareness of regulations 58
  class position 114
  disclosure notices (ASADA) 56–7
  gender 41
  independence 12, 60, 62, 65, 72, 155
  lack of trust in 38
  marginalization 71
  public scrutiny 6–7
  relationships *see* relationships
  reporting requirements 55, 56
  responsibilities 3, 5–6, 34, 49, 61, 65, 128,
    144, 146–7
  rights and duties 34
  role in assisting the understanding of REC
    members 37
  self-censorship 53
  see also practitioner researchers
educational organizations 84
Edwards, R. 162
Edwards, T. 64
El-adaway, I. 149
elite research 104
Ells, C. 66, 67
empathy 21, 114
empirical data 122, 131
empirical research 63, 71, 117, 153, 154
empowerment 48, 113, 142, 161
equality 42, 98, 99
ethical actions 20, 22, 24, 25
ethical codes 11, 19, 25–34, 30, 41, 96, 154
ethical dilemmas 155
  consent 89
  due to changing ethical standards 10–11
  education-focused neuroscience 68
  ethical principles and negotiation of 39
  need for consideration and judgement 26
  occurrence 5–6
  online research 9
  publication-related 148
  researching with colleagues 115–16
  sensitivity to 154
  variation across place and space 11–14
  vignettes 2
ethical guidelines 32–4, 60, 153–4
  advice in 101
  credit for authorship 147
  critiques of 34–42
  data analysis 119–21
  development of 26–7

ethical guidelines *cont.*
  ethical theories in 25–6
  principles in selected 30–1t
  reporting/dissemination 136, 137, 139
  researchers' obligation to protect
    themselves 76
Ethical Guidelines for Educational Research
    (BERA) 33, 81, 96, 137
ethical issues/concerns 2–3
  access 157–8
  data analysis 117–34, 163–4
  data collection 158–9
  disclosure 57
  dissemination 135–51
  gatekeeping regulations 53–4
  identity, power and positionality 112–15
  importance of 4–5
  key arguments 153–4
  matching, rapport and trust 107–11
  power and reciprocity 159–63
  power relationships 101–7
  research design 59–78
  research methods 7–8, 9, 68, 70–1
  researching with colleagues 115–16
  social relations 156
ethical norms 75
ethical practice 8, 13, 21, 60, 61, 100–1, 153
ethical principles 28–32
  in Belmont Report 27
  ethical theories 26
  internalization 39
  in selected ethical guidelines 30–1t
  value-ladenness 39
  variation in 12
  Western values 13
ethical responsibility 65, 75, 128, 166–8
ethical sensibilities 8, 10
ethical stance 4–5, 110, 138, 162
ethical standards 10–11
ethical theories 19–26
ethical thinking 3
ethics
  of care 20–1
  see also research ethics
ethics approval
  and consent 87, 88
  for difficult areas 155
  documentation 101, 154
  official procedures 33, 34
  perceived as the end-point of ethical
    consideration 38
  qualitative research 67, 159
  regulatory contexts 50, 51, 52, 53
ethics creep 4, 8, 14

Ethics and Educational Research 33
The Ethics of Educational Research 4
ethics ombudsmen 134, 167
ethics review 33
   applications for 37
   and choice of method 66–7
   restrictiveness of 35–6
   undermining of professional reflection 38–9
ethnography 37, 52, 68, 75, 77, 89–90
eurocentrism 132
Europe 30t, 34
evaluation research 7, 72, 131
evidence 63, 121, 125, 130
evidence-based research 147
exaggeration 124, 126, 130
exclusion 29, 113, 161
experiences, different 112
experimental research 7, 66, 68, 69
exploitation 29, 49, 63, 99, 109, 110, 161
exploratory research 51–2

false friendships 110
Farrell, A. 49, 56, 82
Farrimond, H. 124, 134
feminist perspective 98
feminist research 61, 74, 96
feminist researchers 66, 69, 108, 132
fictionalization 141
fidelity 24
fieldwork 76, 103, 161
filiality 25
film 9
financial incentives 97–8
First Nation/Inuit/Métis associations 53
Fisher, E. 56
Fitzgerald, T. 134
Fonseca, L. 37, 54, 154
Foucault, M. 21, 106
Framework for Research Ethics (ESRC) 32, 33
framing 113, 132
freedom of expression 82
freedom of information 56, 57
freedom of will 24
frequency counts, key words 127
friendliness 24
friendships 90–1, 110
funding 6, 66, 69, 146
   see also sponsors

Gallagher, M. 84, 94, 99
gatekeepers 6, 48, 76, 85–8, 157
gatekeeping 36–7, 37, 50–4, 150
Gelman, A. 121
gender 41
gender research 132

gendered experiences 108
Ghana 12, 76
Gibson, M. 75
Gillborn, D. 132
Gillick competence 82, 86
Gillies, V. 13
Gilligan, C. 20
Girls into Science and Technology project 92
Global North 8, 11, 13, 75, 78, 166
Global South 11, 75, 166
globalisation 11
Goldacre, B. 69, 71
'golden rule' 23
good practice 11, 13, 132, 155
Goodwin, J. 10
Gove, M. 122, 126
governing bodies 52
government-held information 57
government-sponsored research 6–7, 12, 63,
   64, 66, 128
Grant, P. 146, 147
gratitude 24
Greece 55
Greig, A. 102
Griffiths, M. 107, 110
group discussions 55
Gustav (case study) 44, 46, 48, 52, 56, 58

Haggerty, K. 4
Halse, C. 38
Hamid, M.O. 40, 41
Hammersley, M. 4, 5, 13, 34, 38, 41, 60, 64, 85,
   96, 99, 131
happiness 22
Hargreaves, D. 132
harm 29, 36, 70, 145
harm prevention 24, 138, 156
Harold, B. 41
Harper, D. 145
Hattie, J. 123
Hawker, S. 76
Heath, S. 67–8, 87–8
Henderson, R. 137, 143–4
Heptinstall, E. 52
Herring, S. 140
hierarchical relationships 12, 76, 156
Higgs, M.D. 125–6
Hinton, D. 10
history (personal) 112
honesty 119, 123, 126
Howe, K. 137
Huberman, A.M. 127
Hudson, C. 77
Hughes, A. 104
human rights 20

Human Rights Act (1998) 81–2
humility 25, 154
Hutchinson, D. 71

identifications 107, 145
identity 9, 12, 112, 115, 143
identity-biography 108
identity-positionality 107, 108, 109, 114, 130
ideological positions 62
incentives, offering 97–8
inclusion 29
independence (researcher) 12, 60, 62, 65, 72, 155
independent choice, children's exercise of 48
Indigenous communities
   codes for working with outsider researchers 129
   concern over data destruction 78
   ethically reflexive research 114
   ethics regulations 53
   eurocentrism 132
   gatekeepers, prison research 52
   imposition of Western research methods 41
   negotiation of consent 83
   ownership of data 13
   participatory approaches 74–5
   permission for data collection 13
   revelation of identity 12–13
   right to full and fair participation 42
Indigenous researchers 41, 114
individualism 13, 41, 83, 156
infantilization 102, 160, 165
inference 126, 133
information age 122, 129
information sheets 95
informed consent 27, 79, 154
   as an ongoing process 89, 140, 143
   autonomy 13
   data collection from social media sites 9
   defined 80–1
   duration of 162–3
   explaining 163
   full participant involvement 98
   for future uses of data 77
   gatekeepers and 85, 86, 87, 88
   liberal individualism 83
   method-specific issues 68, 89–94
   negotiation 83, 104, 156
   pedagogic work of the researcher 49
   provision of research information 94–7
   restrictiveness in the interpretation of 36
   social embeddedness of decision-making 83–8
   value of 99

informed dissent 84, 156
insider research 29, 109, 113
insider/outsider 111, 113, 129, 143, 144, 161
institutional contexts 6
institutional locations 65, 84
institutional pressures 62–3, 81
Institutional Review Boards (IRBs) 27, 58
   see also research ethics committees
institutions, gatekeeping 52–3
integrity 25, 60, 120, 128, 134, 166
intellectual property rights 13, 52, 64, 128, 148
interests (researcher) 47
intergenerational respect 12, 76
internalization, ethical principles 39
international conventions 4
International Journal of Research and Method in Education 35
international pressure, of statistics 122
internet-based research 92–4
intersectionality 113
intervention 6, 128
intervention groups, in RCTs 70, 72
intervention research 22
interview fatigue 66
interview research 10, 73–4, 104, 111, 116
invisibility 65, 155
Iphofen, R. 7, 11, 60, 61, 63, 68, 110, 111, 116, 161
Ireland 69, 70, 72
irresponsibilization 38

Jane (case study) 100, 102, 107, 109
Jeanes, R. 75, 87
jen 25
Jennings, M. 149
Jessop, J. 110, 111
journal editors 150
Joynson, R.B. 123
judgementalism 137–40
judgement(s) 64, 77, 131, 155
justice 12, 24, 27, 29

Kant, I. 23, 24
Karnieli-Miller, O. 163
Kay, T. 75, 87
Kelly, A. 92, 96
Kenyon, E. 76
key concepts 127
key words 127
Kidman, J. 12, 83
knowledge 21, 69, 80, 108
knowledge holders 53
Kromrey, J.D. 117, 134
Kvale, S. 127

lack of capacity 82
Ladner, J.A. 112–13, 133
Lalancette, H. 68
Lambert, M. 73
language background 149–50
large samples 124–5
large-scale online surveys 93
Lather, P. 97
Lauren (case study) 152, 154
learning, virtue ethics 25
learning difficulties, capacity to consent 83
legal context, of consent 81–3
legislation 4, 12, 30, 50–8
less capacity 82
li 25
liberal individualism 13, 83, 156
life history research 52
limited disclosure 95–7
lived identity 107
lobbying 52
local elders 53
location of research 65, 75–7, 84
Locke, J. 20
'logically will' 23
longitudinal research 68, 89, 157
looked-after children 52–3, 87
loyalty 25, 105
Luke, A. 63

McCormack, M. 90
Macfarlane, B. 25, 101, 123–4, 124–5, 130
Maguire, M. 67, 110
'majority rules' approach 22
Malin, M. 139
mandatory reporting 55–6, 137
manipulation 102, 109, 123, 162
Mansaray, A.A. 105, 106
marginalization 71, 113
marginalized groups 112, 142, 166
Mark, M. 72
Marsh, H. 148
matching 108, 110, 113, 114–15
maturity, and ability to express oneself 48–9
Mauthner, N. 4, 61, 77
May, T. 112
mean (statistical) 121
meanings, testing emergent 127
median (statistical) 121
Mellor, J. 114
member checking 134
merit (research) 32, 60
message boards (internet) 93
methods *see* research methods
Miles, M.B. 127
Mill, J.S. 22

mindfulness 166, 167
minorities, research with 108, 112
minority researchers 113
misconduct 34, 120
misrepresentation 103, 119
misuse of data 122, 129
mobiles telephones 10
mode (statistical) 121
modernist self 13–14
monitoring procedures 64
Moore, M. 24
moral being 21
moral intuition 24
moral obligations 23, 76, 145
moral perspective 168
moral regard 145
moral responsibility 65
moral self-cultivation 167
Morrow, V. 84, 156
Moses, M. 137
multi-disciplinary research 75
mutuality 109

'naming, shaming and framing' 113–14
national differences 11–12
National Health and Medical Research Council
   (Australia) 32, 42
national legislation and regulation 50–8
National Offender Management Service 52, 54
*National Statement on Ethical Conduct in
   Human Research* (Australia) 31–2
natural rights 20
negotiation
   of access 6, 96, 104, 157
   of consent 83, 104, 156
   of contracts 64
   intellectual property rights 128
Netherlands Organization for Scientific
   Research 146
neuroscience, education-focused 68
New South Wales 50, 51
New Zealand 12, 30, 34, 37–8, 41, 53, 55, 83
No Child left Behind 63
Noddings, N. 20
non-disclosure 137
non-elite research 104
non-maleficence 24, 28, 142
non-partisanship 133
normative response 163
normative stance 61, 62
Norway 55
'nothing about us without us' approach 112
novice writers 150
Nutt, L. 5
NVivo 134

objective approach 131
OCAP 53
O'Connor, H. 10
Office for Standards in Education (Ofsted) 132
omission of data 124
1,000 page question 127
O'Neill, J. 36, 37–8
online research 9, 72–3, 92–4
open-mindedness 154
openness 115
oral consent 94
O'Regan, C. 70, 72
other 113, 132
outsider *see* insider/outsider
overt political position 155
ownership of data 13, 53, 128, 162–3

paper-based questionnaires 73
parental consent 41, 52, 86, 87–8, 92, 94, 158
parents
   interpretation of children's best interests 47
   role, children's consent 86
Parker, D. 111
partial truths 96
participant observation 90–1
participants
   autonomy 28
   children as 48
   confidentiality compromised by 9, 10
   empowerment 48, 113–14
   ethical commitments in reporting 136–45
   feminist social research 74
   gatekeeping by 52
   gender 41
   inviting full involvement of 98–9
   lack of control over, after publication 144
   member checking 134
   perceptions of judgmentalism 138–40
   performances of a 'modernist self' 13–14
   presenting information to potential 94–7
   protection 28
   in RCTs 70, 71
   re-imagining 114, 161
   and relationships *see* relationships
   revelation of identity 9, 12
   review of articles and papers 134
   right to identification 145
   selection of 27, 29
   withdrawal from research 157
participation
   children's right to 37
   contrasting perceptions of 40
   declining 6, 76, 80, 85, 86, 156
   exclusion/inclusion 29
   incentives and 97

participation *cont.*
   rates 63
   tension between protection and 53
participatory action research 48, 91–2
participatory research 37, 47–8, 74, 140, 145
partisanship 132, 133
Pascoe, V. 52
paternalism 47, 165
'pedagogic work of the researcher' 49
perceptions
   of ethics of randomization 70
   of judgementalism 138–40
   misrepresentation of children's 103
performance metrics 148–9
performative representation 141–2
personal ethical perspective 20
personal information 54, 55, 57
personality (reviewer) 150
Phan, L.H. 149–50
philosophical objections, research ethics
      regulations 35
photographs 9, 55, 145
phronesis 25
pictorial representation 49
Piper, H. 35, 37
plausibility 127
Pole, C. 88
policing, research perceived as 7
policy 6, 63
political commitment 66
political debates 62
political expediency 130
political ideology 70, 155
political objectives 61
political views 133
Pollard, A. 89
poorly designed research 60
Pope, C. 144–5
positionality 103, 107, 108, 109, 114, 115, 130,
      141, 160
positioning 113
positivism 63
posts (social networking) 93
power 115
   differentials 9, 74, 97, 102, 104, 106
   ethical issues 159–63
   Foucault on 21, 106
   and knowledge 109
   structures 88
   of visual data 129
power relationships 79
   choice of topic 61
   and consent 81, 91
   construction and reading of texts 141
   cultural norms 12

power relationships *cont.*
  declining participation 6
  ethical judgements 77
  Global North/South 166
  qualitative research 115
  researchers and participants 101–7
  two-way nature of 84
  vulnerable groups 160
practice
  education research and 6
  unethical 29, 149
  see also ethical practice; good practice
practitioner research 63, 67, 159
practitioner researchers 5–6, 91, 101, 110
prejudice 142
pressure(s)
  on choice of method 66–7
  on choice of topic 62–3, 155
  on design of research instruments 72
  governmental 12
  of statistics 122
  of time 160
  to consent 84
  to sculpt documentation 154
pride 24
prima facie duties 24, 28
principalist approach 27, 28
prison research 51–2
privacy 49, 51, 54, 55, 57, 128
private-public distinction 9, 10, 92
probability (statistical) 125, 142
productive power 21
professional associations 32, 33, 153
proof (statistical) 125
protection 42
  from exploitation 49
  tension between participation and 53
  through informed consent 81
  vulnerable groups 28, 53
  see also self-protection
pseudonyms 144
public figures, anonymity 105
public use data files 58
public/private distinction 9, 10, 92
publication-related dilemmas 148
publications, quality of 149
publicly funded research data 57
publishing 164–5
pure data 133

qualitative data 55, 77, 112
qualitative research
  consent 89
  data analysis 126–9
  difficulty in pursuing 12

qualitative research *cont.*
  ethical issues 7, 68, 159
  perceived as scientifically 'soft' 63
  political commitment 66
  position/identity 108
  power relationships 115
  regulatory context (NSW) 52
  research ethics committees 8, 37, 67
  researcher-researched relationships 68
  see also individual methods
quality
  of data 81, 88
  of publications 149
  REC attention to 32
quantitative data 54–5
quantitative research
  data analysis 121–6
  data quality 88
  favouring/privileging of 8, 12, 60, 64
  government funding and 66
  perceived as unbiased and truthful 63
  see also individual methods
questionnaires 72–3, 84

Radel, K. 52
Raffe, D. 62, 64, 72
randomization 70–1
randomized control trials (RCTs) 7, 8, 62, 66,
  69–72
Ransome, P. 33, 131
rape research 97
rapport 108, 109, 110, 111, 115
rational agents 23, 28
rational knowledge 69
rationality 24
reciprocity 25, 42, 97–9, 159–63
reflection 38–9
reflexivity 3, 25, 38, 106–7, 114, 141, 154,
  162, 167
refusal to participate 157
regulation 4, 12, 27, 34–5, 50–8
Reiss, M. 138–9, 140, 141, 143, 144
relationships
  adult-child 85, 87
  care ethics 20, 21
  ethics approval 52
  hierarchical 12, 76, 156
  researcher-participant 98, 99, 101–7
  researcher-researched 61, 68, 90–1, 101, 109,
    110, 112
  researcher-respondent 81
  see also power relationships; social
    relations
reliability 119, 124
reparation 24

reporting
  directness and simplicity in 125
  mandatory 55–6, 137
  selective 124
  see also dissemination
representation 116, 118, 122, 141–3
  see also misrepresentation
representativeness 97
research agendas 64
research design 59–78, 159
research ethics
  approaches to 5
  engagement with 19
  English language literature 14
  regulation 4, 27, 34–5
  ubiquity of forms and processes 43
  universal 11
  see also ethical codes; ethical guidelines;
    ethical principles
research ethics committees (RECs) 20, 27
  attention to quality 32
  and choice of research method 67
  critiques of 34–42
  ethical review and approval 33, 34
  parental consent 87
  questioning of research approach 8
  scrutiny of benefits and harm 29
research findings
  dissemination *see* dissemination
  judgements 131
  see also data; evidence
research information
  child-friendly 49, 94
  differing interpretations of 139
  and informed consent 80
  in participant observation 90
  presenting to potential participants 94–7
research instruments, design 72–4, 159
research methods
  acknowledgment of limitations 146–7
  and child competence 103
  choice of 8, 66–72, 158
  ethical issues 7–8, 9
  imposition of Western 41
  and informed consent 89–94
  methodological gatekeeping 37
  technology and changes in 9, 10
Research in Schools and Early Childhood
    (RISEC) 50, 51
research technique 60
researchers
  feminist 66, 69, 108, 132
  indigenous 41, 114
  self-protection 76
  see also education researchers

resident ethicists 134, 167
resoluteness 25
respect 12, 25, 42, 103, 138
  for children's views 47–9
  for persons 23, 27, 28, 80, 139, 140, 165
  violation of intergenerational 76
RESPECT project 30
response rates 87–8, 110–11
responsibility(ies) 3, 5–6, 12, 34, 42, 49, 61, 65,
    75, 126, 128, 144, 146–7, 166–8
restricted settings 54
restrictiveness 35–8
results, use/misuse 129
retrospective consent 96
'reverse image' searching 145
reviewers 150
Rex, L. 11–12, 61–2, 63
Riddell, S. 96
right(s)
  indigenous peoples 42
  of reply 140
  researchers 34
  to confidentiality 11, 54, 64
  see also children's rights; intellectual
    property rights; natural rights
rights-based theories 20
rigour 119, 127, 128, 131, 133, 155
risk(s)
  of data misuse 122
  government-commissioned and sponsored
    research 64
  of harm 145
  restrictiveness in the interpretation of 36
risk assessment 27, 29
Rogers, B. 63
role models 25
Ross, W.D. 24, 28, 29
Ruane, J.M. 118, 121, 154

safety (researcher) 76
Sam (case study) 135, 137, 138, 144, 150
sample size 124–5
Sara (case study) 59, 60, 62
Saunders, M. 114
'Scared Straight' programme 70
scepticism 7
scholarship 142, 149, 155
school-based research 37, 56, 76, 77, 83, 84,
    88, 156
Schrag, Z. 34
Schutt, R.K. 128–9
scientific gloss 126
Scott, C.L. 37, 54, 154
second-wave feminism 113
selection of subjects 27, 29

selective reporting 124
self, ethics of care 20, 21
self-censorship 53, 105
self-criticality 140
self-determination 53
self-improvement 24
self-protection 76
sensitive data 58
sensitive topics 65
sensitivity 154, 162, 168
Setyowati, R. 49
Sevati (case study) 117, 118, 119–20, 123,
    130, 134
shaming 114
shared enterprise, research as 74, 98
Siegelman, S. 150
significance (data) 124, 125, 163
Sikes, P. 35, 37, 65, 155
sincerity 25
situatedness 38, 115
'skewing' of data sets 130
Small, R. 26, 27
small-scale research 12, 63, 160
Smith, F. 103
Smith, G.W.H. 129
Smith, T. 41
social class 114–15
social context 84
social embeddedness, decision-making 79–80,
    83–8, 156
social media sites 9, 93, 166
social relations 21, 108, 156, 166
social research 4, 11, 34, 54, 74, 87–8, 112
  see also education research
Social Research Association 32, 76
social responsibility 126
social science research 4, 7, 154, 156, 159
socially excluded individuals/groups 161
Song, M. 111
sponsored research 6
  see also government-sponsored research
sponsors
  choice of research topic 64
  contract negotiation 64
  favouring/privileging of quantitative
    research 60, 74
  pressure from 63, 72
  responsibilities to 146–7
stakeholders 22, 23
State Education Research Approvals Process
  (SERAP) 50, 51
statistical analysis 124, 126, 163
statistical significance 124, 125, 163
statistics 118, 121, 122, 124, 125, 126, 142

status-power differentials 104
steering groups 162
Sterba, S.K. 121
stereotypes 113, 142, 143
stigma(tization) 68, 84
structural/material differences 112
Styles, B. 71
subjectivity 116
subpoenas 56, 57
subterfuge 137
summaries 127
super-masculinisation 69
supervisors 54, 148
support groups 162
support networks 52
survey research 7, 72–3, 84, 93, 156
sympathy, towards political views 133
systematic approach 131, 134

taken-for-granted beliefs/assumptions 65
Te Riele, K. 140
teachers
  status and authority 41
  see also practitioner researchers
team compact 75
team research 74, 75, 156
technical rationality 63
technical role 147
technology 9, 10
telephone interviews 10
temperance 24
'test' connotation, survey research 84, 156
testing (data) 127
Tetteh, P. 12
text-based methods 67
theatrical representation 141–2
theory-free data 133
Thorne, B. 81
time pressure 160
timely reporting 147
Tooley, J. 132, 133
topic, choice of 61–5, 155
Torgerson, C. 70
Torrance, H 7
Traianou, A. 4, 5, 13, 34, 38, 41, 64, 85, 96, 99
transformation 161
transparency 126
*Tri-Council Policy Statement: Ethical Conduct
    for Research Involving Humans* 53
trimming (data) 124
trust 21, 38, 105, 149
trustworthiness 141
truth/truthfulness 21, 24, 96, 141, 142
Tuck, E. 48

Understanding Science Lessons 138–9
unethical practices 29, 149
United Kingdom
  critique of education research 132
  data management plans 77
  ethical approval 34
  ethical guidelines and principles 30, 31t,
    32–4
  increasing interest in experimental
    methods 69
  legal context of consent 82
  policy emphasis, commissioned research 63
  promotion of RCTs 70
  public scrutiny of research 6–7
  regulatory context 51, 52, 54, 55, 57
  research ethics literature 14
  school-based research 76
United Nations Committee on the Rights of
  the child 46, 47
United Nations Convention on the Rights of
  the Child 4, 20, 37, 45–50, 53, 81
United States
  ethical approval 34
  ethical guidelines and principles 27, 30, 31t
  parents' interpretation of children's best
    interests 47
  policy emphasis, commissioned research 63
  privileging of quantitative research 11–12
  promotion of RCTs 69, 70
  regulatory context 55, 57–8
  research ethics literature 14
Universal Declaration of Human Rights 49
universal ethics 11
universal moral principles 27
universalizability 23
upwards research 104, 105
utilitarianism 19, 21–3, 26, 35
utility, definitions 22

validity 127, 141
value assumptions 131
value positions 130, 155
value-based decisions 158
value-laden language 68

value-laden principles and procedures 39
value-neutral approach 62
values 13, 33, 64, 103, 131, 153, 166
Viete, R. 41, 149
virtue cultivation 39
virtue ethics 19–20, 24–5, 38–9
virtues 24, 25
visual data 126, 129, 166
  see also photographs
visual methods 9, 37, 49, 60, 68, 144–5
voice 82, 141–3, 150, 161
voluntary consent 34, 80, 81, 96
vulnerability 53, 160–1, 165
vulnerable groups 28, 29, 93, 154, 160
  see also children; indigenous communities;
    minorities

Walford, G. 104, 105
Walkerdine, V. 107–8
Walsh, L. 142
well-being 154, 156
Weller, S. 162
Wenar, L. 20
western ethical codes 41
Western norms/values 13
What Works Centre 69
White, J. 134
white sociologists 112–13
white supremacy 132
White, V. 141
Why Educational Research Matters (BERA) 7
Widiyanto 49
Willis, J. 114
withdrawal from research 103, 157
Wollcott, H. 140
Wood, B. 9, 12, 83
working group (BERA) 33
writing up 164–5
written consent 39, 40, 94

yi 25
youth participatory research 47, 143

Zambia 75, 87